Please remember that this is a library book,
and that it belongs only temporarily to each
person who uses it. Be considerate. Do
not write in this, or any, library book.

Traveller in Space

Traveller in Space

In Search of Female Identity in Tibetan
Buddhism

June Campbell

GEORGE BRAZILLER
New York

First published in the United States in 1996 by
George Braziller, Inc.

Originally published in Great Britain in 1996 by
The Athlone Press

Cataloging-in-Publication Data for this title
is available at The Library of Congress.

For further information, please address the publisher:

George Braziller, Inc.
60 Madison Avenue
New York, New York 10010

Jacket Design by Mark Hammer
Typeset by Bibloset
Printed and bound in Great Britain by
Bookcraft (Bath) Ltd

ISBN 0-8076-1406-8

FIRST EDITION 1996

Contents

Acknowledgements

I am grateful to the following people who have helped me realise this project. First of all, I wish to thank Benedetta Gaetani for helping to create the circumstances in which I could find time to write, and also for her valued friendship, encouragement, and financial support during the years in which this work was brought to fruition. I also thank Frances, Alastair and Elison Campbell for their support over many years, and Sophie Bentinck, Joaquin Canizares and Jennifer Batty for their very helpful individual contributions in supporting the development of my work. I am grateful to Valerie Allen and Angela Smith of the English Department at Stirling University for appreciating my writing, and to Mary Daly for encouraging my work. My thanks also to Maria Phylactou who provided very helpful comments on the text, and advice on editing, and to Brian Southam of The Athlone Press for recognising that this book was worthwhile.

Glossary

Amitabha   The Buddha of Pure Light, one of five primordial Buddhas of the five directions, whose family colour is red, and whose symbol is the lotus.

Bön   The religion which existed in Tibet prior to Buddhism, and whose main structures and iconography were adapted by the Buddhists.

Buddha   The historical figure of Prince Siddhartha Gautama, otherwise known as Sakyamuni Buddha, born in India in 583 BC. Lived and preached throughout India and Nepal, reaching enlightenment under a Bodhi tree at Bodhgaya in Bihar State, India.

Chenrezig   The central Tibetan deity, the Buddha of Compassion, who is said to be incarnate in the Dalai Lama. His mantra *Om Mani Padme Hum* is to be found carved in stones, placed in prayer wheels, and recited daily by all Tibetans. Also known by his Sanskrit name Avolokiteswara.

Dakini   The female deity who is represented in the iconography as naked and dancing, and whose role is traditionally to clear obstacles on the religious path, and provide insight into the nature of mind. She may appear as human, taking a variety of forms, from crone to virgin or sexual consort. Her name literally means sky or space-goer.

Dharma   The teaching of the Buddha, the doctrine, or law.

Dharmadhatu   The ideal realm of the Absolute.

Dolma   The Tibetan 'mother goddess', also known by her Sanskrit name, Tara.

Emptiness   The central concept of the Mahayana traditions, known in Sankrit as *sunyata* and in Tibetan as *tong pa nyi* which proposes that all phenomena are without substantiality, and non-dual in nature.

Hinayana   The Sanskrit term for the Tibetan *Thegpa chung chung*, literally 'small vehicle', which describes the major traditions of Buddhism otherwise known as *Theravada*. These traditions are practised in countries such as Sri Lanka and Thailand and favour monasticism and the gaining of merit through meditation and good deeds, as the basis of Buddhist practice. They reflect most closely the original teachings of the Buddha

Karma Action, or the law of cause and effect.

Kuan-Yin Chinese lotus goddess and goddess of compassion.

Lama The name given to a priest in the Tibetan Buddhist tradition, usually a *tulku* (recognised reincarnation), but also given to one who has shown great scholarship or success in meditation.

Mahayana The Sanskrit term for the Tibetan *Thegpa Chenpo*, or 'great vehicle', which describes the traditions of Buddhism practised in Japan, China and areas of Southeast Asia, and which hold to the doctrines of emptiness and compassion. Practitioners of this tradition vow not to enter into the state of *nirvana* for the sake of all sentient beings.

Mantra Sanskrit formula which is repreated or chanted, and which relates to a particular deity.

Mahamudra Sanskrit term for the Tibetan *Chaja Chenpo*, which is considered to be the highest realisation of the Tibetan tradition, in which the meditator experiences 'one-taste', i.e. no differentiation between mind and phenomena.

Mudra Sanskrit term which signifies both a gesture, and a female consort.

Padmasambhava 'Lotus Born' teacher who is said to have introduced Buddhism into Tibet. Known in Tibet as *Guru Rinpoche* (Precious Teacher).

Prajnaparamita Name of the Buddhist Sutra which expounds the teaching on emptiness. Also applied to the Great Mother, as the embodiment of emptiness.

Sakti Female principle or power, also sexual consort

Sutra The name given to the discourses thought to have been given by the Buddha himself.

Tantra Ancient practices which involved yoga, sexual ritual and meditation, central to certain forms of Hinduism and to Tibetan Buddhism.

Tulku A child chosen to be enthroned in a position of religious power, in the belief that he (rarely she) is the reincarnation of a lama who has died, or of a divinity.

Vajrayana   The Sanskrit term for the Tibetan *Sang Nga Dorje Thegpa*, 'the adamantine or diamond vehicle', the tradition of Buddhism practised in Tibet which incorporates the Hinayana and Mahayana, together with Tantric Buddhism.

Introduction

Before embarking on my search for female identity in Tibetan Buddhism, it is necessary to present to the reader the context of this work, together with the theoretical approaches which I have used in writing it. On the face of it, a study of a particular aspect of any religion may seem straightforward enough, but in this case, the complexities are many. First of all, despite the fact that Buddhism has become popular as a religious practice in the west, the teachings of Tibetan Buddhism are little known generally, and are often the subject of much imaginative speculation and misunderstanding, because of what has been written about Tibet, its landscape, religion and people, in the past. Secondly, although the major focus of the book is a search for female identity in Tibetan Buddhism, this does not mean that the book is purely about specific female symbols, or indeed about the lives of specific women, but rather it examines the historical and institutional context of the religion, as a means of analysing and understanding the Tibetan religious *philosophy* of the female. As part of my analysis I have had to take into account the contemporary encounter of Tibetan Buddhism with the west, and the implications of that encounter, particularly in the light of the importance placed by Tibetan Buddhists on the centrality of sexual imagery in their religious icons and texts.

There can be few people in the west who, on hearing the name of Tibet, do not conjure up pictures in their minds of vast mountainous landscapes, mysterious Buddhist monasteries and magical rituals. I was certainly one of them, and at the early age of ten decided that one day I would travel to Tibet and become a Buddhist. As it turned out, only one of my wishes came true, for in 1959 the Chinese Government annexed Tibet and it became virtually closed to outside visitors, and the Tibetan religious traditions were severely repressed by the communist regime which replaced the ancient theocracy. At the outset, however, the heads of the four main schools of Tibetan Buddhism (the Nyingma,

Kagyu, Sakya and Gelug) fled into exile in India with about 80,000 followers, and there they established new monasteries in their refugee communities which kept alive the spirit and traditions of their homeland. Two young Tibetan lamas of the Kagyu lineage eventually found their way to the United Kingdom, and in 1967 opened the first Tibetan religious centre in the west, in the borders of Scotland, where I met them the following year, and became a Buddhist by 'taking refuge'.[1] Shortly afterwards, I set out for the foothills of the Himalayas to a nunnery run by a small community of Tibetans in exile and it was there that I began my studies of the Tibetan language and the philosophy of Buddhism, known as the *dharma*. Much later, in the 1970s, I travelled throughout Europe and North America as a Tibetan interpreter, providing the link, through language, between my lama-guru and his many students. Subsequently he requested that I become his sexual consort, and take part in secret activities with him, despite the fact that to outsiders he was a very high-ranking yogi-lama of the Kagyu lineage who, as abbot of his own monastery, had taken vows of celibacy. Given that he was one of the oldest lamas in exile at that time, had personally spent fourteen years in solitary retreat, and counted amongst his students the highest ranking lamas in Tibet, his own status was unquestioned in the Tibetan community, and his holiness attested to by all. As I describe in Chapter 6, these events took place under unusual conditions, and were to have a profound effect on my whole relationship with the Tibetan Buddhist religion.

Since these early days, hundreds of dharma centres have been established by Tibetans all over the world, their assets running into billions of dollars,[2] and their prominence ever increasing as the teachings of Buddhism gain popularity in the west. This process, set in motion by the Chinese political actions of the 1950s, gave people across the world access to a religious tradition which had been largely hidden for centuries by the geographical inaccessibility of Tibet. What was particularly remarkable about this series of events was that in a relatively short space of time, the highest Tibetan lamas in exile managed to establish alternative sources of income and support across the globe, in sharp contrast to many other political refugees all over the world who have faced a more terrible fate. One of the reasons for the extraordinary success of the Tibetans in gaining financial support from westerners was the upsurge of interest in the west in the Buddhist religion. The Tibetans capitalised on this, not only in order to open the doors of their traditional Buddhist way of life to those who sought that knowledge, and certainly not solely as a proselytising exercise (for strictly speaking they do not believe in missionary work), but in order to keep their own culture and belief system alive outside of Tibet. While the Chinese zealously imposed their values and the principles of communism on the non-secular society that was Tibet, the Tibetans in exile, alarmed at the prospect of the destruction of their culture, set out to sustain their tradition outwith its societal context. This situation led to the establishing, by the diaspora, of the unusual structures and institutions of Tibetan Buddhism not only in many developing countries in Asia, but also within the context of many western societies throughout the world. This unique juncture of events which involved the movement of people, ideas, institutions and culture across continents, brought about a moment in the history of the Tibetan civilisation of the last thousand years, in which, at worst, the extinction of its ancient culture was faced, or at the very least the social structures and geographical grandeur of Tibet and its landscape would no longer be the primary context in which Tibetan Buddhism thrived.

In considering the potential value of my study of Tibetan Buddhism, it is certainly the case that the promotion of any religious system, which purports to contain truths of universal relevance, outside of the cultural environment in which that system first evolved, is a subject worthy of debate. Furthermore, as I hope to show, the particularly unique relationship between the institutional structures of their society, their religious beliefs, and the consequential effects on notions of female identity, make this debate very interesting, and all the more so since many western men have achieved positions of power within the Tibetan Buddhist institution. The historical events of 1959, which eventually brought about the widespread study of Tibetan Buddhism by westerners, meant that the teachings of the lamas began to be transmitted in cultural environments vastly different to the ones visited by earlier western Tibetologists and orientalists. For the Tibetans, however, there was naturally a problem in the transmission of their teachings outwith their societal structures, a problem which had the potential to lead to enormous cross-cultural misunderstandings and misgivings.

As a largely oral tradition, (indeed the name of one of the schools – the Kagyu (Tibetan *ka.rgyud*) – literally means 'lineage by mouth'), the Tibetan religion was always under the threat of degeneration, once its institutions left Tibet. This threat hovers over all fragile, oral cultures, for as John Potter has remarked 'Oral cultures are capable of immense sophistication, and tend to become visible only when they come into contact with the literate genres that are destined to replace them'.[3] The Tibetan culture may not have been totally 'invisible', although some might argue that it was, but it was certainly remote, and as such did not come into contact with many areas of the world until it was forced into the international arena when the Chinese attempted to replace the religious culture with the dogmas of communism. As for the question of the western 'literate genres' with which it has come into contact, it remains to be seen whether 'replacement' or evolution of the Tibetan Buddhist culture will take place. What is sure is that those aspects of the religious tradition which find little resonance in the mores of western society will be discussed, criticised, debated and perhaps even attacked,[4] whilst those aspects which may add something to the contemporary understanding of human nature will be valorised, or 'revalorised', as the feminist-Buddhist Rita Gross has attempted in her book on Buddhism.[5]

There is no doubt that the greatest danger to their cultural tradition is the threat to the continuation of their religious institutions whose traditions have depended on the very old practice of selecting a child to replace a dead lama of high status, and for that child to be considered his 'incarnation'. These reincarnate lamas, (known as *tulku*s, Tibetan *sprul.sku*) who hold immense spiritual and political power, maintained their status in Tibetan culture through the common belief in their actual divinity. It is these positions which will certainly be under threat should the practice, already begun by the Tibetans themselves,[6] of choosing western boys (or even girls as is suggested by some feminist Buddhists)[7] to be enthroned as the reincarnations of dead Tibetan lamas, and to head Tibetan Buddhist monasteries and religious centres throughout the world, continue or increase. Additionally, there is a possibility that the global forces of secularism and materialism may overpower the spiritual dimension of the oral tradition which rested comfortably in the high plateaux of Tibet, and that the Tibetans themselves may be willing participants in a process which ultimately swallows up their culture. If Tibetan lamas themselves succumb to the pressures of western materialism, or if the highest positions of power are gradually taken over by western 'incarnations', there seems little doubt that the traditions of the Vajrayana[8] will alter radically.

THE BASICS OF TIBETAN BUDDHISM

Clearly, it would be impossible here to examine the many and varied facets of Tibetan Buddhism in any great depth. However, for those completely unfamiliar with the teachings of this form of Buddhism, I will set out the most basic elements of the religion, specifying those areas which make it so different from other forms of Buddhism, and highlight the points which I consider the most relevant in the context of this book. The first few chapters of the book will then elucidate the unique features I discuss here, and place their development within an historical context. Certainly there are many aspects of Tibetan Buddhism, the Vajrayana, which are familiar to people who know anything about Buddhism in general – e.g. the belief in *karma*, in reincarnation, in the practice of non-violence to all living beings, in the non-existence of a distinct self, and in meditation as a means to achieve spiritual realisation. These beliefs and principles are upheld by all Buddhists in the many countries which practise Buddhism, but each tradition developed in a different way, and placed emphasis on different aspects of the teachings which the Buddha himself was said to have transmitted.

Most people are also aware that Buddhism has a very strong monastic tradition, and that this tradition reflects the emphasis which Buddhists often place on the renunciation of desire as the key component in religious practice. Monasticism became the main basis of the *Theravada* tradition which is found in countries such as Sri Lanka and Thailand, but was also a major component in the other traditions, including that of Tibet which had a monastic and a lay priesthood. The position of Tibetan Buddhist nuns, however, was traditionally one of inferiority, partly because the female lineage which allowed for full ordination did not evolve in Tibet, and therefore their status was lower than that of the men, and secondly because few women were given access to the scholarly tradition.

Buddhism itself is founded upon The Four Noble Truths of the historical figure of the Buddha, who began his life as an Indian prince, and after many years of ascetic practice and meditation achieved 'enlightenment' under a bodhi tree at Bodhgaya, in the Indian state of Bihar, in the fifth century BC. He stated, after his 'enlightenment', that all life is unsatisfactory, that the cause of this is desire, that the cessation of desire brings about unlimited happiness or nirvana, and that the path to achieving enlightenment, free of suffering, is to follow his eightfold path. The path itself sets out certain moral, ethical and spiritual guidelines for achieving liberation from the cycle of existence (*samsara*), where that liberation is also characterised by complete knowledge. This is all reflected in the title 'Buddha', which has the same meaning in its Tibetan form, Sanje (Tibetan *sangs.rgyas*), the two syllables of which mean 'completely purified'.

Tibetan Buddhism, however, contains a second strand of teachings which it has in common with the traditions of other countries such as Japan and Korea. This aspect of Buddhism relates to a belief in the existence of 'bodhisattvas' (Tibetan Changchub Sempa, *byangs.chub.sems.pa.*) or saintly practitioners who renounce their entry into nirvana for the sake of all sentient beings, and thereafter are reborn again and again, taking any expedient bodily form in order to hasten the enlightenment of others. A central aspect of Tibetan Buddhist meditation is the engendering of such an attitude for the sake of others. Of the texts which make up this form of Buddhist practice, known as the Sutra path, whose main focus is altruism, the corpus known as the *Prajnaparamita* has a major place in Tibetan Buddhism, teaching as it does 'a nonsystematic religious philosophy, fervent in devotion and rich in poetic expression, centring on the notion that all is Emptiness'.[9] One of the most interesting philosophical schools concerned with Emptiness, or the non-substantiality of all phenomena (even mind itself), is the Madhyamika, the 'middle way', whose major proponent, an Indian philosopher Nagarjuna, stated that 'any philosophical view could be refuted, [and] that one must not dwell upon any answer or description of reality, whether extreme or moderate, including the notion of "one-mind"'.[10]

Philosophies such as these underpin the techniques of meditation which Tibetan Buddhists enter into as part of the more advanced forms of practice such as the *Mahamudra* (Tibetan Chaja Chenpo, *phyag.rgya.chen.po.*), which seeks to develop a realisation of the nature of mind itself. But before embarking on such kinds of meditation which aim to reach the depths of human insight and understanding, certain preliminary practices, together with the necessity of complete devotion to a lama or guru, are considered essential. It is in these areas of the Vajrayana practice, which relate to the ancient and complex Hindu philosophy known as the 'Tantra', that one finds the unique nature of Tibetan Buddhism, which differentiates it from the other forms found elsewhere in the world. The Tantric aspect of the Vajrayana involves a rich and colourful pantheon of deities in its iconography, and teachings which are considered extremely risky to undertake, yet so efficacious if practised correctly, that they are reputed to lead to enlightenment in one lifetime. In essence, the Buddhist Tantra makes use of the notion that to *enlist* the passions in one's religious practice, rather than *avoid* them, is a potent way to realise the basic non-substantiality of all phenomena.

The Buddhist Tantric deities are invoked and visualised in meditation, and practitioners identify with them in such a way as to enable them not only to be released from the limitations of ego-clinging, but also to transmute the various mind poisons into various forms of wisdom or enlightenment which the deities represent. This kind of practice is reputed to help break the boundaries between 'self' and 'other' and ultimately between all dualities which are experienced as part of mundane existence. The highest form of such realisation is said only to come about through the secret Tantric practices which involve sexual relations, and which are depicted iconographically in many religious paintings and images. Amongst celibate practitioners, and the 'not-so-advanced', these actions are visualised in the mind during meditation, as a way of experiencing the 'non-dual' through the images of the dual.

On becoming a Tibetan Buddhist, most lay practitioners receive some basic teachings concerning faith, non-violence and karma, and may be given a simple mantra to recite in order to increase compassion towards others. The most commonly recited mantra is *Om Mani Padme Hum*, whose meaning I discuss in some detail in Chapter 3. Those who seek to practice meditation at a more advanced level must undergo a rigorous training which involves four foundational practices, each of which must be done 100,000 times. The first involves a metaphorical enactment of the devotion and submission of the practitioner to the central pillars of Tibetan Buddhism, which are represented by the lama-gura in a deified form, the Buddha, his teaching, the community of practitioners, and the deities who make up the protectors and guides whose purpose is to clear obstacles on the path. The submission to and veneration of them is carried out by the performance of 100,000 actual body prostrations and recitations of a prayer. This practice normally takes some time to complete, but is usually undertaken over several months. The second foundational practice is the recitation of 100,000 mantras of the deity Dorje Sempa, together with a visualisation which is aimed at purifying previous negative karma accumulated over many lifetimes. Finally the lama himself is worshipped in a devotional prayer which is recited 100,000 times, in order to increase faith and total submission of the ego to the religious lineage of which the lama is a representative. According to the Tibetan belief, all teachings which are given by the lamas of the lineage are said to have been transmitted in an unbroken oral tradition which began with the Buddha himself, and all of which therefore originated in India.

Following these events, the practitioner is then considered a fit vessel for receiving more elaborate and detailed teachings, and is also eligible for 'initiation' into the Tantric practices whereby identification with the divine and transcendental bodies of deities may be carried out in meditation, in order to develop insight as to the nature of the mind. In tandem with these kinds of practices, the initiate may undertake special forms of developing the mind through concentrative meditation, the enhancement of deep insight and the development of discriminatory awareness. It is within the framework of the more advanced teachings that the notion of the lama or guru becomes crucial in Tibetan Buddhism, and the nature of guru-devotion potentially problematic. In a preface to the Mahamudra teachings of the 9th Karmapa Lama, it is written,

Guru-devotion involves both your thoughts and actions. The most important thing is to develop the total conviction that your Guru is a Buddha. . . . If you doubt your Guru's competence and ability to guide you, your practices will be extremely unstable and you will be unable to make any concrete progress.[11]

Whilst the Tibetans themselves rarely have a problem with this kind of approach, because of their own cultural background in which the lamas were held in awesome regard, in a western context the concept of viewing any human as totally divine poses problems, and this is especially so if the lama invokes the use of sexual relations with a student as a means of either furthering his own practice, or alleging spiritual benefit for the woman concerned. Leaving aside for the moment the question of what so-called 'advanced' sexual practices actually entail, the difficulties for any student involved in Tibetan Buddhism are highlighted in this statement by the Tibetan lama Beru Kyhentze Rinpoche on the importance of guru-devotion,

If your Guru acts in a seemingly unenlightened manner and you feel it would be hypocritical to think him a Buddha, you should remember that *your own opinions are unreliable and the apparent faults you see may only be a reflection of your own deluded state of mind*. Also you should think that if your Guru acted in a completely perfect manner, he would be inaccessible and you would be unable to relate to him. It is therefore out of your Guru's great compassion that he may show apparent flaws. This is part of his use of skilful means in order for him to be able to teach you. *He is mirroring your own faults*.[12] (Italics mine)

The consequences of the failure to see the guru as Buddha are also elaborated by Kyhentze, when he points out that the adherence to a view of lama-as-Buddha most certainly brings the practitioner closer to enlightenment, whereas any nega-tivity directed towards the lama-guru results in going further away from enlightenment and in 'intense suffering' for the stu-dent.[13] As Kyhentze is at pains to point out, guru-devotion is much more essential in the Tantric path than in the Sutra path, and is therefore considered the central pillar of the Tibetan Vajrayana.

THE CONTEXT OF THE DEBATE ON GENDER AND TIBETAN BUDDHISM

In order to enter the debate on gender, sexuality and religion in the field of Tibetan Buddhist studies, I have drawn upon several disparate bodies of knowledge, and in particular have utilised the theoretical approaches of feminism and psychoanalysis, alongside my knowledge as a Tibetan scholar and translator. This work follows the interpretative books of Robert A. Paul, who made an orthodox Freudian analysis of the Tibetan religious culture, in *The Tibetan Symbolic World*, and of Peter Bishop who intuitively realised the imaginative role which Tibet has played in the minds of westerners, in *The Myth of Shangri-La* and *Dreams of Power*. Bishop in particular was aware of the cross-cultural dimension in his work, and as a Buddhist saw the need for debate between east and west, if Tibetan Buddhism were to be of value: 'Tibetan Buddhism' he wrote, 'must be in contact with the pathologies of the West if it is to have any real effect'.[14] Both these books, whilst fascinating and instructive, failed however to consider in any depth the problem of female identity, concerned as they were with the male-dominated power structures of Tibet and the psyches of men. Instead, the problem area of women in the Tibetan system and the symbolism pertaining to them has been taken up by western Buddhists who have presented two different and fairly conservative perspectives. Firstly, autobiographical accounts of the lives, works and historical significance of Tibetan women practitioners (e.g. Tsultrim Allione's *Women of Wisdom*, Hanna Havnevik's *Tibetan Buddhist Nuns*, Keith Dowman's *Sky Dancer*), and of Tantric female 'masters' (Miranda Shaw's *Passionate Enlightenment*) certainly address the question of the recognition of the contribution of women and their insertion into the historical accounts of Tibetan Buddhism's evolution. What they show is that there is evidence that the status of women was once different within Tibetan Buddhism from what it is now, and that women have, despite the social difficulties of their lives, been diligent scholars and practitioners. What they fail to convey, however, is the process by which many of the very *early* achievements were eroded and how the female became 'fixed' in a different and inferior position which was reflected both in the textual philosophy and her position within the religious institutions.

Secondly, other writers have exposed the anomalies in the

Tibetan system *vis-à-vis* women's position, taking a feminist stand-point in their critique of the institutions and of the philosophies, which though patently egalitarian in nature, do not translate into the social and religious structures of Tibetan society. Rita Gross's work, *Buddhism after Patriarchy*, whilst not exclusively dealing with Tibetan Buddhism, does however raise many of the issues which I discuss here, principally those of the philosophy concerning gender in the Vajrayana, and the future of Tibetan Buddhism in its meeting with western culture, particularly feminist thought. Gross proposes 'a feminist revalorization'[15] of Buddhism through the insertion of women into the historical framework, valuing the 'feminine principle', and reassessing the key concepts in Buddhism concerning gender. She also puts forward her 'solution' to the woman question, by proposing androgynous institutions as a way in which Buddhism could be assimilated into the ethos of contemporary western culture.

Whilst I review some of Gross's ideas in this work, my contribution to the debate is not so much about uncovering women's history, or in finding strategies for equality, but rather in questioning the notions of female identity and subjectivity, as found within the Tibetan tradition, and trying to relate these to the contemporary western debate on gender, sexuality and religion. My project has been twofold. Firstly I wished to enter the debate which became inevitable when westerners gained full access to the secret world of Tibetan Buddhism, and to do so by using not only my knowledge and experience of Buddhism and the Tibetan language, but also my understanding of certain western theoretical perspectives. Given the serious questions which have been made public concerning the role, power and status of Vajrayana lamas in the west, and their potential abuse of that power, I wanted to offer an analysis of the institutions of Tibetan Buddhism, which might facilitate cross-cultural debate. This kind of debate would involve the different meanings which can be attached to the teachings of Tibetan Buddhism, and the dynamic which occurs between different cultures *where the encounter between them involves teachings which relate to gender difference and sexuality.*

Secondly, the focus of my attention, the quest for female identity in Tibetan Buddhism, is based undeniably on my own position and past experience as a woman within Tibetan Buddhism and is the expression of a kind of female desire which seeks *to name itself*. As someone who initially left her homeland in an idealistic search for spiritual meaning, my own position as a female in an environment dominated by celibate men, led me to reflect on the religious 'truths' and symbolism concerning the female, that were presented to me in the Buddhist context. In this book I have tried to make sense of the notion of female identity as an important aspect of comparative religious study and of cross-cultural debate, and have chosen to use the metaphor 'traveller in space' in order to reflect the different layers of meaning which emerge when a search for female identity is undertaken.

The title of the book therefore, can be read in different ways. Primarily it is a translation of a Tibetan word which portrays the essential female aspect within the religion, and in Chapter 7 I explore its etymology in some depth. In addition, however, woman as a 'traveller in space' can be read in western historical terms as a non-fixed subject, who has been largely hidden from history, lacks real equality, and is unable to be located in the 'space' of philosophy. Her position, therefore, whilst absent from major patriarchal discourse, is none the less not static, for women participate in the endless journey of humanity alongside men, and do so through the unique perspective which having a female body brings. Finally, the term 'space travel' in itself suggests something not just of space and its vastness, but also of time, particularly of the future. Space travel implies the exploration of unknown territory, which takes place in a future dimension which itself is outwith the bounds of ordinary human knowledge. This exploration of the unknown is akin to the metaphysical journey which is involved in all endeavours of the human spirit, when individuals attempt to understand the realms of the human psyche, or the unconscious. Such exploration in the somewhat risky areas of the unknown signifies dimensions of reality with which we have barely begun to come to grips, and emphasises the intimate relationship between the human body and the powers of the mind to create these journeys.

In the past, westerners projected their fantasies of the unknown and the undiscovered onto places such as Tibet, and it is no coincidence that the early explorers identified and were particularly excited about the Tibetan yogis who were said to have been adepts at *lung gom* (air meditation), which supposedly gave them the power to travel rapidly over the earth without touching the ground. In many accounts of Tibetan life, early western writers recounted stories of how lamas could 'fly through space'. The romanticism of this idea fitted well with other notions of 'Shangri-La', which represented the ultimate fantasy of having the ability to be in a place where the unknown could be known, and the physical body transcended. But another aspect of the power to travel in space is the commonly perceived association with the breaking of barriers ('space – the final frontier') and the ability to communicate at levels different from those we know now. In the future, 'virtual reality', the communications 'net' and the 'superhighway' promise to make us all 'travellers in space', or at least give us multiple possibilities concerning 'identity'. We are now facing a technological revolution which may be a part of that journey into unknown territory, where it is conceivable that the female symbolic, *as it has been articulated so far*, and as a manifestation of a dying world-view, will finally disappear along with other detrimental barriers between beings of all kinds.

A final consideration on the context of the cross-cultural debate is the question of 'orientalism' and the dangers which emerge when a study such as this is undertaken. In his book *Orientalism*, Edward Said criticises the role of those in the west who have written of the orient in such a way as to promote 'racial, ideological, and imperialist stereotypes'.[16] He clearly identifies the 'powerful series of political and ultimately ideological realities (which) inform scholarship',[17] and concludes that it may be in the field of the 'human sciences' that the insights which are lacking in traditional orientalism may be found. Said points out the kinds of ideologies which posit the notion of the 'other' as alien, and therefore inferior, as manifesting in the orientalist tradition in splits of east/west, north/south, have/have-not, imperialist/anti-imperialist, and white/black. He does not include in this list, however, the question of the gender split as equally significant.

None the less, in his analysis of the 'orientalist' view of women, he concedes three important points. Firstly, that orientalism was 'an exclusively male province';[18] secondly that the women described by orientalists were subsequently and inevitably 'the creatures of a male power-fantasy';[19] and thirdly, that orientalists linked 'the

Oriental . . . to elements in Western society (delinquents, the insane, *women*, the poor), having in common an identity best described as *lamentably alien* (italics mine).[20] Peter Bishop also takes up this point by describing the orientalists' view of the orient as 'feminine', and Tibet in particular as 'a symbol of Otherness'.[21] As a woman writer, my position enables me to counteract all these approaches to some extent, and I have made extensive use of the human sciences in order to redress the balance of the orientalist approach which, according to Said, 'failed to identify with *human* experience' (italics mine).[22]

In this context I would present my work as an analysis of the dynamic *between* people, cultures and belief systems, and would suggest that my position as a woman, having experienced the limitations and authority imposed by patriarchal modes of thought in the west *and* with the Tibetans, is recognised as a significant factor in this study. As I have pointed out, the situation concerning study of the Tibetan religious institution is complex, for in taking the unusual step of deliberately placing westerners in positions of power within these institutions, through 'recognising' western boys as incarnations of recently dead Tibetan lamas, the Tibetans themselves have shown that their desire to integrate Tibetan Buddhism into the west is very serious indeed. By so doing they initiated a process which has inevitably brought about a debate on the evolution of their unique system in the west.

THEORETICAL APPROACHES

The two main strands of theory which have informed my work are feminist thought and psychoanalysis, both of which have different and separate histories, yet have also found a convergence in the work of contemporary theorists, such as Luce Irigaray, Julia Kristeva and Hélène Cixous, although all of them find the use of the word 'feminist' problematic.[23] I have used their work primarily because it provides a certain context within which the more complex questions of female identity can be addressed, and because each of them has articulated, in their own very different ways, the enormous difficulties involved in any kind of search for 'female identity'. In order therefore to locate the theoretical perspectives which I have used in this work, it may be useful first of all to contextualise them within the evolutionary processes of the two 'waves of feminism', which brought about different manifestations of feminist theory, and then to specify the particular aspects of their approaches which I found useful.

The 'first wave' of feminism attempted to *locate* women in history, and also sought to establish equal rights for women through parliamentary, constitutional, political and institutional change. This movement had its roots in the liberalism of the nineteenth century, and was strongly identified with Marxist ideology. Its impetus challenged, with some success, all the powerful western institutions and male edifices of its time – in education, law, politics and, to some extent, religion. The so-called 'second wave', on the other hand, was born largely after the political movements of the 1960s, and was heavily influenced by the writings of Freud and by twentieth-century socialism. These dual influences created an analytical and aesthetic ambience in which many feminists withdrew their demands for a place in historical or linear time, in order to create a uniquely female space, where female identity was not required to be projected and justified, as in previous times. The second movement, having developed a different concept of itself, its subjectivity, and therefore its relation to temporality, reflected a growing distrust of political initiatives and solutions. Its main preoccupations became, according to Kristeva, specificity and difference, as opposed to equality, and brought with it more global awareness and concern for socio-cultural cohesion through the recognition and acceptance of wider issues, to do with reproduction, life and death. These moral issues related more specifically to the survival of the species than to the earlier universal and nationalistic concerns over the modes of production in society, and were linked to an upsurge in interest in marginal movements concerned with such things as spirituality and ecology.

Kristeva's critique of the two movements notes that the first movement was constructed within the confines of history, linear time, the symbolic order of the patriarchy, and therefore of language, whilst the second movement attempted to place itself outside the patriarchal order of its time by seeking to establish a radical change in gender relations, and an entirely new language in which women's experiences and desires would be inscribed. In her essay *Women's Time*, Kristeva maintains that, in the end, both movements achieved limited success, because each contained within it a relationship to the symbolic contract,[24] which was ultimately self-defeating. The first movement invested in the social order by pursuing positions of power for women, but nothing changed as these women were ingested into the system, and in some cases ended up becoming 'the pillars of the existing governments, guardians of the status quo, the most zealous protectors of the established order'.[25] On the other hand, the second-wave feminists, by focusing on the specificity of the female subject, through writing, representations, and a devotion to archaic images of the maternal, failed to acknowledge the multiplicity of background, experience and need to be found amongst women themselves. Nonetheless, the impact of the two waves of feminism had a considerable effect on the institutions of western society and on issues concerning gender relations.

In her vision of the nature of the future debate on feminism, however, Kristeva proposes a 'third wave' or a 'third attitude'[26] in which a new generation may be able to adopt a new position, which, though different from the first two waves of feminism, nevertheless would not reject them out of hand, but encompass their ideals within the philosophical debate on gender and difference. At the heart of her argument is the importance of the psychoanalytic view of sexual difference, and therefore of the relationship between the psychopathology of the individual, and society. Her hope is that through the convergence of the third attitude together with an enactment of both kinds of approach to women's relationship to the symbolic order, i.e. the insertion into history, and the identification with all marginal movements, 'the very dichotomy man/woman as an opposition between two rival entities may be understood as belonging to *metaphysics*' (italics original).[27] Furthermore, her view of women's special relationship with the semiotic leads her to suggest that all forms of academic and aesthetic practice which expose the socio-symbolic order as a 'sacrificial contract',[28] which women 'are forced to experience . . . against their will',[29] would change the very future of the species.

The work of Luce Irigaray, which also uses a psychoanalytical approach, is primarily concerned with *difference*, and of the importance of the accession by women to female subjectivity. She exposes the double bind which is present when any attempt to define 'woman' is made, by demonstrating that to do so would be to remain within the context of the phallocentric system of representation, but to fail to do so would allow for anything to be projected on to her. Whilst many seek to accuse Irigaray of 'essentialism' in her work (because of her quest for female genealogies and the acknowledgement of female *difference*), these accusations are counteracted by her strategic proposal *not* to reverse the current ideologies in order to favour women, nor even to elaborate a new theory, but rather to engage in a process of 'jamming the theoretical machinery itself'.[30] Women, she suggests, should not join logical discourse about the category 'woman' but repeat and interpret the ways in which the feminine is always depicted as a lack or deficiency. This kind of approach, which attempts to 'slip' the oppositional dualities inscribed in language and patriarchal philosophy, would come about, she maintains, by the disruption of dichotomies. It would bring about an argument in which 'Nothing is ever to be *posited* that is not also reversed and caught up again in the *supplementarity of this reversal*' (italics original).[31] Once engaged in this kind of discourse, she says, 'There would no longer be either a right or a wrong side of discourse, or even of texts'.[32] Both Irigaray and Hélène Cixous imagine a potential relation between the sexes which does not deny difference. Cixous places her psychoanalytic emphasis on women's sexuality, and its omission from patriarchal discourse. Her response to the question of female equality is to propose new kinds of discourses which can be expressed through 'feminine' writing. 'For Cixous the Unconscious is always a cultural phenomenon . . . a product of a masculine imaginary'.[33] Her work therefore makes a link between culture and sexuality, and the need for expressions of the female libido in all aspects of culture, particularly writing.

The theoretical approaches I have taken in this book reflect the main concerns of these three philosophers. I have attempted, in accordance with Kristeva's view, to adopt a 'third attitude' by including perspectives which are drawn from the first two waves of feminism, but are located within and alongside my metaphysical argument about female identity. These perspectives include: a critique of patriarchal institutions, the insertion of female experience into history, and the acknowledgement of archaic images of the maternal. They form not only part of the debate on female specificity and difference, but are also the means through which the metaphysical questions concerning woman and man can be addressed, particularly through the writing of a 'feminine' imaginary. It has not been my aim to undertake a 'reconstruction' of Buddhism in order to establish female equality within the institutions of Buddhism, nor to seek to justify that women are as important as men within the Tibetan system, because that work has been undertaken by others. My aim has been to address some of the complexities surrounding the search for meaning in the ways in which female identity has been constructed and interpreted within the Tibetan system, and *why* the Tibetan system has remained theocratic rather than democratic. This has seemed particularly important in the light of Tibetan Buddhism's encounter with the west, and the ramifications of its use of the sexual metaphor, within a different cultural context. Whilst I do include a critique of the institutions, and examine some aspects of women's lives, my main focus has been the metaphysical question concerning identity. My conclusions concerning female equality within Buddhism emerge, therefore, not from finding strategies for adapting teachings to include women and rationalise the gender question, but rather from raising the controversial question of whether *after* patriarchy *any religions*, as we now know them, could possibly survive in a recognisable form.

To begin the task of unravelling the idiosyncracies of the Tibetan view, *vis-à-vis* female identity, I firstly examine the historical links of Tibetan Buddhism with the west and set out some of the problematic areas of female identity as they were commonly represented in texts, including the use of language. In Chapter 2 I begin the search for the roots of female symbolism by examining some of the remnants of historical evidence pertaining to the emergence of Tantric Buddhism in Tibet. I acknowledge the many cross-cultural factors of pre-Buddhistic times, including the impact of many belief systems, not least those from neighbouring Persia, on the development of the first-recorded indigenous belief system of Tibet (Bön), and the adoption of Tantric practices from India. As I show, these influences, themselves arising from the almost universal and ancient cult of the Great Mother, became deeply embedded in cultural practices some of which have survived in diluted, yet recognisable form, till modern times. I argue that because of Tibet's geographical remoteness, many ancient cultural features, which were lost to other traditions, retained their potency in Tibet, and that some of the symbolism pertaining to the female in Tibetan Buddhism has its origins in these pre-Buddhist times.

As an example of the kind of influences which pre-dated Buddhism in Tibet, I trace, in Chapter 3, the evolution of the Lotus Deity, now the most important (and male) deity of the Tibetan pantheon, in his form as Chenrezig. I show how the deity, originally female, and an aspect of the Great Mother, underwent a gender change during the period when Buddhism emerged in Tibet, and as a result changed meaning, iconographically. This, I argue, led to an absence of representations of the essentialist female-as-herself in Tibetan imagery. In order to understand the context in which this important transformation took place, I go on in Chapter 4 to examine the theocracy of Tibet and its unique power structures, the place of women in them, and the relationship between the theocracy and the iconography. I maintain that the introduction of the tulku system of reincarnate lamas in Tibet in the early thirteenth century promoted the idea of the enlightened male subject, to accommodate the doctrine concerning the rule of the 'divine lama-king' and as a result further weakened the potentially positive images of the female in the iconography. In Chapter 5 I look at the symbolic position of the mother of the 'Divine Lama-King', whose representational absence in the system, I argue, is a key factor in its maintenance.

In Chapter 6 I discuss the links between the 'non-presence' of the female-as-herself and the existence of the secret female consort (Tibetan *gsang.yum*.)[34] within the Tibetan theocratic system, taking into account not only the relevance of sexuality to the basic tenets of Tibetan Buddhism, but also the motivating factors which existed in order to perpetuate secrecy. In addition I consider the implications for women involved in secret relationships with lamas, and argue that their collusion, often through fear, enables the system to survive. In Chapter 7 I turn to an analysis of the *dakini* and explore some ideas concerning her so-called 'secret language' and her association with the discovery of secret texts. Through an examination of the symbolic female identity which the dakini purports to represent, I look at the significance of attaching gendered bodies (in this case the female body) to philosophical concepts. These notions are further elaborated in Chapter 8 when I discuss female transcendence, and the ways in which the association of the female with 'otherness' is conveyed through texts and representations. I also address the problem of female subjectivity in Tibetan Buddhism and how concepts pertaining to 'selfhood' are used differentially with women and men. In Chapter 9 the questions which I raise about female identity and difference are set within the context of the debate in the west about female subjectivity, and at the intersection of the debate on culture and gender. Finally I conclude by making a plea for a kind of debate which would take place at the boundary between subjects, of all categories and distinctions, whether human or metaphysical.

Concerning the use of Tibetan texts as sources in this work, I have made considerable use of the *The Hundred Thousand Songs of Milarepa*, a text based on the life and teachings of the eleventh-century poet and yogi Milarepa, as well as the biographical text of his life, *Tibet's Great Yogi Milarepa*, to introduce the historical view of the position of the female in the social sphere and in the religious iconography. These works, alongside the *Tibetan Book of the Dead*, represent three of the most popular texts in Tibetan literature, known not only to the priesthood but also to all practising Buddhists. Their importance cannot be underestimated, for they provided, till the present day, the means through which lay people could understand the significance of the teachings to everyday life, in the case of Milarepa, through folk tales and fantastic myths, and in the case of the *Book of the Dead*, through providing a context to death, with instruction for the dying, and teachings on rebirth and karma. The other texts which I have consulted in the original Tibetan have been largely drawn from the Karma Kagyu and Nyingma traditions.

For ease of reference, and in order to keep the terminology as simple as possible for the benefit of readers not familiar with these areas of study, I have mainly used transliterated Tibetan words, (in the Kham dialect), with the accurate spelling in brackets, but where the Sanskrit term is already in common use, I have either prioritised it or included it, using anglified spelling. In the absence of adequate terminology to express the differences between cultures, I have felt bound by the language which conceptualises 'east' and 'west', despite its problematic and inadequate nature. I recognise that until our conceptual frameworks allow language to move beyond the dualistic framing of east/west, north/south, oriental/occidental, developed/developing, present modes of expression are very limited.

PERSONAL REFLECTIONS, PERSPECTIVES AND INFLUENCES
When I began this book, it was difficult to imagine how I could manage to convey the many and varied strands of thought which have come together to form this particular cross-cultural analysis of a very specific, but I believe fundamentally intriguing, aspect of Tibetan Buddhism. Readers will certainly be able to identify the confluence of personal experience alongside cultural and academic study, and it will be apparent that I have been deeply influenced by the study of quite diverse modes of thought which have emerged from my involvement with Tibetan Buddhism, feminism and psychoanalysis respectively. What may not be so apparent, but which undoubtedly underlies these influences is the cradle of the Scottish philosophical tradition which has nurtured my own personal deliberations, and which has given me, since childhood, an education which emphasised the 'democratic intellect'[35] and egalitarianism. The weaving together of such apparently disparate streams of consciousness has been an essential component in enabling me to express some ideas concerning gender, religion and cross-cultural understanding, and I have tried to do this in the spirit of openness and exchange, in an attempt to contribute something towards the understanding between people of different genders, cultures and faiths.

There are several points I wish to make about my own position in entering this debate on Tibetan Buddhism. Firstly, my role for many years was as someone who helped the transition of Tibetan Buddhism to the west take place. I travelled to India and, after having studied the language and practised all the preliminary meditations and rituals, began working as an interpreter at a time when Tibetan lamas had just begun to travel to the west. This meant that I was present at a moment when the institutions of Tibetan Buddhism had not yet become established in the west, and the Tibetans depended to some extent on the desire of westerners to understand and be a part of their ancient traditions. As a student of Tibetan Buddhism and the Tibetan language I gained access to texts, but more importantly was able to communicate directly with the lamas, and thus moved quickly into the inner sanctum of the religious institution, and was invited to enter the realm of secret relationships with lamas. It was at this point that my involvement ceased to be purely that of the student who receives teachings in a didactic sense, given that I had to cross the boundary into an unknown world of secret religious practices and culturally different relationships. The significance of these events is explored in Chapter 7.

Secondly, I wholly agree with the comment of the psychoanalyst Harry Guntrip on the 'difficult question of the sources of theory'[36] when he states, 'it seems that our theory must be rooted in our psychopathology'.[37] For me this means that I am aware of the interesting relationship between my own personal life experience and the thesis which I have put forward. It also means that I detect in the theory, or philosophy of others, a personal strand which is often excluded by the objectivity demanded of certain modes of thinking, and which denies the relevance of the life of individuals to the societal structures, mores and belief systems which are created by them. To the extent that each individual is limited by both personal experience and the inability to reflect *absolute truth*, the work which I have undertaken here quite clearly is selective and individual. It neither claims truth nor certainty, and does not attempt to be definitive in its conclusions. Often the archaeological journey which takes individuals through the fragmented knowledge of the past can do no more than uncover shards of evidence, through which an understanding of certain aspects of the past might be created, and thus provide some insight into the present. In this book, therefore, I have tried to link the personal experiences of key individuals, both women and men, to the complex belief systems of which they were a part, in an attempt both to recognise the humanity in all of us, and as a way of understanding the meaning of female identity, not only in the Tibetan Buddhist world, but also in the western context.

Chapter 1
When Iron Birds Appear

In Tibet's own history, the movement of peoples across the high plateaux of central Asia took place for thousands of years, especially on the east–west 'silk route' to China, but also northwards towards Mongolia and Russia, and southwards towards Nepal, and that other great cradle of oriental civilisation, India. Around the seventh century the Tibetan empire began to develop, and, notably alongside the political upheavals of the time, a Tibetan alphabet was devised and Buddhism became the state religion.[1] The king credited with the most sweeping cultural developments of that time, Songtsen Gampo, had among his several wives two princesses, a Nepali and a Chinese, and the cultural and religious influences which they brought to the court ensured the further development of Buddhism. Although his expansionist policies and activities put him, according to some writers, in a league with Gengis Khan, his name has largely been mythologised by the Tibetans as a great hero, perhaps even the incarnation of a deity who took form on earth in order to clear away the 'demonic' practices of Bön and bring the true religion to Tibet. This was a time when Indian Buddhists were encouraged to bring their teachings to Tibet, and Tibetans who had travelled to India and Nepal to receive instruction in Buddhism returned to their homeland with missionary zeal, to convert the inhabitants from the indigenous Bön religion to the new faith.

The battles for secular and religious power at that time are well documented in the popular literature, and feature many tales of the subjugation of the Bön priests, whose doctrines were considered inferior to those of the new Buddhists. The biography of the eleventh-century saint Milarepa,[2] for example, contains stories which illustrate how important these confrontations were in the establishment of Buddhism as a moral as well as a spiritual code. In the end the Buddhists triumphed and it became the state religion, although the form it took quite plainly was influenced by the then indigenous traditions of Bön. What seems very clear is that the adoption of Buddhism by the people who held power (for it was a feudal society), involved a process of institutional change, and the establishment of peculiar hierarchical structures in society, whilst the predominant images of Bön's iconography and many of its teachings were retained but adapted. In Milarepa's biography one convert to Buddhism confirms this, 'Outwardly, the practice and words of Bön and Dharma appear alike, but the compassion and grace are different and so are the achievements'.[3] This meant that the imaginal aspects of Tibet's historical religious tradition, which lived in the minds of the people, could not be totally replaced, whilst the power structures could, because there was no political democracy. Buddhism was promoted as a civil code as well as a religious one, and the practices of Bön seen as primitive and inferior, incapable of supporting a great culture. That Buddhist culture survived until 1950 when the Chinese began a policy of annexation, and culminated in the 'Tibetan Uprising' of 1959, and the exodus of many refugees.

Obviously the contemporary situation which has seen the emergence of Tibetan Buddhism from its geographical isolation in the remote regions of the high plateaux of Central Asia, to urban centres in every westernised country in the world, has, on the face of it, few parallels with the gradual development of Buddhism in that country over many centuries. Yet the fact remains that to many Tibetan Buddhists, the karma, or Buddhist law of cause and effect which operated when many Tibetans were forced to flee their country and settle elsewhere, was an inevitable consequence of previous deeds come to fruition, and perhaps an expression of the Tibetan saying, attributed to Buddhism's main founder in Tibet, Padmasambhava, and often quoted, that 'when iron birds appear in the sky, the Dharma will go to the west'.[4] This kind of Buddhist perspective places the evolution of Tibet's religion in a larger context than its geographical location, viewing it as part of a greater process in which humans, at the mercy of karmic forces may be subject to political and social change throughout many lifetimes, whilst the *dharma*, unchanging in nature, becomes accessible to different beings at different times. It is also interesting to note that Buddhism itself had been a leading religion in India for a thousand years or more before it was adopted by the unified Tibet as its official religion, and that for more than a thousand years Tibetan Buddhism remained confined to Tibet and neighbouring remote countries till it was taken to other parts of the world by exiles.

The process of the development of interest by westerners in Tibetan Buddhism did not simply begin however when the Tibetans were exiled from their land in 1959. From the seventeenth century, Tibet was a country which held a remarkable interest for western travellers. Inaccessible and mysterious to outsiders, it was visited by a succession of European explorers and Christian missionaries, intent on studying the local customs and people, or in converting the natives from their so-called 'heathen' beliefs. In Victorian times, fascination with the country and its people reached a high point as the colonial observers, scholars, missionaries and soldiers recorded their journeys, providing us with many valuable records of Tibet, its religion, language and people. The obsession of western travellers for Tibet and all things Tibetan seems to have fitted very well the Victorian penchant for viewing the 'undiscovered', particularly the explorations of the so-called 'dark continents' and the wonders of science, as essentially female. Metaphors abound in the literature of the time. Knowledge was acquired by 'tearing the veil', 'penetrating' the mysteries, and 'raping' nature of her secrets. Tibet was identified with the feminine in the minds of these repressed Victorian travellers, who viewed it as an object of curiosity, and a landscape of secrets, mystery and of the unknown. It offered to them, according to Peter Bishop, 'a kind of imaginal continuity, especially at times of social and individual doubt or uncertainty'.[5]

Whilst the imaginal association of the feminine with the unknown was a common feature of the writers of the nineteenth century, the continuity factor was also significant. There is no doubt, for example, that the *actual* continuity of the Tibetan religious and political system represented a unique form of society, preserved as it was, on account of its geographical isolation, with its intricate structures of civilisation largely unchanged for more than a thousand years. For those early explorers, whose views of culture were blinkered by the arrogance of Eurocentrism, the agrarian-based, tribal communities of Africa and South America, for example, represented the 'primitive'. Tibet, on the other hand, seemed to offer the possibility of so-called primitiveness alongside a recognisable civilisation which consisted of a highly literate culture of philosophy, art and medicine. At the centre of this society were the lamas, with their priest-king the Dalai Lama, who presided over the religious and political affairs of the country, all of which were intricately related to the almost universal practice of Tibetan Buddhism. The fact that Tibet seemed to represent a very obviously patriarchal and hierarchical system of rule, alongside what was perceived by westerners to be its more 'feminine' aspect of 'purity', as a mysterious 'virgin territory', gave it an extra fascination for those western men who wrote about it.

As was soon discovered, any study of the life of the Tibetan people of necessity included the study of the religious system which had remained intact for so many centuries. Early writers took the view that, whilst the society was fairly civilised, the Buddhist religion as practised in Tibet was completely pagan, and they quite openly disdained it, whilst later writers began to analyse some of the more complex ideas contained within the ancient texts and iconography. Interestingly, it was a French woman, Alexandra David-Neel, who provided one of the first sympathetic appraisals of Tibetan Buddhism, for although her account of travel through Tibet disguised as a monk, first published in 1931, quickly went out of print in the United Kingdom, it later became popular, and gave an unusual insight by a religious convert to the life and religion of the Tibetans. It was in the 1930s also that several publications of translations of Tibetan texts were made, and these heightened interest in the meaning of the religion, particularly when Carl Jung wrote the psychological commentary to the *Tibetan Book of the Dead*, and extolled its virtues as a valuable text for westerners. He equated the initiation process associated with the book with western psychoanalysis. Jung's declaration of the value of what until then had almost universally been considered a primitive religion had significant consequences. By then the religion had been considered from both anthropological and psychological viewpoints, and other perspectives were not long in following. In the course of the next forty years, philosophical and theological interpretations were explored by men like W. Y. Evans-Wentz, Herbert Guenther, Anagarika Govinda, and even the Christian contemplative Thomas Merton. Later, when the exiled Tibetans had actually established themselves in the west, an avalanche of commentaries, translations and analyses followed. Eventually, the trend away from the orientalist approach to Tibet was tempered by the exodus of many lamas to India, giving westerners the opportunity to study the religion directly, outwith the social context of Tibet itself.

Evans-Wentz, in his introduction to the English publication of the biography of Milarepa in 1928, draws parallels between the teachings of Milarepa and Jesus Christ, and calls Milarepa 'the Socrates of Asia'. He admits that his task in bringing the work to the attention of an occidental audience was to show that Tibet, at the time of Milarepa, was probably more developed philosophically and religiously than Europe. His wish to, 'help to spread understanding of this *natural law of Universal Brotherhood*' (italics mine)[6] may have seemed at the time like a plea to end colonial attitudes towards the peoples of the empire and beyond, and for peoples of different religions to be tolerant towards one another, but it was never meant to be a proselytising piece of work. The trend to find common ground between western thought and that of Tibet remained a motivating factor, however, in many of the works of the twentieth century (both those written by westerners and by Tibetans themselves) and highlighted the desire amongst certain Buddhists, theologians, psychoanalysts and philosophers to assimilate the teachings of Tibetan Buddhism into western thought, despite the apparent differences in terms of societal structure and philosophical background.[7]

On the surface, these very differences seemed to be attractive. Jung, for example, in his fascination with the *Tibetan Book of the Dead* found it rich in symbolism and psychoanalytic meaning, in contrast with what he called, 'the dreary, half-baked literature of European and American Spiritualism'.[8] A religion which addressed subjects such as medicine, astrology, sex, and the art of dying, in its texts was one which appealed to many who were opening the doors of the 'New Age' philosophies, where the occult, mysticism, healing and world religions often became mixed in a hotchpotch of esoteric ideas. For westerners, the desire to reject the philosophical traditions which were perceived to have led to the values and norms of occidental, materialistic society was very strong, coupled with the motivation to adhere to belief systems which appeared more egalitarian, more compassionate, and more acknowledging of the whole person, mind and body, in a vast, universal context. Not only did this form of Buddhism offer a game-plan for the spiritual progress of the individual, through meditation techniques and moral practices, but it also provided texts whose metaphysical philosophies genuinely seemed to give alternative and enlightening perspectives on the nature of the human condition and in particular the relationship between men and women.

It was no wonder then, that in the 1960s and 70s, so many young and truth-seeking people turned to the Tibetans for spiritual teachings, once the exodus of so many lamas from Tibet had taken place, and they had begun to establish themselves in the west. Just at the moment when the second wave of feminism swept the western world, the New Age cults along with, in particular, Buddhism, took hold of the imagination of the young. It is within this context, that the colourful, different and exciting images of Tibetan Buddhism, together with its texts, which addressed the issues of selfhood, morality and spiritual enlightenment, were presented to westerners as a possible way forward in a dark and troubled world. For many women, the possibility of being part of a tradition which saw equality in different terms from occidental religious systems, seemed to suggest that the limiting nature of gender, as they had experienced it, was truly inconsequential.

However, the particular system which is Tibetan Buddhism has, like other patriarchal systems, a historical context, which undoubtedly has determined its position philosophically and socially, on the role and status of the female. This aspect of the religion has never been examined in much depth by either Tibetans themselves, or by western scholars. For converts to the religion, therefore, it was initially easy to ignore some of the ramifications of the lack of status given to women, and the ways in which the representations of women in many of the texts appeared less than favourable. It was also quite easy for the lamas themselves, given such a new and enthusiastic audience of potential converts, to underestimate the complexities of the motivating factors which westerners had in pursuing Tibetan Buddhism as a religion to which they could belong. Little of the societal context of the Tibetans and their religion was known, and in particular the role and place of women in the society was hidden because of the fact that the first wave of Tibetans to teach publicly in the west were all men, and many of them celibate monks.

Gradually, it became apparent that there was an absence of Tibetan women in positions of authority, and that certain elements of popular mythology and folklore contained references to women which raised questions about the Tibetan Buddhist system. But what were these initial questions, and what were the common perceptions of the role and place of women in Tibetan Buddhist society and in particular the role of women within the religious establishment? It is known that a patriarchal theocracy existed for at least nine hundred years, until the time of the Chinese annexation of 1959. It is also known that the status of women in Tibetan society was ambiguous, given that there existed a degree of sexual freedom for both men and women, and the widespread practice of polyandry alongside that of polygamy. These social norms, which are associated with the acceptance by Tibetans of matrilinear customs, survived to the present, allowing, for example, rich Tibetan women to maintain the right to carry their own family names after marriage, inherit property, and marry two or more brothers at the same time in order to keep property in one family. Sexual freedom, however, was not without its consequences, for as Indra Majupuria notes in her book, *Tibetan Women*, in the case of adultery, there is historical evidence to suggest that a woman could be legally killed by her husband, providing 'he immediately takes the dagger or sword to the magistrate with a silk scarf tied at its handle'.[9]

Majupuria, however, prefers to explain the position of women in pre-communist Tibet as being governed by their class status, rather than by the religious structures which, as I argue, operated to disadvantage women socially and politically. According to her, the general religious view was that, 'women were greatly respected and enjoyed a great deal of freedom . . . there is a great significance of Mother and the Dakini principles'.[10] Despite this assertion, however, she is unable to explain why women had no place in the hierarchical theocracy, and very few, apart from relatives of the Dalai Lama, or members of the small but powerful aristocracy, held positions of social power. Majupuria's notion is that the religious system and iconography, as somehow separate from the social and

feudal structure of Tibetan society, upheld the images of women
as exalted and equal, and thus conferred *relative* freedom on Tibetan
women. This is the very idea which Anne C. Klein ponders in
her essay about the failure of Tibetan Buddhism to translate its
'principles of egalitarianism' to the role and position of women
in society. Her conclusion is that,

> failure at any level – public or private – to emphasize personal
> appropriation of the inner religion as the starting point for social,
> symbolic, and other permutations of religious perspective is a
> major factor impeding full translation of, for example positive
> female symbolism into full social equality for women.[11]

Klein's inconclusive analysis, which upholds the view that there
are positive images of the female upon which societal equality
could be based, fails to acknowledge the other key elements in
the debate as to why Tibetan Buddhism, in exile in the western
world, is still predominantly patriarchal.[12] This is the debate into
which I have entered, by exploring the relationship between the
historical, theocratic and iconographical factors in the development
of the imagery of the female within Tibetan Buddhism.

One of the fundamental areas in which gender bias is expressed
in societies is language, and this is no exception in Tibetan.
Alongside the development of the Buddhist Tantric philosophy
in Tibet, the invention of a Tibetan alphabet and the subsequent
emergence of a written language capable of translating the most
complex of Sanskrit Buddhist texts, heralded the beginning of
Tibet's great Classical Period. The written Tibetan language, with
its alphabet of five vowels and thirty consonants,was devised in the
seventh century by the scholar Thonmi Sambhota, who returned
to Tibet after a long period of study in India. Based on the
Sanskrit alphabet, Tibetan, whose dialects are spoken from Nepal
to Mongolia, has, unlike Chinese, letters rather than characters.
According to the lexicographer Jäschke, the achievements of early
Tibetan scholars were extraordinary, for they had to 'grapple with
the infinite wealth and refinement of Sanskrit . . . save the
independence of their own tongue . . . and . . . produce translations
at once literal and faithful to the spirit of the original.'[13]

The Classical Period, also known as the Period of Translations, lasted until the sixteenth century, and during that time all

Tibetan texts consisted of either religious, historical or legendary subjects. This canon of work was added to later when cultural influences from China precipitated a study of Chinese literature. With political power held in the hands of the Buddhist clergy, whose theocratic rule lasted for well over a thousand years, it is unsurprising to note that Tibet's literature was, until the Chinese annexation of 1959, exclusively religious (even medical and astrological texts are contained within the religious canon). For this reason, it is only to these religious texts that one can turn to investigate the images of women, and use of language in relation to the female. In contrast to other cultures, where secular and religious texts can be compared to show changing attitudes, and to highlight the differences between popular culture and religious doctrine, the Tibetan model only allows for a religious perspective. Because of this, the separation of religious and secular life is impossible, and the consequent anomalies between the religious view of 'woman' and her actual societal position, made more acute.

In Tibetan texts, in addition to the divine aspect, the female also appears as human and in demonic form. The language itself illustrates her position and role, with its etymology demonstrating a clear difference in the perception of the social roles of men and women. In Tibetan there are considerably more words for 'woman' than for 'man'. Like English, the most common word for 'man', *mi* (Tibetan *mi.*), has been used in the spoken idiom and in the literature to signify both 'man' and 'person'. The literal translation of the few other words for 'man', seem value-free descriptions – *kyepapo* (Tibetan *skyes.pa.po.*), he who has birth; *kang nyimi* (Tibetan *kang.gnyis.mi.*) two-legged person; *gonag* (Tibetan *mgo.nag.*), dark-head.

In contrast, the many words for 'woman', often imply a given status and a description which places woman *in relation to man*. Chandra Das cites twenty synonyms for 'woman' in his *Tibetan–English Dictionary.*[14] The two most common words are *kyemen* (Tibetan *skye.dman*) which means 'inferior birth', and *pumo* (Tibetan *bu.mo.*) which means 'female man'. Other synonyms for 'woman' include *tsamdenma* (Tibetan *mtshams.ldan.ma.*) 'she who has limitations'; *chingchema* (Tibetan *hching.byed.ma.*) 'she who shackles'; *dodenma* (Tibetan *hdod.ldan.ma.*) 'she who has lust';

gaweshi (Tibetan *dgah.wahi.gshi.*) 'the source of pleasure'; and
tobmema (Tibetan *stobs.med.ma.*) 'she who is without semen'
(or strength). Chandra Das points out the ambiguity of the
etymology of another word, *pumeh* (Tibetan *bud.med.*), which he
acknowledges may mean 'cannot be dispensed with or forsaken'[15]
from the root *bud.*, 'to cast out', and *med.*, meaning 'not', but also
cites another meaning as 'one that cannot be left outside the house
at night'.[16] The verb, however, has other equally valid meanings
and can be read as 'to set free, to set at liberty, to allow to pass'.[17]
It is therefore possible when read in this way, that *bud.med.* could
also mean 'not set free', 'unliberated' or 'blocked'.

In Milarepa's biography, examples can be found of a range of
images of woman, from human to demonic and to divine. In
general Milarepa disparages women, their nature, appearance, and
the role they play in the life of the religious practitioner. 'Woman
is always a trouble-maker . . . the primary source of suffering',[18] he
warns (male) practitioners. Of woman's ability to attract men he
cautions, 'At first the lady is like a heavenly angel . . . middle-aged
she becomes a demon with corpse's eyes . . . at life's end she
becomes an old cow with no teeth.'[19] Of her role he is equally
scathing, 'At her best, she may serve and devote herself to others, at
her worst, she will bring mishap and disaster.'[20] In the text, women
themselves subscribe to this position, 'Because of my sinful Karma
I was given this inferior [female] body',[21] declares a young woman
when she approaches Milarepa for Buddhist teachings. In these
examples, the practitioner of Buddhism is implicitly male, the
woman implicitly 'other'. While the male strives for perfection,
the woman acts as obstacle and deterrent, or as an inferior being.

In many of the Buddhist scriptures there are numerous examples
of teachings which pair together the female and the demon as
beings which potentially cause difficulties for the 'practitioner'
on the path. Robert Paul notes the connection between these
categories, 'In general it may be said that the demons, the passions
and women are conceptually related, and thought of as opponents
of Buddhism, and of patriarchal unity.'[22] Milarepa constantly warns
of the destructive powers of women, admonishing his followers
to reject their seductive charms, and become meditative hermits.
Even a demon, who is subdued by Milarepa after she emerges from
a crack in a rock, is told that she is in an unfortunate rebirth, *not*

because of her demonic form, or because of living in a rock, but that 'Because of your evil habit propensities formed in the past, and your vicious doings in the present . . . you were born as a *lower form of woman*' (italics mine).[23] In the relatively tormented world of demons, Milarepa is at pains to point out that the female demonic status is inferior to that of the male.

Despite these clear-cut views of the female (in whatever form) as polluting and inferior, Milarepa's biography also contains quite contradictory statements concerning 'woman'. When he meets women whom he considers fit vessels for his Buddhist teaching, he confirms the Buddhist view of 'woman' as nothing more than a category, and a manifestation of dualistic thought. 'Though . . . born in a female form, which is considered to be inferior, never-theless, so far as the Ālaya [Store] Consciousness is concerned', he maintains, 'there is no discrimination between man and woman.'[24] Furthermore, he acknowledges, in accordance with the Tantric tradition, the absolute necessity of a sexual relationship with a woman to the (male) practitioner, if he is ever going to realise the highest teachings of Buddhism. 'It is said in the Supreme Tantra, [That the qualified yogi] should attract the maids of heaven. . . . It also says that of all services the best is Karma Mudra.'[25]

Elsewhere, the fourteenth-century philosopher Longchenpa states, 'Since enlightened understanding does not come without resorting to a *mudrā*, we are fettered to the triple world without such understanding' (italics original).[26] Similarly, the Indian mystic Naropa writes, 'Without Karma Mudrā, no Mahāmudrā',[27] thus confirming the concept that for the male practitioner, enlightenment is impossible without sexual relations with an actual woman, as opposed to a visualised, imaginary sexual relationship in meditation practice. All these examples demonstrate the wide range of pronouncements regarding 'woman', something which clearly is not reciprocated in relation to 'man'. It is for this reason that the idea of a special 'view' on 'woman', which occurs throughout Tibetan Buddhist philosophy, is worth scrutiny, for in the absence of gender-bias language, or an analysis of the polluting qualities of 'man' to women practitioners, or the specific declaration of 'man' as an irrelevancy in gender terms, Tibetan Buddhism quite clearly uses the language of sexist polarities, and the privileging of the male, to describe its teachings. In order to begin the process of tracing some of the deeply held views on the nature of women, and the identity of the female within the religious context, I want to examine some of the historical influences on the development of Buddhist thought in Tibet, and to uncover some of the archaic images of the maternal and of the female which still find resonance in the contemporary Tibetan view. In the next chapter, therefore, I will look for evidence of the kinds of female images which pre-dated Buddhism and which lived on in the minds of people through folklore and mythology. In order to do this, I will examine some of the early influences which came together to create the unique character of Tibetan Buddhism, including those which may have been indigenous to the high plateaux of Asia, and those which entered Tibet from other cultures.

Chapter 2
Archaic Female Images and Indigenous Culture

Although most Tibetan Buddhists would argue that the form of Buddhism practised by them is altogether comprehensive, including teachings drawn from all the major schools of Buddhist thought, it does nonetheless contain quite specific forms of practice which are not to be found in the more orthodox forms of Buddhism as taught for example in Thailand, Japan or Sri Lanka. The rationale given by Tibetans on this issue is that the Buddha revealed different levels of teachings, which he maintained would be appropriate for people of differing abilities and understanding. Tibetans believe that there are in fact 84,000 different forms of teaching, and that the teachings and methods of the *Vajrayana* represent the highest form of Buddhism, because in essence they give the means by which an individual could become enlightened in one lifetime. The classic example of a practitioner who is said to have achieved Buddhahood in one life is Milarepa, who in one of his songs proclaims, 'the Diamond Vehicle . . . abounds with skills and means; it is the easiest, fastest and most versatile Path leading towards Buddhahood'.[1]

Yet the most compelling aspects of Tibetan Tantric Buddhism, which characterise its unique form, appear to have their roots in the mixture of traditions and beliefs which pre-dated the official establishment of Buddhism as the state religion in AD763, and which owe their survival, I believe, as much to the physical landscape of the country as to anything else. The particular features to which I refer are yoga and meditational practices involving a pantheon of peaceful and wrathful deities; Tantric rites and initiations; the tulku system of reincarnate lamas; and secrecy as a major factor within the whole system. Supported by a range of religious texts and iconographical images, which are part of this complex system, Tantric Buddhism offers a variety of ideas about the role and philosophy of the female, both in terms of the place of women within its theocracy, and the esoteric meaning of female being. Just how radical, innovative or even relevant these philosophies are to contemporary women practitioners is an issue which bears close examination, particularly as these teachings are now most frequently presented outwith the social, political and cultural context in which they developed. It is only by building a picture of that historical context and by showing how it played a part in promoting certain anomalies concerning the status of the real and symbolic female, that an understanding of the mythologies and beliefs concerning female identity in Tantric Buddhism can be achieved. In order to clarify the various components which contributed to the complexity of the Tibetan religious belief, and in order to make links with the development of female identity in the philosophy, I have traced several distinctive aspects which have their roots in ancient times. These themes are categorised under the headings : (i) Early religious influences and the shamanic component, and (ii) The waning power of the Great Mother and the Threads of Tantra.

EARLY RELIGIOUS INFLUENCES AND THE SHAMANIC COMPONENT
When Buddhism was established in Tibet in the eighth century, it was recorded that the legendary Indian yogi Padmasambhava spearheaded the movement which led to the conversion of the people to a new religious form of Buddhism as taught by the Buddha himself. However, the indigenous belief system which it sought to overthrow (Bön) was by no means simply a primitive form of shamanism, as is often reported. The traditions of Bön are so strikingly similar to those of its successor that there is little doubt that Bön was a form of Buddhism, brought to Tibet, as its many texts testify, at an earlier time, through the western rather than the southern route. Textual sources refer to the areas of Zhang–Zhung (Tibetan *zhang.zhung*), which has always been associated with an area to the west, and perhaps bordering on what is now Pakistan, and Ta–Zig (Tibetan *stag.gzig,*), which is a corruption of Tajik, and the name given by Tibetans to Persia, as the significant places associated with the beginnings of the Bön religion. More specifically these names are thought to refer to Sogdiana and Bactria. Whilst it is possible that Buddhism entered western Tibet hundreds of years

before Padmasambhava's missionary efforts of the eighth century (and indeed Bön texts confirm the existence of Indian Tantric thought as well as the basic tenets of Buddhism), it is also possible that other religious influences came into Tibet around the same time, and that various strands of thought combined to produce the indigenous practices which were subsumed under the name Bön.

According to the Russian academic Kuznetzov, Bön was introduced to Tibet in the fifth century BC, when there occurred a mass migration of Iranians, from Sogdiana in north-east Iran, to the northern parts of Tibet. The theory is that they brought with them their religion, an ancient form of polytheistic Mithraism, and the Aramaic alphabet, named after Aramaiti, the Iranian Earth Goddess.[2] This is an interesting proposition, given that Buddhists have always maintained that the Tibetan alphabet was devised by Sanskrit scholars at the time of the state establishment, whereas Bön texts ascertain the existence of a written language long before this time. These texts maintain that many translations were made into different Indo-European languages, and the teachings of Bön thus spread right across the Middle East and Asia. Texts of the sixteenth-century Buddhist philosopher and scholar Taranatha refer to the founders of Bön as being of Persian origin, and name Mathura as being one of them. In Bön texts the name Mura is given. In the Tibetan biography of Shenrab, who is said said to have been the original founder of Bön, his origins are recorded as being in Iran-Elam and his name given as Mithra. Furthermore one of the epithets of Bön's founder as it appears in its Tibetan form, is Tsug Pu (Tibetan *gtsug.phud*), meaning 'the crown of the head', which approximates with the actual meaning of the word 'Mithra'.

If indeed ancient traditions of both Iran and India reached Tibet and influenced the already existent practices of shamanism which were certainly a common feature of all the peoples of Northern Asia and America in early times, then the curious combination of aspects of Indian Tantra, Buddhism and Iranian cults such as Mithraism, provide clues as to how the representations of the female developed. Certain myths appear to have common roots. The Tibetans for example, believe that their race came into being when a monkey married a goddess who emerged from a rock, whilst in Mithraic myth the Iranian Mithras was born from the Rock Mother (*Petra Genetrix*). The name of the principal Iranian

deity Ahura Mazda is to be found in Bön texts. Indeed Chandra
Das translates a phrase meaning 'the language of Ahura' (*aura trita*,
Tibetan *a.u.ra.bri.ta*) as 'the language of the demons',[3] implying
the Buddhist view of the ancient deities as 'demons'. The roots of
Mithraic belief are to be found far back in the annals of prehistory,
in the worship of the Sky Goddess Mitra, references to whom
can be found in the history of north Mesopotamia around the
fourteenth century BC, and whose predominance as the central
female deity either resulted in, or was due to, a social system
in which female identity was highly valued.[4] Her worship in
later times was connected to the Anatolian cults of the Mother
Goddess Ma, but as time went on a gender transformation seems
to have taken place, and Mitra became the male Indo-Iranian
Sun God Mithra, who according to Mithraic myth, *took as his
consort* the Anatolian Mother Goddess Ma. This phenomenon, of
gender transformation and reversal of roles, as I shall later show,
was not restricted to the Middle East, but seems to have taken place
throughout the whole sub-continent of India, and also in China
where confusion over gender transformations of popular deities still
exists to this day.

Devotion to the goddess, however, was maintained in different
forms, in both indigenous Bön and subsequent Buddhism, but
particularly important is her form as the central figure representing
female energy. In Sanskrit she is known as the *dakini*[5] whilst in
Tibetan, her name *khandro* (Tibetan *mkha.hgro.*) literally means
'sky-goer', or 'traveller in space'. Her dynamic presence is a
particular feature in the biographies of all the famous practitioners
of the Tantra, appearing as she does to help the acolyte on the
path, by clearing obstacles, challenging an intellectual approach,
and uniting in sexual union with the male practitioner in order to
provide the means whereby he can realise the highest truth. Her
further association with charnel grounds links the dakini to several
ancient goddesses whose powers over life and death are described
in the texts of many traditions. Astarte, for example, as one of the
most ancient forms of the universal great goddess, was worshipped
by the Iranians in her form as Anahita, and was characterised
by her powers of creation, preservation and destruction. One
of her epithets was 'Queen of the Stars'. Her image, found in
Sumeria around 2300 BC, is recorded by Barbara Walker as being

'identical with Kali's love-and-death sacramental posture, squatting on top of her consort's body'.[6] In the Bön pantheon she has a manifestation in one of the chief goddesses, Kaladugmo (Tibetan *mkhah.la.gdug.mo*), whose name means 'fierce sky goddess'. At the beginning of many prayers in Tibetan Buddhist texts she is invoked directly as *Ma Namkha* (Tibetan *ma. nams. mkha*), which literally means 'Mother Sky'.

As Mithraism developed, however, it became, according to Pythian-Adams, 'a system solely and entirely devoted to the needs of the Male'.[7] Barbara Walker describes it as ascetic and anti-female, 'its priesthood consisted of celibate men only . . . women were forbidden to enter Mithraic temples'.[8] A male cult developed: women were forced to worship separately, and this they did by continuing the tradition of the early Aryan religions in their worship of the Great Mother, often apart from the male tradition, but sometimes incorporated into it, as a cult. If the influences of Mithraism were indeed brought to Tibet around the fifth century BC, then it is possible that by that time its institutional and masculist tendencies were already existent, and that these factors had an impact on the beliefs and practices of the indigenous shamans. It is certainly the case that both in Bön and in its successor Tantric Buddhism, there is evidence of these two distinct features – the traditions of shamanism which were at one time almost universal, and the mytholologies of the more formal religious rituals of Mithraism. Mircea Eliade, in a work on shamanism, acknowledges these two strands as 'the still scarcely studied problem of the similarities between the Tibetan and Iranian traditions'.[9]

Many of these similarities are to be found in the belief systems concerning the religious cosmologies. The descriptions of seven, nine or sixteen heavens in Bön, is characteristic of the 'Babylonian idea of seven planetary heavens'.[10] These numbers appear again in the groupings of early Tibetan Buddhist deities, described by de Nebesky-Wojkowitz as '"brotherhoods" and "sisterhoods" comprising mostly thirteen, seven and especially nine members'.[11] Not only were the numbers seven and nine significant in the rites of Bön, but they were also the numbers most often used by shamans. Siberian shamans for example, believed in seven sisters who guarded the Earth, and who were devoted to the seven stars of ursa major. The frequently described 'seven bone ornaments' worn by yogic practitioners of Tantric Buddhism are the same as those worn by the Siberian shamans. Even the most orthodox Buddhist myths seem to reflect the preoccupation with the ancient magic qualities of the number seven. In Mithraism, the soul of man at his birth was thought to pass down a seven-gated staircase. The Buddha at his birth took seven steps. According to Mithraic belief the initiate had to climb seven rungs of a symbolic ladder, through seven planetary heavens towards perfection, whilst the Buddha was said to have passed through seven heavens on his way to enlightenment.

Central to the practice of Mithraism, (and the Gnostic tradition), was the essentiality of a 'master' to the acolyte in his quest to realise perfection. The master's role was to test the acolyte and to help him destroy the negative influences of the ego in his quest for self-knowledge. As part of his progress on the path to perfection, he would also be expected to maintain secrecy within the 'brotherhood'. These elements are equally strong in Tantric Buddhism and clear examples can be found in the many biographies of Tibetan practitioners, for whom devotion to the 'guru' was paramount, and vows of secrecy within the Vajra Brotherhood equally important for his spiritual health. In addition, several other mutual features are striking. In both traditions there is no one divine book; the mystical geometry of the mandala (in the Buddhist case) and the rotas-sator (in the Mithraic case) were highly significant in mapping cosmic reality and symbolism; and whilst the priesthood in Mithraism wore red or purple robes, the Tibetan priesthood wore dark red or maroon.

Shamanism was, of course, practised widely across the world, and there are clearly many similarities between the rituals of native North Americans, Inuit peoples, and the nomads of Siberia and Tibet. With its primary focus on initiatory rites concerning death and resurrection, numerology, the influence of the sun and moon, and a belief in the soul (Tibetan la, *bla.*) as being related to certain animals or birds, shamanism offered a view of the world in which the boundaries between death and birth could be bridged. The use of sound, particularly the beat of the drum, together with incantations of spells and rhythmic rituals involving dance and an 'altered consciousness' all survived the transition from shamanism to Buddhism in Tibet. Furthermore, ceremonies which involved cemeteries, the wearing of bone ornaments, and the ritual offering of flesh to the spirits, also survived in different forms after the advent of Buddhism. Evidence of the particular cults associated with bones, particularly the skull and the femur, is to be found in the art of Tantric Buddhism and in many of its lay and religious dance forms. In an account of the life of Padmasambhava, he is described as dancing on the roof of his house 'clad only in seven ornaments of bone'.[12]

The significance of this description lies not only in the fact that the costume is shamanistic, and not Buddhist, but also in the reference to the number seven which, as an important shamanistic number, links the missionary of the new faith with the old traditions of Tibet's indigenous religion. It is interesting to note that in the mythical accounts of Padmasambhava's subjugation of the demons of the old religion, he is described as gaining power over the twenty-eight (four times seven) *jukar* (Tibetan *rgyu.kar.*), 'the lunar mansions which are represented in the shape of twenty eight goddesses'.[13] Literally meaning 'the moving stars', the *jukar* not only symbolised the movements of the moon through its various constellations, but by association the female, and the influences of the female monthly cycle of twenty-eight days. It seems very likely, given that Astarte, as the main female deity of ancient Persia whose name appears in Bön texts, and who was thought to rule the stars, would indeed be the object of Padmasmbhava's suppressive missionary zeal.

Another fascinating feature which Mithraism and Tantric Buddhism had in common with shamanistic cults is the significance attributed to horn and bone, with their magical properties and centrality in the overall philosophy. This belief appears to have originated in the devotion to the horn, particularly that of the cow or ox. According to Marija Gimbutas, the great goddess of antiquity was both ox and moon. The horns symbolised the crescent moon, and even the shape of the skull was said to be associated with the shape of the uterus, and thus with the female menstrual cycle. At Çatal Huyuk the goddess images were 'shown in a more stylised version with the bulls' horns emerging from her womb'.[14] The ancients clearly placed the ox or the cow, and later the bull, at the centre of goddess worship, as the embodiment of

the fertility of the Earth, who in the Indus civilisation was 'related
to the horned goddess of the tree, who more than once appears
with a cow's mask, hooves and tail',[15] a belief shared with eastern
Europeans who also associated the Mother Goddess, tree and bull.
The sacred tree was of course a motif which appeared in the
myths of many religions, including the Egyptian, Judeo-Christian,
and Hindu traditions. In Tantric Buddhism, it is still the central
image in paintings depicting lineages of lamas, who are shown
superimposed upon a huge tree, surrounded by the Three Jewels
of Buddha, Dharma and Sangha, together with the dakinis and
dharma protectors.

It is therefore an astonishing *reversal* of her role and symbolism
which takes place with the advent of the Mithraic belief that the
bull had to be sacrificed in order that spiritual perfection could
take place. 'To kill the bull (the fleshly soul) is the stipulation of
the path, in order that the spirit may be restored to consciousness
by the stroke of his tail'.[16] From an object of veneration to a ritual
object of sacrifice, the bull became in Mithraism a representation
of corporeality and the lower self. The act of killing became the
means whereby the life-force was engendered, through the power
of the bull's body, to create fertility. In ancient Iran, the belief
was that once the bull was sacrificed its seed rose up to the moon
and brought fertility of the crops.[17] Plants were thought to have
come from the dead bull's body; vine from the blood; and animals
from the semen. In many astrological traditions the bull, Taurus, is
associated with springtime, and the renewal and growth of nature.

Perhaps the most telling connection between the killing of the
bull or ox and the ascendency of official Buddhism in Tibet is the
story concerning the killing of the last Bön (often described as
anti-Buddhist) king in AD842. Langdarma (Tibetan *glang.dar.ma.*),
whose name literally means 'youthful ox' (*glang.* also means the sign
of the zodiac Taurus), is the slain bull, by whose death the true
religion can become established. The symbolism, however, was not
rejected totally in the subsequent development of the heterodox
form of Buddhism which then took over, for in religious paintings,
stories and myths, the importance of the horn recurs, particularly
the yak horn because of its indigenous importance in Tibet. In
one of Milarepa's stories, the linkage of the yak horn with the
death of a 'fearful old woman'[18] is made when he miraculously

shrinks the size of his body and goes inside a yak horn in order to display his powers to his student Rechungpa. Later they meet the old woman who refuses them alms, then dies outside their tent that night. Finally they carry her corpse and bury it in a swamp, converting her soul through prayers to Buddhism.

As a symbol of fertility, the 'horn of plenty', the cornucopia, was initially associated with the white moon-cow goddess, but came to symbolise procreation. It is seen frequently as one of the offerings made before the throne of a deity in Tibetan scroll paintings. In Europe as well as Asia, the belief was that the horn emerged from the head and thus was made of the same substance as the brain, which in turn was associated with semen and life-giving forces. In Tantric Buddhism both the skull and femur are employed as ritual implements in ceremonies and in worship. In particular, the thigh bone of a 16-year-old virgin is thought to be the most auspicious bone to be used as a trumpet, *kangling*, (Tibetan *rkang.gling.*) in rituals. Coincidentally, the Greeks also held the thigh bone in high esteem, particularly its marrow, again linked with the 'seed' of being, or life-force. The Latin word *femur* has the same root as *feminus*, 'that which engenders'. In Greek, Hindu, Egyptian and Jewish ancient cultures there are legends concerning the extraordinary powers of the thigh bone, which was said to have birth-giving properties and when used as a ritual implement to have the power to bring the dead back to life.[19] The right thigh of the male was said to be 'a seat of fertility' in Hindu myth, and certain practices which involve the release of blood from the right thigh have been documented in studies of goddess worship in India.

The skull is equally important in Tantric Buddhist rituals. Not only is it carried by many deities (including the *dakini*) as a skull-cup, *topa* (Tibetan *thod.pa.*; Sanskrit *kapala*), filled with blood or *amrita* (the fluid of life), but is also filled during certain rituals with fluids which symbolise menstrual blood, semen, urine, faeces or saliva, which are then made as offerings to wrathful deities.[20] These practices can also be found in Bön rituals and are in all likelihood linked to the shamanistic practices which once were spread from the Atlantic to the Pacific. The Greeks, for example, thought that the head was sacred, and the seat of the soul. The fluid surrounding the brain, believed to be the same as semen, was considered to be the seed of life and therefore an important element to be preserved. The Greek word meaning semen or genius connects the brain fluids with procreativity. Whilst the Greeks believed that self-castration would lead to the retention of the life-force, the Tibetan Tantrics believed (and still believe) that the physical witholding of the semen in sexual intercourse would lead to long life and enlightenment. These particular practices, shrouded in secrecy in Tantric Buddhism, yet central to its yogic traditions, have a direct link to the traditions which preceded Buddhism. Having as its stated aim the liberation of the mind in one lifetime, Tibetan Tantric Buddhism skilfully mixes the philosophies of Buddhism with the Tantric yoga and shamanism of its ancient past, to achieve 'the spiritual revalorization of prehistoric customs entailing human sacrifices and the cult of skulls'.[21] Mircea Eliade suggests that the connections between skull hunts and human sacrifices in Assam and Burma have been linked to 'a matriarchal ideology that still survives in Tibet and the Himalayan regions'.[22]

THE WANING POWER OF THE GREAT MOTHER AND THE THREADS OF TANTRA

Riane Eisler supports the view that sacrificial acts associated with rituals and burials, which can be dated at their earliest as far back as the fourth millenium BC, were a phenomenon related to patriarchal rule, and not to earlier societies which, whilst sometimes categorised as 'matrilinear' or 'matriarchal', had simply at their centre the worship of the Great Mother. Her argument is that such societies were peaceful, agrarian, and life-loving, and emphasised partnership rather than dominance as a cultural norm. Given Tibet's geographical position, it is easy to see how the remnants of very ancient belief-systems which favoured matrilinear norms and the importance of the Great Mother could have survived, alongside later adaptations of these systems. Whilst not completely replacing the old traditions, the new ones, themselves influenced by the patriarchal norms of Persian cults such as Mithraism and other reformed cults which filtered through to Tibet from the western borders, were incorporated and later further reformed by the traditions of monastic, mysogynistic Buddhism.

In an insightful essay on the *sinmo* (Tibetan *srin.mo.*), the mythical Tibetan demoness who had to be subdued in order for Buddhism to become established in Tibet, Janet Gyatso proposes that the demoness's supine presence in art and in literature represents actual forces which had to be put under control in order that the patriarchal imperatives of Buddhism might prevail. Her femaleness was necessary, she argues, because the subjugation of the land as Mother Earth was inevitable, societal patterns of matrifocal and matrilinear customs had to be wiped out, and the early patriarchal view of 'that which is uncontrolled and threatening as feminine'[23] had to be established. Gyatso is convinced, 'the *Srin-mo* does not primarily represent woman, but rather a religion, or more accurately a religious culture and world view that is being dominated'.[24]

If Gyatso's thesis is true, then it is possible to argue that in addition to the religious symbols changing in Tibet in accordance with the patriarchal imperatives which placed the male Buddha as central in the iconography, then the status of women may have been gradually affected in the social sphere. This is what Gyatso implies in her study of the *sinmo*, whose mythical proportions as the evil force of primitive religion represented not only an outdated way of thinking, but quite possibly a completely different way of living. This meant that when the changes came about which were to affect a whole world view involving the male Buddha as the central image of power and enlightenment, the old deities were banished along with the implications of replacing ancient female deities with male ones. Just as the worship of the Great Mother had represented a primitive form of recognition in humanity that, in nature, the female was the originator of life because of her ability to give birth, so the recognition of the symbolic male as pure and omniscient introduced the notion of *culture*, and the male power to create it.

Before the evolution to patriarchy where a hierarchical structure of divine and earthly power was regulated, it is likely that woman's subjectivity was established through her biological functions. With the gradual ascension of the male to divinity, first as the son, then the consort, and finally in his own right, the images of the female as all-powerful faded, just as her role in religious ritual and her secular position were eventually determined by the new priesthood. That there is a connection between the gender of deities, their place in the minds of the faithful and the actual lives of the people who worship them, seems beyond doubt. In the case of the *sinmo*, upon whom the Buddha is represented as sitting, the significant factor should not necessarily be the *gender* of the sitter and the sat-upon (for in other representations one can see female or male deities standing, sitting or dancing on both male and female bodies), but *what* the vanquished actually represent. Most often that which is subdued beneath the body of the deity represents a particular defilement, or the power of the ego, or sometimes death itself. In the case of the *sinmo* however, whilst her presence may have represented a certain belief system, it is clear from what Gyatso implies that she also represented a whole world view, one which was seen as being the antithesis of Buddhism, and one which was represented by the female body. It may well be that Buddhism triumphed over the primitive world view which held the Great Mother in primary esteem, but the image also suggests that, societally, the female had to be subjugated *in order for patriarchy to survive*.

From the outset, when Buddhism was officially adopted in Tibet, it is clear that the influence of Tantra from India was already a significant part of native belief through Bön, and was crucial to the development of the kind of Buddhism which then evolved. The etymology of the word Tantra is similar in Sanskrit and Tibetan. In Sanskrit, the word means loom, or warp, but is also understood as the principle underlying everything. In Tibetan, Tantra is known as *ju* (Tibetan *rgyud.*), which means thread, string, or 'that which joins things together'.[25] Whilst there are obvious similarities between the two concepts, it is interesting to note that in very early Bön times, the Tibetans had 'only a very primitive method of recording their thoughts by means of knotted strings'.[26] These strings, as a means of communication, often formed the basis of covenants between people. Even today, knotted strings are given by lamas to their disciples as a means of protection against evil. In the old Bön traditions of spell-casting, multi-coloured threads were often made into very intricate designs, known as *doe* (Tibetan *mdos*) and, depending on their size, were either worn round the neck or placed outside dwellings as a form of protection and blessing. Two of the most common patterns used as protective devices were the sky and the tree symbols, which connect the practice to the ancient traditions of shamanism.

Evidence for the existence of Buddhist Tantras in India is dated as early as the fourth century, when the amalgamation of the ancient Hindu Tantras with Buddhist thought began to emerge. Bhattacharyya, in his study of Tantra, describes it as being comparable with the philosophy of Pythagoras. In essence, he states, the Tantric maxim is, 'That which is not of the body is not of the universe',[27] and that the matter from which the body and the universe is composed is the female principle, known in the Hindu tradition as *shakti*, or power, and in the Tibetan tradition as *yeshi* (Tibetan *ye.shes.*), or wisdom. Bhattacharyya writes, 'Wisdom, conceived as the Female Principle, and the means of its attainment through the male, are to be combined in *one's self* for the purpose of liberation which is perfect enlightenment through the practical experience of the Female Principle'. (italics mine).[28] The emphasis in Tantra on the centrality of the female principle can be traced historically to the pre-Vedic period of India, when devotional activities were focused upon the worship of the Great Mother, and women in general. In one of the early Hindu Tantras, the *Kularnava*, it is stated that, 'every woman is born in the *Kula* of the Great Mother and hence she must be regarded as an object of veneration' (italics original)[29] (*Kula* being the Sanskrit word for family, or race).

Alongside the devotional aspect, however, the practice of sexual rituals, necromancy and ritual murder were also associated with the Tantra. Although Indian Tantra is thought to be very ancient, some argue that the influences of these particular features were of another origin, perhaps entering the sub-continent from Iran, western Asia and China, at a time when ancient cults of mother goddesses and associated practices were prevalent in many places, from Greece, across Anatolia, to Syria and Persia. As I have already suggested, however, these kinds of practices were already debased forms of goddess worship, brought about by the demotion of her centrality to that of consort or mother of male deities, and the promotion of sacrificial rituals in her name. In Asia, the Great Mother cults and worship of the female may well have taken place at a time when women participated more in religious affairs and when there possibly existed a female priesthood. Miranda Shaw, in her study of early female Tantrics, agrees with this, pointing out the affirmation of the female in Tantric texts, and also the autonomy of the woman practitioner who 'chooses when and on whom to bestow her blessing'.[30]

Shaw too highlights the gynocentrism in ancient texts, which suggest that 'women do not need to take any special measures to meet the approval of men'[31] and that women were 'astute and indomitable'[32] and were not 'characterized as passive or victimized sex-objects'.[33] Shaw's main argument is that women in the Tantric tradition of ancient times were equal partners to men. Battacharyya, however, goes further by arguing that although modern Tantra is male-dominated, 'there is reason to believe that once it *belonged* to the females' (italics mine).[34] His view is that,

> The leading part played by women in religious life, their identification with the Mother Goddess, the symbolisation of various concepts and relations ascribed to women . . . the insistence on the cult of sex and the female organ as the sole seat of all happiness, the function of women as priestesses . . . the concept of the supreme being as a Female Principle, etc., must have a social basis.[35]

As far as the Tantric tradition in India was concerned, this is all the more likely because, symbolically, the Tantric non-Buddhists assigned the dynamic aspect to the female and the passive to the male, the complete reverse of the assignation made later in Tibetan Buddhism. It therefore makes more sense to theorise, as Bharati does in his work on Tantra, that in India the dynamic female was conceptualised because of a different concept of the female in society. Of the Hindus, who allocated the dynamic to the female, he writes, 'it seems probable that the matrifocal atmosphere in which they flourished (Bengal in the East, Oddiyana in the west – the latter being linked with an Amazon-like tribe in legend) was indirectly conducive to assigning the *dynamis* to woman'.[36] There is certainly some evidence even amongst tribal communities today which shows that many of the traditions associated with worship of the female generative organ, the *yoni*,[37] exist alongside matrilinear customs and matrifocal marriage.

In Tibet it appears that societal structures which were predominantly matrifocal, or matrilinear, did exist in very early times. This means that because they preceded the rule of Buddhism it is likely that ideas concerning the association of the dynamic aspect with the female may have been indigenous before the reverse symbolism emerged. The Chinese annals of the Sui and T'ang dynasties record some evidence for supporting the view that women's power in society was recognised as valid and followed a unique pattern of traditional rule. The annals record at least three 'Kingdoms (*sic*) of Women', in what was later to become known as Tibet. One of these was Nu Kuo, which was situated in the Tsung-ling mountains in the north of Tibet. The 'kingdom' had ten thousand families and produced copper. Its queen was said to live in a nine-storied house and have hundreds of female attendants, and she held joint rule with 'a little queen'.[38] Women were reported to 'hold in light esteem their husbands',[39] and on the death of a queen two women were chosen from her clan to succeed her. The Chinese records also show that every new year men or monkeys would be sacrificed, and a divination ritual performed after the sacrifice, to establish the potential for a fruitful year by examining the innards of a pheasant. The kingdom of Nu Kuo was apparently known at the Tibetan court up until AD586, three hundred years before the establishment of Tantric Buddhism as a state religion.

The second documented queendom was that of Tung Nu Kuo, situated in the east, said to be ruled entirely by women, and consisting of eighty towns with forty thousand families and an army of ten thousand. The queen, who lived in the K'ang-Yen valley, was described as wearing black or blue robes, and having a similar entourage of female attendants to that of her counterpart in the north. In the event of her death, it was noted, twenty or more people followed her to the tomb. The country was described as cold, the people grew barley and had herds of horses and sheep, and gold was mined. Rich women had male servants who painted their mistresses' faces black, a custom which lasted into the nineteenth century among certain Tibetan women. As in Nu Kuo, it was written that the women 'do not esteem highly the men'[40] who, according to custom, took their mother's name. The main task of the men was to fight when necessary and work the land, while the women held government.

Other remnants of ancient matrifocal rituals and symbolism have been found. On the north-west frontier region between Tibet and India, A.H. Francke found evidence not only of the worship of the *yoni* amongst Tibetan Buddhist peoples, but also of human and animal sacrifice associated with the burials of important leaders. On his visit to Poo, on the north-west frontier of Tibet, at the beginning of the twentieth century, he observed inscriptions of passages from the Mahayana text, the *Prajnaparamita*,[41] addressed to the *Yum Chenmo* (Tibetan for the Great Mother), on *Mani* walls.[42] He writes, 'It is not unremarkable that we should find here a prayer addressed to *the wife of Śiva*, for the festival of Shar-rgan which was distinguished by a human sacrifice, was apparently celebrated in her honour' (italics mine).[43] According to Francke, human sacrifice at this particular festival in the name of the goddess had taken place almost within living memory, and certainly up until the eighteenth century. He quotes a local Tibetan saying which implies human sacrifice in the worship of Tara, one of the manifestations of the Great Mother. 'When I (Tārā) came here from India, [I used to receive] a calf three years old and a child of eight years of age.'[44]

In this example, it is clear that an indigenous goddess named Tara is associated with human sacrifice, a Hindu god, and the Buddhist deity Prajnaparamita. It is unlikely, given the history of the region, that the Tara to which these people referred is the same deity as the Tara known to Tibetans as Dolma and normally regarded by Buddhists as the Mother of Compassion. The Tibetan Buddhist Tara is associated with Chenrezig, the god of compassion, from whom she is said to have been born. Under Buddhist rule, with its emphasis on non-violence, and its opposition to all manner of sacrifice in religious ritual, the Tibetan Buddhist Tara would not have been worshipped in this way. It is much more likely, as Bharati suggests, that the Hindu Tara was 'simply the wife of Śiva . . . an entirely different deity',[45] and one whose name was retained by custom, but whose meaning was changed with the influx of Buddhist thought. Bharati goes on,

> the name is a common epithet of all great Hindu goddesses, and we find it in the *Sahasranāma*, in the 'Invocation of the thousand Names, of Lalitā (Śiva's spouse proper), or Sarasvatī, and of Lakṣmī; neither of them bears any relation to a Tibetan or Vajrayāna Buddhist goddess'.[46]

Given her great stature within Hindu thought, it is also imaginable that she would become associated with the Yum Chenmo, or Great Mother, who was conceptualised in Tibetan Buddhism as

Prajnaparamita. The rituals and traditions of Poo therefore, reflect very clearly the ways in which deities were confused with one another, and adapted in meaning, but not necessarily in name, to fit the changing trends in the belief systems which met at certain geographical points. In one of the Indian texts, the *Sammohatantra*, it is recorded that many centres of Tantra existed across central and eastern Asia, in such countries as Persia, Medea, Iraq, Nepal and China. Although certain basic aspects of the ancient Great Mother cult can be seen to be common to all these countries, it does appear that the main features of the Indian Tantra are those which were adopted most strenuously in Tibet, to be amalgamated with not dissimilar concepts whose roots were firstly in shamanism and later in Bön. 'Buddhist tantrism has borrowed many of its lesser deities from Hinduism, or at least from the large stock of deities present in areas which nurtured Hindu, Buddhist, and aboriginal Indian mythology.'[47]

The most vital elements of the ancient Tantra were the symbolism of polarity which designates male and female with opposing, or complementary attributes; the doctrines concerning death and reincarnation; the practices of yoga, sexual ritual and symbolic sacrifice; the centrality of the guru; the symbolism of the iconography and language; the importance of the *mantra*;[48] and the essentiality of initiation and secrecy in the successful achievement of spiritual progress. However, before examining how these concepts were adapted and promoted in a new form under Tibetan monastic rule, I want to show how one of the ancient female goddesses reached a changed apotheosis in the institutionalised form of Tibetan Buddhism, and how that changed the question of an 'essential' female identity.

Chapter 3
The Lotus Deity – A Lost Goddess

At the centre of the complex system of beliefs and philosophy which is Tantric Buddhism, there exists a powerful iconography of carved images, *ku* (Tibetan *sku.*), and painted scrolls, *tangka* (Tibetan *thang.ka*).[1] These representations make up a pantheon of deities, male and female, peaceful and wrathful, who are worshipped for the specific qualities they are said to embody, and are used not only as decorative features in colourful temples and shrines, but also as objects of mental visualisation in the specific meditational practices of Tibetan Yoga. Surprisingly, images of the historical Buddha are far outnumbered in the iconography by the images of Tantric deities, including the mythical Buddhas of the five directions, who form an important part of the philosophy of the Vajrayana. The most popular deity in the whole of Tibetan Buddhism and the patron deity of the country is, however, Chenrezig (Tibetan *spyan.ras.gzigs*, Sanskrit *Avolokiteswara*), the so-called 'God of Compassion', who is said to have his earthly incarnations in the human form of successive Dalai Lamas.

Throughout the geographical area in which Tibetan Buddhism is practised, devotion to Chenrezig is manifest everywhere, through the construction of walls of stone carved with his mantra ('*Mani* walls'), and through the universal recitation of his mantra, which is undoubtedly the most significant and widely used devotional prayer in the Buddhist world. The prayer is usually printed on large drums which are spun round by devotees, as well as inside the smaller prayer wheels which Tibetans traditionally carry and keep spinning. The importance of Chenrezig, therefore, in the minds of faithful, is not only as the tangible manifestation of continuity in their social system through the power of the Dalai Lamas, but also as the *essence* of the Mahayana Buddha-Dharma and its stress on compassion. The origins and mythology surrounding Chenrezig are however, quite obscure and by no means simple. The Indian god Avolokiteswara, who is considered to be the equivalent of Chenrezig, emerged in India, according to Diana Paul, around the fifth century, and, as 'the chief assistant to the Buddha Amitābha, escorted the faithful to the Pure Land along with Amitabha's other chief assistant, the Bodhisattva Mahāsthāmaprāpta'.[2] It is Paul's contention that this deity was always male, yet De la Vallee Poussin states that Avolokiteswara was worshipped in India in female form before her introduction to China in the first century as the female Kuan-Yin. It is known that in the seventh century he appeared as the male Chenrezig in Tibet. Paul does however acknowledge the links between the Indian Avolokiteswara and the Chinese deity Kuan-Yin, who always took female form, but argues that the puzzling change in gender *from male to female*, which occurred when the deity became prominent in China, is rationalised in Mahayana literature by the advancement of the idea of the ultimate 'asexuality' of Bodhisattvas.

The asexuality ascribed to Bodhisattvas meant that gender transformation was feasible, because 'the sutras . . . claimed that all notions of sexuality, either male or female, were mental attachments contradicting the Buddha's teaching that all phenomena are Empty'.[3] As a result, representations of the denied, or hidden sexuality of the physical body, were put forward, both textually and iconographically, and in the case of the Buddha himself this was achieved by the 'concealment of the male sexual organ'.[4] Despite this symbolic representation of asexuality, which appeared to place gender as an insignificant factor in the quest for Buddhahood, transformation from female to male was still considered desirable, because even at the level of Bodhisattvahood, masculinity was the preferred state of physicality. Paul writes,

> It is only when sexuality remains a criterion for enlightenment that feminine images of Buddhahood are untenable. The enduring association of the feminine with sexuality becomes a 'double-edged sword' in images of Buddhahood. *When sex is conceived as an important factor for attaining Buddhahood, the perfect sex is always masculine.*[5] (Italics mine)

By rationalising gender transformation in these terms, the problem of what Paul calls 'the tensions between misogyny and egalitarian ideals'[6] in Buddhism were addressed, but in a way which still

perpetuated dualistic notions of gender, which ultimately privileged the male. Paul's examples show that representations of
Bodhisattvas and Buddhas either emphasise maleness, promote
asexuality, or incorporate the female into the male to produce
images of androgyny, but tend to exclude images where the
female body and sexuality stand by themselves. This missing
fourth dimension is alluded to in another of Paul's observations
on the alternative states for achieving enlightenment, when she
writes that, 'There is a specific sutra which states that a Buddha
appeared in a land of women and in a female body became
a Buddha'.[7] Despite this rare reference to an essentialist vision
of the female as complete in herself, and capable of corporeal
Buddhahood, Tantric philosophical texts tend to deny the female
as a viable 'Buddha-subject' in her own right by theorising in terms
of gender. Paul sums it up when she notes the genderisation of
concepts occuring in certain Mahayana texts,

> The male state of mind, that is, the Bodhisattva and Buddha
> state of mind, understands the teaching of Emptiness. The
> transformation from female to male symbolized the state of
> transition from ignorance to the Perfection of Wisdom which
> is Emptiness.[8]

In the Tibetan iconography, an examination of the origins of
Chenrezig as the single most important deity reveals the 'gender
problem' as a relevant factor in the evolution of their belief
system, for it is not only possible to make historical connections
with other deities of other traditions, but also to surmise the way
in which his gender is an important signifier of the changing
meaning, through time, of certain religious symbols, and their
relationship with the social reality. Unlike Diana Paul, I believe
that the male Bodhisattva Chenrezig had his origins in a female
deity, of great antiquity and universal significance, and rather than
transforming into female in China, actually retained her original
gender categorisation there, whilst transformations were taking
place in neighbouring Tibet and India. The deity which emerged
in Tibet, whilst embodying attributes of the earlier female, actually
subsumed her symbolic meaning, and did, as Diana Paul describes,
embody the three essential characteristics of a Bodhisattva, that is,
male in body, asexual in nature, and androgynous by character.

Alongside him a symbolic 'daughter' Dolma carried forward the mother symbolism, but in a less prominent position.

There seems little doubt that the promotion of Buddhist philosophies, which theorized the possibility of gender change as an attribute of Bodhisattvas, explained these confusions of gender and exchanges of roles in a philosophical rather than an historical context. Nonetheless, some commentators do recognise that certain 'autonomous'[9] deities did develop in the Buddhist cults of the fourth century. These deities, whose 'independent development outside the Buddhist tradition, (were) subsequently incorporated by Buddhist practitioners',[10] most frequently had their origins in the much older Hindu tradition. Even in China, Taoism seems to have carried forward archaic images, 'As is well known, symbols such as the Mysterious Female and Mother Earth are fundamental to Taoism, representing essential pragmatic aspects of the teaching.'[11] In the Tibetan case this process was considerably affected by its geographical position, sandwiched as it was, strategically, between several great civilisations. When the male god Chenrezig gained ascendency in the minds of the faithful, his qualities and attributes were set out in such a way as to fulfil the criteria required by the Mahayana teachings, and his status as a Bodhisattva, while replacing primitive mother goddesses, *but not the symbols associated with them*. In this way continuity would be achieved, and a new order created, but one in which the meaning of the earlier essentialist symbols of the deity would be considerably weakened for women.

The importance of these transformations cannot be underestimated, because what they represent is a shift in consciousness from a so-called 'primitive' belief in the essential be-ing,[12] sexuality and divinity of the female, in her personification as the Great Mother, to a position in which the female became not only of secondary importance, but also categorised relationally and sometimes *in symbolic opposition* to the male. This dualistic position, characterised by the goddess's existence as defined by her relationship to the male, gave rise not only to an androcentric view of philosophical matters, but also to the loss of symbolic relationship between females, and thus the loss of potential divinity through the female, *as and by herself*. As various writers have noted, this has led, in tandem with the social structure which supports such a belief system, to a problem in female transcendency. Luce Irigaray states categorically, 'there is no longer any spirit of divinity circulating between mother and daughter, between woman and woman'.[13]

The evolution of Chenrezig, however, has to be seen in the context of the symbol most closely associated with him – *the Lotus*. This universal symbol, whose images are to be found far back in the depths of antiquity, links Chenrezig with the ancient Lotus Goddess of the past. Her existence, in various forms, can be traced as far back as 2500 BC, when images of her were made during the great Mohenjo-Daro civilisation of the Indus. Joseph Campbell writes of her, 'She is a special aspect or local development of the Mother Earth of old: the great mother goddess of the Chalolithic period, who was worshipped over a wide area of the world.'[14] The Mother Goddess, whose image has been found in caves in Utter Pradesh, India, and carbon-dated to 20,000 BC, is very ancient indeed. Her later association with the lotus can be seen from lands as far afield as the Mediterranean, the Black Sea, and the valley of the Danube, replicating the features of an early Sumero-Semitic goddess of Mesopotamia and pre-Aryan times.

In Asia, the symbol of the lotus represented female sexuality, so much so that images of the lotus (Sanskrit *padma*) were understood as alluding to the vulva. Always associated with fluid, because the lotus vegetates from its own matrice without earth, it was the symbol of 'the productive powers of the waters'.[15] Indian myths describe the white lotus and white elephant as figures which arose out of the churning of a milky ocean at the beginning of time. The first elephant, known as Airavata, 'born of she who is possessed by fluid',[16] later came to symbolise fertility and abundance, as well as its association with the female. In ritual festivals in India, devotees of the Mother Goddess seeking to invoke her powers to bring the rains, and increase fertility, follow a white elephant, painted with sandalwood, and accompanied by men wearing women's dress, in order to 'do honor to the cosmic female principle, the maternal, the procreative, feeding energy of nature'.[17]

Clearly related to notions of fertility, and to the generative powers of the female, the Lotus Goddess Padma came to represent essential female being. Many of the themes of the original myth of the creation appear in the story of the conception of the historical Buddha, Gautama, in the womb of his mother, Queen Maya. In the legend, the queen prepares for a full moon festival by giving money to the poor, taking vows of self-discipline and then retiring to bed. Once asleep, she dreams of being taken to the Himalayas, the traditional abode of the ancient gods, where she is bathed in a lake by the queens of the rulers of the four directions. They then lay her on a bed inside a golden mansion, set on a silver mountain, and the Buddha-to-be enters the mansion in the form of a white elephant bearing a white lotus in its trunk, and enters her body through her right side. The next morning, when the queen tells her husband of the dream, and he summons 64 priests to make an interpretation, their first words, as though anticipating the assumption drawn from so much female symbolism, are, 'Do not be anxious, the embryo is not female, but male, and a superior being'.[18]

In India, the ascetic branches of Buddhism attempted to get rid of the ancient lotus imagery, but their zeal was unsuccessful when 'a few centuries after Buddha's time, the most prominent figure on Buddhist monuments was again Padma, openly displaying her genital lotus'.[19] Later, the actual sexual imagery of a female deity displaying her own sexuality in a unitary image would largely be replaced by the *yab-yum* images of male and female deities in sexual union, and the lotus itself given a symbolic position on Tibetan Buddhist images. In China she evolved to become the goddess Kuan-Yin, who pre-dated the emergence of the deity as male in Tibet. Diana Paul views the female Kuan-Yin as a deity who has undergone gender transformation. 'It is not at all evident how this intriguing transformation from male to female took place',[20] she writes, yet does not take account of the possibility that Kuan-Yin may have remained true to her original gender, and that the transformation was the one which took place in Tibet and India, from female to male. She argues that Kuan-Yin's origins could have been either as a combination of the ancient Taoist 'Queen Mother of the West' and the Indian Buddhist figure of Avolokiteswara; or as an extended form of Tara, his Tantric Buddhist consort. Certainly the boundaries between all these deities seem very fluid and their individual evolution may have depended upon social and geographical factors which influenced how their meaning was established in the different iconographies of different cultures. The clues to the evolutionary process which took place are, however, to be found in the similarities which emerge in the legends and myths regarding all these deities, and in particular the stories concerning all three phases of development, the ancient female, the incorporated female, and the primary male.

The Tibetan deity Dolma, for example, was linked in legend to Chenrezig. She is said to have been born from him, in a lotus flower which grew in a lake formed by one of his teardrops. As a myth, this account of the birth of a goddess demonstrates a strange reversal of roles, in which a male deity 'gives birth' to a female, through the only body fluid directly comparable with water (or the sea) – the original source of the lotus itself. In a similar way the Hindus themselves reversed their early symbolism regarding the goddess Padma, by representing the lotus as emerging from Vishnu's navel. But as Joseph Campbell has noted,

> (because) the primary reference of the lotus in India has always been the goddess Padma, 'Lotus', whose body itself is the universe, the long stem from navel to lotus should properly connote an umbilical cord through which the flow of energy would be running from the goddess to the god, mother to child, not the other way.[21]

The mythological origins of Kuan-Yin as the leading lotus deity of China has similar interesting parallels with many of the features attributed to the latter-day male god Chenrezig in Tibet. Her existence as a figure of mythology, named Miao-Shan, was said to have been in the Chow Dynasty, around 696 BC, although some records date the legend as early as the Chin T'ien epoch of 2587 BC.[22] It is said that as a young woman she wanted to become a nun against her father's wishes, and went to the monastery of White Sparrows in order to meditate. To show his displeasure at her not marrying, her father ordered that she be decapitated. The sword used to do this, however, was said to have broken into a thousand pieces when it struck her, so she was strangled, and her soul after reaching paradise re-emerged, and was transported on a lotus flower to the island of *P'oo too*. Later, when her father fell ill, he dreamt of a doctor who told him that his only cure would be to obtain medicine made from the hand and eye of a living person. The doctor was in fact his transformed daughter, who had gained powers through eating a magical peach, and she cut off her arms and plucked out an eye, in order to cure him. In gratitude, the father made a statue of her, which had one thousand arms and eyes. On confessing his evil deed in murdering her, the daughter's response was simply, 'Will you now force me to marry?'[23] Later she gained many disciples, one of whom, a fish, gifted her with a magic pearl for saving his life.

In the myth of Miao-Shan, it is clear that the daughter struggles against patriarchal imperatives in order to attempt to fulfil her own spiritual destiny, but that ultimately it is her sacrificial act of love *for the father* which carries the meaning of her altruistic compassion. In this kind of patriarchal myth, the father is the key point of reference in the daughter's choice of action, because it is *he* whom she disobeys, it is *he* who kills her, and it is to *him* that she sacrifices her body in an act of love. There is no doubt that the story would have carried quite a different meaning had her *mother* killed her and she had sacrificed her body for the sake of her mother. Instead, Miao-Shan's tale illustrates the options open to women under a patriarchal system in which she must either submit herself to the institution of marriage, or reject it openly in an act of defiance of societal norms, and thereafter suffer the punitive consequences. Furthermore, after having undergone a symbolic 'annhilation' in society through her actions, (as symbolised by her strangulation) such a woman is obliged to show her compassion for her oppressor by sacrificing her body (and thus its sexuality) in order to be rehabilitated in the eyes of man, and take up a new position in which he can worship her. Julia Kristeva has analysed this paradoxical scenario as it affects women today:

> woman is presented with a clear-cut choice: either she remains identified with the mother, thus ensuring her own exclusion from and marginality in relation to patriarchal society or, repressing the body of the mother, she identifies with the father, thus raising herself to his symbolic heights. Such an identification, however, not only deprives woman of the maternal body, *but also of her own.*[24] (Italics mine)

There are several other interesting aspects to the Miao-Shan story. To satisfy his anger the father attempts to sacrifice her by decapitation, in an act which reverses the genders of the participants of the beheadings made in the name of the great angry goddess of antiquity, Kali. Once dead, however, Miao-Shan's plucking out of an eye, and mutilation of her own body, symbolically remove two signifiers of woman's power – the fearful all-seeing eye (represented in myths by such goddesses as Medusa, or the Indian Minaksi-Kali, the 'Fish-Eyed One', or the Tibetan one-eyed goddess Ekajati), which has the power to destroy, and female beauty itself which has the power to tempt men. In many ancient cultures, the *evil eye* was identified as female, associated with Kali, and thought to be capable of looking into the souls of men. In India itself, the symbol of the *yoni* was used as an amulet to ward it off. In the myth, not only is Miao-Shan obliged to remove an eye as an offering to the father, but later she is gifted back eyes and arms by her father, as symbolic attributes which signify not the power of destruction and evil, but rather the all-seeing power of *goodness*.

In the legends of many ancient goddesses, the two features of beauty and magnetic eyes are frequently represented together, but in later myths and in the accounts even of the lives of female Christian saints, they are described as obstacles to *woman's* spiritual life, which require to be 'removed' before she can pursue her ambitions in peace. Frequently these myths describe the self-effacement of women in terms of the benefit for women themselves who, by carrying out such acts against themselves, are freed from the restraints of patriarchal imperatives to marry, and thus can follow a religious life. But the other aspect of sacrifical acts against the body is the requirement by women to undertake such gestures 'for the sake of the father', in other words for the sake of society, which, under patriarchy, obliges them to place their powers secondary to those of men, and to give up the female body and its sexuality in order to gain an equal status with men in the religious domain. These imperatives were born not only out of men's discomfort at being unable to control beautiful women who chose to follow the spiritual life rather than marry, but also out of the requirement for female sexuality to be negated *unless it was under the control of men*. The myths which emerged in the transitional period between the ancient worship of goddesses as primary, and the later worship of gods as primary (such as that of Miao-Shan), illustrate this new order under which the old attributes were reversed and redefined under religious patriarchal rule.

One last note concerning the legend is the intriguing insertions of references to the ancient deity most closely linked with female generative powers. When Miao-Shan 'comes back from the dead', she does so by eating a magical peach, which in Chinese mythology represented the female genital, whose juice was thought to be the elixir of life. The Chinese believed that there existed a magical peach garden, *situated to the west*, which was ruled over by the Great Mother. Later the story tells us that a disciple, a fish, gives her a magical pearl, a jewel always known to be sacred to the Goddess of the Sea, whose body, in Chinese myth, was the gate (the 'pearly gate') through which all passed at birth and death. 'The ancients gave all pearls the feminine connotation, saying they were made of two female powers, the moon and water'.[25] That the donor of the pearl is a fish is also related to its ancient symbolism. 'A world-wide symbol of the Great Mother was the pointed-oval of the *yoni*, known as *vesica piscis*, Vessel of the Fish. . . . The Chinese Great Mother Kwan-Yin ("Yoni of yonis") often appeared as a fish-goddess'.[26] The myth of Miao-Shan therefore confirms the importance of the maternal for women, emphasising that women's powers come from the mother, although in patriarchal societies this must be hidden, and the mother denied.

It is very evident that the story of Miao-Shan incorporates significant references to the culture of the past, while describing the requirements for harmony in a new social order. In this way, in a manner not unlike the Hesiodic myths, the Chinese myth becomes an important signifier of historical change, which carries forward in the minds of the people the memories of the past, together with the reality of the present, in a kind of universal unconscious. Miao-Shan's story reminds us of the magical quality of the time in which the relationship with the Great Mother was primary, and describes the violence which is an inevitable part of the establishment of patriarchal rule *by force*. René Girard supports this argument that all societies are based on some kind of sacrifice, whose violence is mediated by religion, but Luce Irigaray goes further in pointing out that the initial sacrifice in all structured societies relates to the mother, and thus to fertility. 'The suppression and incorporation of the maternal genealogy by the paternal genealogy leads to a non-respect of fertility'.[27] In Miao-Shan's legend there is a clear rejection of motherhood, so that she may achieve spiritual progress, a theme which is repeated in many later Buddhist stories which involve women, even those who, as mothers already, feel obliged to give up their roles in order to attain spiritual enlightenment.

Despite the antiquity of Kuan-Yin's legend in her form as Miao-Shan, many remnants of this old story have been preserved in the present-day image of the male Buddhist god, Chenrezig. She was known as 'she whose eyes see all things', and 'Great Mercy', while Chenrezig's name in Tibetan literally means 'all-seeing', and one of his epithets is 'Great Merciful one'. Miao-Shan lived on the island of *P'oo too*, while Chenrezig is said to reside in the *Po to la*, the name also given to the Lhasa palace of his alleged incarnation on earth, the Dalai Lama.[28] Miao-Shan is depicted wearing white robes, and was worshipped in her form with one thousand arms and eyes. Chenrezig is white in colour (despite the anomaly of belonging to the red Buddha family), and has a form which has a thousand arms and eyes. Miao-Shan had a magic pearl, a magic fruit, and was transported to *P'oo too* on a lotus. Chenrezig holds a pearl rosary, a lotus, and a magic round jewel in his four-armed form, and is said to have been born from a lotus flower.

In both China (Kuan-Yin) and Japan (Kannon) her name literally means 'looking at the sounds' and she has forms which carry a baby, or hold a round object said to be a fruit which represents fertility. Getty, in her study of the deity, noted that,

> The common people pray to the divinity as 'goddess of mercy' while the priests and the more educated classes worship the god as a masculine deity, for he is believed to dwell on the right hand of Amitābha . . . where no woman, without attaining merit, can enter.[29]

Amitabha, as the Buddhist deity who oversees the Pure Land of Buddhas of the West, may well have been an adaptation, in legend, of the Taoist Queen Mother of the West, re-cast as the male Buddha in an all-male Pure Land (of the Western Direction), for it is evident that, with the advent of Buddhism, many of the ancient and central deities did re-emerge as male. Evidence of this possibility comes directly from one of the Buddhist Sutras, the aptly named 'Lotus Sutra', where Amitabha is actually represented momentarily as female and as a mother figure, all the more puzzling when one considers the dogma surrounding the belief that meritorious beings are admitted to his Pure Land in male form only.

As I have already mentioned, in Tibet itself, the role of principal Mother Buddha was taken by Dolma, most commonly worshipped in her green form, but also in her white form as the consort to Chenrezig. Twenty-one (seven times three in magic numbers) forms of Dolma are acknowledged. Dolma too is marked by the signs attributed to the early legendary form of Kuan-Yin – she has eyes in the palms of her hands and soles of her feet, and holds a lotus flower. In Japan she is portrayed holding a blue lotus or a pomegranate. In her white form as Junguli, she is invoked to cure snake bites, and holds a white snake in one of her four hands. In Japan the Snake Goddess is an emanation of Sarasvati, who is worshipped as a white snake, and it is thought her worship may have originated from a sixth-century legend that there existed, to the north of China, 'a Kingdom of women who took serpents for husbands'.[30] At any rate, it is well known that the sexual energy aroused in Hindu Tantric practice through the use of a *sakti* is known as *kundalini* and represented as a serpent.

All these kinds of associations, legends and myths clearly mark the lotus deity as a primordial symbol of female sexuality and procreativity. The subsequent gender change and incorporation of the female into the male points to an evolutionary development in society which involved the suppression of female sexuality as the primary object of worship and veneration, and a move from mother worship and superstition to the more organised rationality of the law of the father. Further evidence of the change in gender of the lotus deity, and the suppression of the female is to be found in the meaning of his mantra, *Om Mani Padme Hum*. Popularly translated as 'Hail to the Jewel in the Lotus', it is frequently interpreted as alluding to Tantric sexual practices, with 'jewel' being interpreted as the phallus, and 'lotus' as the vagina. Many Tibetan scholars have disagreed with this interpretation, however.

In the first place, whilst *padma* clearly does refer to the vagina, it is not convincing that *mani* should be interpreted as 'phallus'. In some Sanskrit dictionaries *mani* does carry the meaning of 'glans penis', *but interestingly also carries the meaning of clitoris*.[31] In almost all instances of what Bharati calls Tantric 'intentional language',[32] where a metaphor for phallus is used, it is written as *vajra* in Sanskrit, in Tibetan *dorje*. *Mani*, however, literally means 'pearl', 'jewel' or 'gem' in Sanskrit. The Tibetan equivalents, *mutig* and *norbu* do not carry the connotation of phallus, but rather link the deity with its more ancient form and the legends concerning pearls and jewels. A. H. Francke, in his article on the meaning of the mantra, points out that the 'e' of *padme* is the 'vocative case of a feminine noun ending in 'a'.[33] He argues that the mantra is addressed to a female deity called *Manipadma* – 'the deity *of* the jewel-lotus' (italics mine)[34] – or the Goddess Pearl-Lotus, an epithet which could easily be applied to Kuan-Yin and the ancient forms of the female deity who pre-dated Chenrezig. Read in this way the invocation would be a powerful mantra to the essential sexuality of the female, i.e. the deity of the clitoris-vagina.

This point is further substantiated by the ancient writings of Longchenpa, who verifies that in order to address one's tutelary deity, 'You should invoke his (*sic*) name in Sanskrit prefixing it with the syllable Om and letting it end with Ah or Hum'[35] Francke however goes further and proposes that other mantras which seemingly refer to male deities use a similar vocative case and are therefore addressed to a female, e.g. those of Manjusri and Vajrapani, who are often found in triadic occurrence with Chenrezig. His suggestion for this anomaly is that the mantra may have been addressed to the deity's consort as she was regarded as more powerful, but it seems more likely that when the zealous missionaries of Indian Buddhism sought to establish their faith in Tibet, they had as their goal the obliteration of all signs which were linked in the people's minds with the 'old religion'. As part of this process, these ancient mantras were simply transferred to male deities after they had undergone their sex change. In India similar processes occurred. According to the Hindu belief, the waters of the earth are female and maternal, and the cosmic lotus which emerges from the ocean is called 'The Highest form of Earth' or 'The Goddess Moisture'.[36] It is personified in myth as the Mother Goddess through whom the absolute moves into creation. As Joseph Campbell has pointed out, the Mother Goddess of ancient India, on whom the Buddhist deity Prajnaparamita was modelled, and later shown sitting on a lotus with a lotus in her left hand, 'was removed from her Lotus and

Brahma seated in her stead'.[37] The reason for this event, he claims, was 'the arrival of the strictly patriarchal warrior-herdsmen'[38] who proceeded to install their own patriarchal gods. Whilst Campbell acknowledges the return 'to its archetypal nature'[39] of the goddess Kuan-Yin in China, he also perceives the decline and loss of the fertility aspect, and in particular the specificity of a female gender in the Tibetan representation of the lotus deity, who was then worshipped as male.

That the male deities Chenrezig, Manjusri and Vajrapani may have had original form as female deities is an interesting proposition, especially as their triadic form, still frequently seen, would have been akin to the many manifestations of the triple goddess worshipped elsewhere in the ancient world. Some commentators, however, have tried to argue that the triadic occurrence of deities is symbolically phallic and that the so-called 'femininity' of some of the qualities and aspects of male deities is due to the evolution of a male diety in whom the mother imago is *embodied*, rather than replaced. In this way, Chenrezig has been described as, 'a desexualized mother',[40] '*at worst a female*, and at best an *asexual* youth' (italics mine).[41]

These kinds of images, which appropriate and incorporate the female, together with the use of derogatory language ('at worst a female'), underline the subtleties which a contemporary Freudian interpreter of Tibetan iconography employs in order to rationalise the historical and iconographical place of the female as inferior. In Mary Daly's interpretation of the Dionysian myth, she discusses a similar example of the incorporation of the female into the male, by comparing and contrasting the ways in which Apollo and Dionysus are viewed in Greek mythology, and as modern symbols within Christian theology. Whilst Apollo is seen to represent rampant masculinity, whose influence has been supreme throughout modern history, Dionysus, like Chenrezig, embodies the mother imago, and is himself described as 'feminine' in nature. Like Chenrezig, he is born from a part of the body of a male (father) god – the thigh of Zeus, after Zeus had destroyed Semele who was carrying him. There is a suggestion that some Christian theologians now advocate the return of Dionysus as an ideal model of androgyny, in whom the female has been incorporated, but Daly warns of the dangers of women being seduced by such an image, which she suggests can ultimately lead to madness. She goes further, 'we can well be suspicious of male fascination with the all too feminine Dionysus, for his mythic presence foreshadows attempts *to eliminate women altogether*' (italics mine).[42]

In the Tibetan case, one begins to see how this process evolved, first from an incorporation of the myth of the lotus deity, her features, and even her most basic attribute, her birth-giving powers, into a male counterpart, then in the diminution of her role *as herself* to the relational role of mother or consort of the male. Other female deities, who once represented aspects of female divinity, such as wrathful destructive powers, suffered the same fate, thus ensuring that in the iconography only male subjectivity was prioritised and addressed. Male deities, such as the Buddha, retain their integrity as central subjects, and are never described as 'consorts to' a particular female deity, whilst female deities, sometimes worshipped in their own right, are nonetheless always labelled in this way. Even the iconographical images always show the male as subject, face showing, and the female consort, in sexual union with him, with her back to the viewer.

In the iconography of Tibet the image of the lotus has found its way into the representations of all deities, by forming the seat on which the Buddhas, gods, goddesses or lamas sit. As if the symbolism of this act were not enough, the lotus is employed also as an icon by which purified males are completely free from the taint of female presence. In the religious texts, to be 'lotus-born' is the equivalent of being enlightened, or having been born from purity, rather than of the world. This is the particular epithet of Padmasambhava (Tibetan *Guru Rinpoche*) who reputedly introduced Buddhism to Tibet and whose name in Sanskrit alludes to his status as having originated from a lotus (Sanskrit *padma* – lotus). This myth, in line with many myths concerning the birth of the 'hero', dissociates the male from the human mother by attributing his birth to the miraculous, outwith the sphere of the female; in this case the vagina being represented, as in ancient times, with the lotus flower. A contemporary analyst of the symbolism of the mandala, points out this very fact when he puts forward his view of the symbolism of the lotus circle which is found in representations of the Tibetan *mandala*. According to him, the lotus circle represents the purity of birth of Padmasmbhava, a reincarnation of the Buddha. Whilst the Buddha's birth is described as 'not sufficiently pure on the female side', the birth of his later Tibetan incarnation had to be 'improved upon with further developments'.[43] In other words, not only is the conception of a Buddha deemed to be a symbolic affair, but the actual passage of birth, through the medium of a real woman's body, had to be replaced within the Tibetan system by pure symbolism.

The transformation of the Lotus Goddess into a male god under the Tibetan Buddhist system, was, however, only one aspect of the diminution of her status, for it is also apparent that she became associated with a new and different manifestation of the Great Mother within the Tibetan Buddhist iconography. As Prajnaparamita (Tibetan *yum.chen.mo.*, 'great mother') some characteristics of the old goddess remain, but as Campbell has pointed out concerning this adaptation, 'The ancient pattern of the goddess Lotus . . . has undergone a radical transformation of *meaning*' (italics mine).[44] It is this change in meaning, in addition to the change in form, which determines Tibetan Buddhism as particularly patriarchal, creating, as it does, a system in which the seemingly exalted status of the female in the iconography is not replicated within society. In his observation of this phenomenon, Campbell explains the transfiguration as being from 'maternal goddess of earthly goods and happiness, of fertility and earthbound life' to 'the highest representative of world-transcending wakefulness'.[45] As grand as this may sound, it is important to realise that the transcendency which is inferred by this definition is ultimately of value only to the male, by whose definitions the goddess has come into being. Seen always from *his* perspective and always relationally, the female deity lacks the substance and the subjectivity granted to the male. Thus it transpires that in the loss of the apparent essentialism of her meaning as primordial creator and mother, the Great Mother was reduced, under a new system, to a representation which ultimately served social and political interests, and in particular the interests of the male priesthood.

Chapter 4
Monasticism and the Emergence of the Lineage of the Self-Born

The state establishment of heterodox Buddhism in Tibet ensured that the worship of ancient gods and goddesses would gradually be supplanted by a new social and iconographical hierarchy, brought into being by the all-male priesthood of lamas, who soon were to hold political as well as religious power. With the development of various sects, amongst whom both political and spiritual rivalry grew, the monastic hierarchy sought to establish itself alongside the traditions of older beliefs where the lay aspect of religious life was emphasised.[1] Monasticism, however, whilst dominant, never completely replaced these older ways, but was able to co-exist alongside secular traditions, so that in Tibetan society both lay and celibate lamas held positions of great authority. In effect, only one out of the four major schools consisted wholly of a monastic tradition of succession, and it was from this school, the Gelugpa, that the position of Dalai Lama, as the politico-spiritual leader of the Tibetans, evolved.

There is no doubt that the people of Tibet held the lamas in great esteem. Their power base was established principally on the strength of the intricate institution which developed over the centuries and which led to the virtual deification of certain high lamas and their subsequent successors. This system of succession by reincarnation, the tulku (Tibetan *sprul.ku*)[2] system, ensured a particularly unique means of accession to power by the lamas, in social, political, spiritual and esoteric aspects of Tibetan life. Its adoption by all the major schools of Buddhism in Tibet was significant in the promotion of patriarchal ideals in which male power, both secular and spiritual, was central to society. Furthermore, the central and powerful role which the lama held, not only in the social and religious structures of society, where the theocracy developed, but also in the philosophical and iconographical aspects of the religion itself, ensured that notions of male superiority were embedded in all aspects of Tibetan life.

The lama's role in Tibetan society was multifarious. In many respects his activities were akin to those of the shaman, who as an intermediary between the divine and the profane had the sole power to initiate his followers into the mysteries of the spiritual life, and also help them to pass from this life to the next. Like the shaman too, the lama was frequently called upon by his followers to dispense medicines, perform acts of exorcism and divination, recite incantations, and undertake rituals with bone instruments and sacred objects. Even the shamanistic practice of falling into trance-like states in order to commune with spirits of a different dimension, was retained by the Tibetan Buddhist state through the establishment of official 'oracles' whose role was to take possession of the spirit of a deity, and make pronouncements about the future.

Whilst oracles were thought to have the ability to commune with deities, some lamas were deemed to *be* those deities, and were worshipped as their embodiments on earth. Not only could a lama be a shaman, healer, teacher and holder of spiritual power (Tibetan *dbang.*), which would only be transmitted through religious initiation, but he could also be the donor of divine and spiritual grace. This was certainly the case with the heads of the major schools, who were variously seen to be incarnations of such deities as Avolokiteswara, Padmasambhava, or Manjusri, in addition of course to being incarnations (tulkus), or even 'aspects' of previous famous lamas.

The title 'lama' (Tibetan *bla.ma.*) is only given to those who fall heir to it through reincarnation, or who merit it through many years of study or meditation practice. It has always been equated, however, with the Sanskrit term *guru*, whose esoteric importance in Tantra is emphasised in all the texts. Whilst textual references may infer that the esoteric meaning of the guru is more complex than simply the adoration of one man, some commentators, although keen to underline the synonymity of the word *guru* with *lama*, fail to look further. 'It is unfortunate that both the Tibetan term *bla-ma* and the Sanskrit word *guru* have been horribly misused, be it out of ignorance or self-aggrandisement . . . The word *bla-ma* stands for the Sanskrit word *guru* which has two meanings of 'weighty' (heavy) and 'light' (ethereal). As there is an abundance of capabilities there is weightiness, and as there is no limitation by evil there is lightness. This meaning also applies to primordial pristine cognitiveness'.[3] Whilst this writer may be intrigued by the etymology of the Sanskrit word *guru*, and at pains to make much of its deep meaning, he seems particulary reticent about exploring that of 'lama'. With its definitively feminine ending, its etymology is unambiguous. The syllable 'la' (Tibetan *bla.*) means superior, and it can also mean soul or life; while the syllable 'ma' (Tibetan *ma.*) is conclusively the word for mother, and as an ending denotes the female in many words. Several Tibetans lamas have confirmed to me that the 'ma' in lama refers to the mother, and that the explanation for this title is that the lama is viewed as the highest form of motherhood. In Chandra Das's *Tibetan–English Dictionary* there is an acknowledgement of the literal translation of the word lama as 'soul mother', or 'the all-sustaining mother of the universe.'[4] He also quotes a Tibetan saying, 'previous to the lama, even the name of the Buddha did not exist.'[5]

This saying could have an historical as well as a symbolic meaning. At its most mundane level, it may mean that the lama (i.e. the male priest) came into existence concomitantly with the advent of state Buddhism. On the other hand, given its ambiguity, it may mean that, prior to the worship of the Great Mother, language and patriarchal religion did not exist. Given also the overwhelming evidence which points to the establishment of patriarchal rule in the ancient world some time during the Bronze Age,[6] and the worship of the Great Mother which preceded that rule as far back as the palaeolithic period at least, then it does seem possible that prior to her worship patriarchal language associated with the process of 'naming' did not exist, and certainly there would have been no concept of a supreme male deity. On a final level of symbolic interpretation, the saying bears close resemblence to the psychoanalytic theory which proposes that any human's relationship to the maternal is primary, and precedes entry into the symbolic order where language and the 'word of the father'[7] come into existence. In accordance with the Tibetan proclivity for threefold or sometimes even fourfold explanations of 'outer', 'inner' and 'secret' meanings, this saying can be read in different ways.

In the *Tibetan–English Dictionary*, Das also points out that Tibetan scholars themselves have alluded to pre-Buddhist Hindu influences in the etymology of the word, which strangely has a female suffix. It certainly seems doubtful that the word 'lama' was coined after the state introduction of Buddhism in the eighth century, when there already existed a patriarchal lineage of royal succession. If the word was ever meant to refer to the male priesthood it would surely have been *lapa*, using the male ending *pa*. My conclusion, therefore, is that the word was in use in Tibet before the introduction of the hierarchical theocracy of 'lamas', and referred possibly to the female Tantric priests of ancient India, or to the shamanistic practitioners who worshipped the Great Mother in pre-Buddhist times. This unusual carry-over of usage of a female term for the established male priesthood provides further evidence of the significance of the female at a different time in Tibet's history.

The priesthood, established firmly by the thirteenth century, by which time the unique incarnation system of succession had taken hold, formed the basis of the feudal social system, which governed Tibet for over seven hundred years. With the decline of the pagan societies whose traditions, as I have shown, often featured women as powerful figures, and whose marriage customs incorporated both polygamy and polyandry, the Buddhist system, or 'Lamaism', created a very different form of rule. In her article 'Primordial purity and everyday life', Anne C. Klein ponders on the reasons why women did not have equal status with men in Tibetan society and in the Tibetan Buddhist institution. Citing examples of women's situation at home, at work, in education, in religious life, and the position of the female within the iconographic symbolism, Klein concludes that 'Tibetan society, especially where political or economic power accrued, was intricately hierarchical'[8] and 'wherever hierarchical structures were emphasized, as they were in Tibet's monastic order and theocratic political system . . . women were excluded from power'.[9]

Klein's argument, however, is that there *do* exist within the iconography images of the female (particularly those which depict the association of the female with primordial purity, or emptiness), which predetermine the potentiality for female social liberation. However, as I shall show, the interdependence of the secular and religious spheres in Tibetan Buddhist society, together with

the strong historical influences of shamanism, Bön and Tantra,
combined to create a religion and iconography in which the images
of the female were ambiguous to say the least, and not necessarily
positive, given the *change in meaning* which arose when the old
views of the natural world were replaced with the sophistication
of the hierarchical system of Buddhism which developed. The
interrelationship between the secular and the religious structures
of Tibetan society and the central position of Buddhism as the
arbiter of culture, is clearly one of the aspects of Tibetan civilisation
which sets it apart from many other cultures. It is difficult to find,
for example, much evidence of a secular tradition in art, music
or literature, given that the thread of Buddhist mythology runs
through everything.

The tulku system, however, is by far the most powerful aspect
of the way in which Tibetan Buddhism evolved. Despite being
a patriarchal system of rule it nonetheless incorporated several
female 'tokens' by which it vindicated itself from charges of
exclusivity. Established by the followers of Dusum Khyenpa, the
first Karmapa Lama, at the beginning of the thirteenth century, it
was soon adopted by all the other sects and spread throughout the
Tibetan Buddhist world, to countries such as Mongolia, Bhutan
and Nepal. The system ensured that Buddhist lamas who died were
'reincarnated' in male children, who were then taken as young boys
(tulkus) and enthroned as the head of the monastery which they
were said to have previously ruled. The system was supported by
the Buddhist belief in reincarnation, which postulates that there
are six realms of existence[10] and within these realms any sentient
being (i.e. a being with a mind) may be reborn after death. The
place of birth is dependent on the actions or karma, (Tibetan *lay,
las.*) of the individual during his or her lifetime. Buddhism views
liberation from the cycle of death and rebirth as the goal of the
practitioner, the ultimate state being called nirvana. However of
all the realms, the human realm is seen as being the best, because
it is believed that it is only in the human condition that one
can achieve Buddhahood and liberation from the wheel of life,
or samsara. In addition, the Tibetans believe that the acquisition
of a 'precious human body' also entails not being born with a
disability of the senses, and not being born into 'primitive tribes
to which no religion has appeared'.[11]

It is not surprising therefore, that Tibetan peasants quite readily accepted the tulku theory, as it was applied to Tibet. The theory proposed that the lama, (or guru) who inevitably headed their community, and whose power was manifested in his considerable knowledge, wealth and prestige, was, if not an incarnation of the Buddha himself, then at least a spiritually advanced being, perhaps a Bodhisattva[12] who would have the wisdom and means to choose his next rebirth through his miraculous powers of meditation. Equally unsurprising would be the fact that he would choose to be reborn amongst them, rather than as any other human being in any other country, or as any other being in any other realm.[13] Given Tibet's isolation, and isolationism, few other alternatives could have been thought possible. The powers bestowed on such a male child 'discovered' in this way were therefore quite unique, and his elevation to the status of 'divine' immediate.

As an alternative to local kingships, the Tibetan tulku system allowed for the transference of local power on the death of the lama of a monastery to a child, usually unrelated by blood, and more than often under the age of five. By the seventeenth century the system was adopted to establish wide-ranging temporal power in the form of the Dalai Lamas who, as heads of the so-called Yellow Hat Sect, the Gelugpas, manoeuvered themselves into a position of political power through negotiations with the more powerful sovereigns of China and Mongolia. One Tibetan has described the system as combining, 'popular democracy with metaphysical monarchy'.[14] Whilst it is deeply inaccurate to suppose that the power to choose new incarnations lay anywhere outside a small élite of lamas who previously were close to the deceased, and could never therefore be classed as democratic, the idea of a metaphysical monarchy is one which bears closer examination. Indeed, one commentator who has theorised on the nature of the Tibetan system, Robert A. Paul, sees a parallel between the ancient idea of 'the divine king' and the Tibetan tulku system which, in his view, represents a contemporary version of it. He maintains that 'political and sacred authority are always accompanied by Oedipal symbolism',[15] and sees the Tibetan system as simply another manifestation of the universal law which says that men must rule, and that to do so they must compete with other men over their access to, or control over, women. Using both the historical argument which compares Tibetan traditions with those of other cultures, and the psychoanalytic argument which examines the underlying motivations which influence how patriarchal institutions and societies are organised, it is easy to see how such a phallocentric view could be upheld. There are certainly some of the features of the divine king myth present in the Tibetan system. For example, in the legends of many cultures the divine king is represented as an archetypal figure who, in a variety of guises, is seen as sacred, and as the embodiment of continuity, structure and value in society – qualities which require to be maintained despite the inevitability of his death. This facet is to be found in the tulku system.

Furthermore, the association of certain features of the traditions surrounding Mother Goddess worship, with a male succession to power, strongly suggests that the tulku system could simply be an adaptation of the divine king legends. In the Celtic European practices of the 'divine victim', the king, as the god incarnate and consort to the queen, was worshipped for a set period of time, then sacrificed and replaced by a younger man. This practice later evolved into the sacrificing of animals or symbolic objects at certain times of the year, so that the king himself would not die. In the Tibetan system, whilst the dying lama is not sacrificed, the requirement that there be continuity of his spirit, which is determined by esoteric rituals which predict the whereabouts of his soul after death, ensure that the 'king' does not truly 'die'. Similarly it is known that 'human sacrifice . . . is everywhere characteristic of the worship of the goddess',[16] and as I have already shown there is certain evidence for both sacrifice (both human and animal) and goddess worship in the history of Tibet and its early empire. Other aspects of these ancient practices seem to have their parallels in Tibetan mythology. For example, in the early Bronze Age mythology of ritual regicide, 'the king was identified with the dying and resurrected moon',[17] whilst in Near Eastern civilisation 'The leading concept was of a goddess of an eon mathematically marked by the passages of seven spheres, and the king, ritually slain, was the incarnate god, her ever-living, ever-dying spouse.'[18]

The number seven, as I have shown earlier, was often viewed as magical, was associated with the phases of the moon, and appears frequently in these kinds of mythologies, both in the Bön and Buddhist traditions. It is recorded for instance that, in ancient times, a white horse and seven sheep were sacrificed every year in the seventh moon, at Karma Tang, at the source of the Yellow River in Tibet. The universal king of Tibetan Buddhist mythology is said to have had seven jewelled companions. Most interesting of all are the references, by several Tibetan scholars, to the fact that in 'prehistoric' Tibet the seven mythical kings of the Yar-Lung thrones had a sacrificial death when their sons reached thirteen years of age. If this is indeed true then it is easy to see how the idea of the ever-living 'divine king', with whose mythology the Tibetans were already familiar, could be adapted, under the new system of Buddhism, to accommodate the monastic order of lamas and their wish to rule.

The question of whether or not the whole notion of male power and divinity, which has its roots in such myths as these, can be said to have both universal and timeless qualities is, however, much more controversial. Not only that, but the significance of the proposition that male power and divinity are related to universal norms which dictate that men establish (and have always established) their societal position *vis-à-vis* their particular relationship with their fathers, and thus the so-called Oedipal struggle, has a direct bearing on how women fit into that view of the world, and how indeed the female is represented within that system of thought. By analysing in more depth the historical roots of the Tibetan system, which still appears to promote 'divine kingship', I aim to show the evolutionary quality of the marginalisation and degeneration of the importance of the female within the system. In addition, I argue that there are no such things as universal and timeless categories which place the male as subject, and female as object, but rather that philosophical thought concerning such matters depends on, or is closely related to, ever-changing social structures for their development and promotion.

As I have shown clearly, many of the rituals and practices which are widely acknowledged as being historically associated with matrifocal societies did indeed exist in Tibet (some even into modern times), and it is therefore inaccurate to conclude that the system of patriarchy which now exists arose from universal and historical constants in the lives of men. This is not to say that the traditions which preceded the patriarchal sytem of rule by lamas (Lamaism) were superior *per se*, but rather to view the development of the system within a much wider historical context, which helps to elucidate the paradoxically ever-changing continuum. Failure to acknowledge the existence of the very powerful traditions relating to the Great Mother, and their subsequent adaptation under different social and cultural conditions, produces a one-sided view of reality, a view in which notions of dualism are simply strengthened by privileging the male over the female. It is entirely possible that the Tibetan religious system, now freed from the geographical constraints of an isolated Tibet, will yet undergo further changes to accommodate both western philosophy and the presence of women in a different societal context.

If the tulku system retains aspects of the divine king myth, which may have grown out a very different cultural context, it does not, however, ascribe the same value to the female as once must have existed when the Mother Goddess reigned supreme. As has been noted, the Tibetan tulku system, which contains spiritual and secular power within the hands of the lamas, has its roots in religious ritual and initiation which passes, 'from "senior male" to "junior male" disciples, and which results in a lineage or descent system.'[19] The system itself, as an invention of the patriarchs, is crucial to the maintenance of the whole religious and social system, which 'carries patriliny a step beyond, by negating the need for sexual reproduction altogether, thus *excluding the need for females* in the system' (italics mine).[20]

In ancient times, in most societies, royal or sacred lineage was determined through kinship and sexual reproduction, but in the Tibetan case the lineage was created solely by the oral transmission of the Buddhist teachings, within which the tulku system played a central role. The tulku, according to Paul, on being recognised as the incarnation of a deceased lama, 'is raised to "Divine King" status, in much the same way as the mythological kings of old, that is, he is perceived as having, thereafter, no bonds in common with other mortals such as kinship, exchange or alliance. He has no royal house, and no need for marriage or children, as *he is his own successor*' (italics original).[21] Unlike other sacred lineages, therefore, there was no 'queen' because most incarnate lamas were celibate monks, and the mother of the child was excluded from the system despite her role in being responsible for bearing the boy child and surrendering him to the system. Her exclusion was not only from power, but also, theoretically, represented an absence within the entire system itself which, though barely acknowledging its need for a female body, could not include her as a potential lineage holder.

The metaphorical denial of the mother, and her sexuality, is a key factor in the maintenance of the system. 'Skeptics may object', Paul states, 'that even a reincarnate lama is, after all, born of a woman. . . . But symbolism can only reduce or conceal, not eliminate, the real paradoxes of existence.'[22] This ambiguous remark, which itself reduces or conceals the actual role which women played in the maintenence of the tulku system, appears to support the exclusion of women from religious or secular power, by promoting the symbolism which facilitates male power within the system as universal, and perhaps itself irreducible. If one views the tulku system, however, as a symbolic enactment of Freud's Oedipal struggle, there are certain elements of that theory which would have to be applicable to its actual structure, so that one could logically conclude that the resolved elements of the struggle can be seen in the complex institution which manifests itself throughout Tibetan Buddhist societies. In the cultural context of historical Tibet, one may surmise that men re-enacted the myths by which senior males must be killed by junior males and yet survive, and vice versa. Through the unique form of succession devised by the Tibetans, this is not only achieved symbolically, but their patrilineal lineage is also ensured *asexually* without the (apparent) use of women. Paul writes,

> The reincarnate lama, then, represents the living proof of the legitimacy of the monk's claim to the possibility of asexual reproduction, *the eternal dream of the male sex.* He represents immortality not of the species, but of the individual . . . the assertion of their ability to create a self- sufficient male world and thus obviate the need for the divisive presence of women. (Italics mine)[23]

Placing the Tibetan monk's fantasies of reproduction and the creation of a homo-erotic world exclusively populated by men as the rationale for the existence of the Tibetan tulku system, Paul clearly demonstrates his use of Freudian theory not only as a theory of individuals, but also as a theory of societies and cultures.

His view is that the perpetuation of the system, which relies on structures which are manifest on the cultural and religious levels within Tibetan Buddhist societies, depends also on psychological factors in individual men.

But what of the notion of a so-called 'universal constant' which proposes that in all societies, at all times, a struggle takes place between younger and older males for power and authority, and *sexual access to women*? This struggle is seen as achieving a symbolic resolution in situations where junior males must kill senior males, and vice versa, yet both must somehow survive. From the male Freudian perspective, this resolution, so vital for *their* well-being and subjectivity, is no more than 'the *phylogenetic* basis of human social organisation in general'.[24] Furthermore, as Paul maintains, 'The individual Oedipus Complex is merely the minimal unit in the nuclear family, of a complex which actually has its roots in the *cybernetic control* of the social system as a whole' (italics mine).[25]

The choice of words used in describing the power ascribed to the complex as experienced by men is interesting. Phylogeny, which is the history of evolution, has its roots in the Greek *phylo*, meaning race, and *genesis* meaning origin. By proposing that the male complex is the phylogenetic basis of everything, the implication is that the male experience is paramount. It alone can be claimed as the ultimate source of all things, and therefore as embodying unquestionable authority. The male Oedipus complex becomes the determining factor in the evolution of all races, implying the universal and evolutionary nature of male power. This power, which crosses all racial boundaries, has as its common bond the struggles between males over their sexual access to women, and the conflict between males for sacred and political authority.

Cybernetic, on the other hand, from the Greek *kubernetes*, meaning a steersman or pilot, describes the manner in which this complex is viewed as *controlling* everything, in a robotic and machine-like way. The view, in this respect, differs widely from, for example, the view put forward by the author of the Gaia Theory,[26] who clearly sees cybernetics as a process of *interaction*, rather than control, in which circular arguments are favoured over linear and mechanical concepts of cause and effect. Although some theorists may like to think of male supremacy as a matter of *automatic* control, the developing view of reality shifts the emphasis from a dominator model to one of co-operation. This view, however, presupposes acknowledgement of the *other* as a complete entity in her own right, something which has not yet been possible under what has been seen as universal patriarchy. The view therefore that the Tibetan system is merely another form of the Oedipal struggle in which men always enact their psychological battles in order to gain power and control over women, whilst convincing in its argument, may not necessarily be accurate when described as a universal constant, either in terms of time or of location. In particular this theory fails to recognise the compliance of women within the system, or their own deeply felt experiences which are equivalent to the male experience of the father–son relationship.

By linking the Tibetan system to the divine kingship myths, and to the Freudian notion of the male psychic struggle for being, one can see quite clearly from Paul's work that patriarchal dominance, as described by men themselves, depends both on historical factors of political power in society, together with individual psychodynamic struggles which pertain to the male view of the world as the male child develops within those male-dominated social structures. Paul is quite right to say that the system engineered by the lamas fulfilled a certain idealised male fantasy in which the masculine element is prioritised, and in which a kind of immortality is granted through social institutions. Of much more relevence to women, however, is the fact that this elaborate system may *owe its very existence* to the complicated devices by which it both makes use of, and excludes or denies, the female.

Through centuries of change in which patriarchal thought has refined its expressions of superiority, the female voice, experience and perspective of 'being' has either been silenced, repressed, overlooked or co-opted in the creation of particular social and philosophical systems. As Luce Irigaray has stated, 'the greatest fault committed by the race of men was to deprive one gender of its ethical consciousness and of its effectiveness as a gender'.[27] In Tibetan Buddhism the exclusion of the female *as the subject of being* is no less remarkable than in any other patriarchal system, but given the wide-ranging philosophy and iconography which purports otherwise, it is important to explore and attempt to understand the mechanisms by which this suppression has taken place.

I have already shown that the manifestations of female identity, as they were reflected in the ancient Tantric texts of India, were not subsequently sustained under the patriarchal lineage system of the Tibetans, where women had no equality within the priesthood. I have argued that the nature of the tulku system, which elevated the male to a central position in the society, was the cause of weakening that archaic position. However, in order to examine the implications of the particular kind of phallocentrism which developed in the Tibetan social, religious and cultural system, it is essential to look in closer detail at the impact of these extraordinary social structures on the individuals who played out their parts within them.

Chapter 5
'Free of the Womb's Impurities' – Divine Birth and the Absent Mother

The very real human drama which took place when a boy child was 'recognised' as being the incarnation of a dead lama, and subsequently taken into the all-male environment of the monastery, is frequently overlooked or given low prominence in the accounts of the lives of lamas. One can only surmise the extent of the pain and the sense of loss which was engendered in these boys when they had to leave their mothers, and enter the world of celibate men, often at tender ages when their own sense of being and relationship was still developing. For the tiny child who was to become the Dalai Lama, found in 1937, before he was three years old, the devastating change in circumstance can scarcely be imagined. The Italian explorer Fosco Maraini described it most graphically:

> From the day of his installation in the Potala an entirely new life begins for this child selected by fortune. Instead of the humble country cottage, the kitchen, the farmyard, the fields and the flowers, the games with little friends of the same age, he now occupies a whole suite in the vast complex of palaces, temples, mausoleums, dungeons, halls, passages, libraries and kitchens of which the Potala consists. His parents are given a suite in which to live, and his father is honoured with the title of *kung*, or duke, but after the first few months both he and the child's mother see less and less of their offspring. The new Dalai Lama, like every other monk, must die completely out of civil life; even his name is changed.[1]

Maraini also refers to the strict rigours of the young Dalai Lama's education as 'a very severe process' in which 'every detail is rigidly prescribed'.[2] Furthermore the penitences, the compulsory attendence at religious ceremonies which lasted for many hours, and the monastic discipline of the community over which he presided, demanded great patience and fortitude on behalf of the young boy. The claustrophobic environment was, 'in short, a whole court with a very rigid and elaborate etiquette, *from which women are completely excluded*' (italics mine).[3]

Of this experience the Dalai Lama comments in his autobiography, 'There now began a somewhat unhappy period of my life. My parents did not stay long and soon I was alone amongst these new and unfamiliar surroundings'.[4] In an account of the 6th Dalai Lama's 'recognition' and removal to the monastery at the early age of two years and eight months, it has been written that, 'Nine years later the mother still bitterly recalled the anguish she felt at this sudden separation.'[5] How much more so for the stricken child? This kind of experience was replicated to a similar degree in many monastic communities in Tibet, where the excessive discipline on young tulkus, already suffering from deprivation of familial relationships and catapulted into the asceticism of monastic life, must have taken its toll on the psychological development of these young boys. Whilst the 14th Dalai Lama himself has memories of being 'terrified',[6] at three years old, of his physically violent uncle, other young monks whom I have known, of lesser status but of equally tender years, were threatened with having their penises cut off if they continued to bedwet, in the harsh conditions of the dormitory.

There were few compensations for such children forced to endure the hardships of this most unusual childhood. Furthermore these hardships did not just pertain, as I have mentioned, to the upbringing of tulkus, but also to the countless young boys who were given by their families at a young age to the monastery. Some estimates suggest that one in three of all male Tibetans were monks, many of whom began their lives in the monastery under the age of seven. Often their only comfort was to be found in relationships which they could form within the confines of their forever-supervised environment. An older monk, such as the one whom the Dalai Lama describes in his memoirs, would sometimes offer physical comfort to the small boy, thus creating an opportunity for closeness. In other cases, and especially with the onset of adolescence, the boys found comfort in one another, very often in order to find an expression for their developing sexuality.

Later in life, in some instances, secret relationships with women were instigated, and these were either of a mundane nature, or incorporated into the spiritual and meditational rituals of the Tantra, which stipulated the use of sexual activity as an essential component of the religious life of advanced practitioners.

The lack of physical intimacy in childhood was not, however, the only facet of the tulku's life which distinguished him from others. Brought up in an atmosphere of adulation, where his position inspired nothing short of awe in others, he was never in a position to define himself in human terms, or strike up his own identity, given that he already carried the name, spirit and responsibilities of a dead, divine lama. In the claustrophobic environment where every small gesture and word was often thought to be 'meaningful', because wisdom and divinity were believed to lie behind them, the child was taught quickly to suppress his own needs and take up the mantle of 'lama', whose role was to become the 'Great Mother' to others. Having been, to all extents and purposes, abandoned by his own mother, this was an ironic position to take up; however, if one considers the degree of 'difference' which such a child must have felt, then an identitifcation with the female, already defined as 'different' in male eyes and ideologies, was not wholly inappropriate. That 'difference' was manifested in the unique environment created around the tulku.

The experience of the very young tulku was characterised by his position as the centre of attention, surrounded by hundreds and sometimes thousands of followers who would prostrate before him, receive blessings by his hand, and never communicate in an ordinary way with him. These actions must have added greatly to the experience of isolation which the child developed, and which had been already established by the sudden detachment from his mother and from women in general. This, together with the monastic attitude to women as being either polluted or dangerous to the monk's essential celibacy, must certainly have bred in the young boy at best an apprehension or fear of women, and at worst a hatred of them. In their theological world too, the monks learned to develop a philosophy of the female, which was graphically portrayed, as I shall show later, both in the language and through the texts and iconography. This philosophy fulfilled the dual function necessary to the monastic male practitioner – on the one hand the denegration of the female as inferior, and polluting, and on the other the idealisation and transcendentalisation of her in order to make use of her imagery in his religious practice.

To begin the complex task of unravelling the psycho-philo-sophical approach to the female, I want to start with the position of the divine son's mother, who as the only woman whose intimacy with the child was predetermined, was of central importance in the development of the ideology concerning the female. The early texts of Bön already describe certain attributes of the mother of divine lamas, which are to be found in later Buddhist texts. For example, in a text concerning the previous lives of Shenrab, the founder of Bön, and the equivalent to the Bönpos of Shakyamuni Buddha, he is described as having once been born in heaven to a goddess, and fathered by a cuckoo. The mother herself proclaims, '*O son born of a virgin woman, You are a shoot grown without a seed being sown*' (italics original).[7] The theme of the virgin mother as significant in the birth of heroes or divinities is not, of course, confined to oriental religions, and is likely to have achieved its near-universal status through the ancient belief of the parthenogenetic powers of the Great Mother. As Marija Gimbutas has written, 'The parthenogenetic Goddess has been the most persistent feature in the archeological record of the ancient world'.[8] Later, when the concept of fatherhood became part of the social consciousness, this motif seems to have been replaced with that of the 'divine' father, often portrayed in religious stories as a mythical animal or bird, and sometimes as the godhead himself.

As far as the mythologies of Buddhism were concerned, the precedent for the absent mother of divine male children was firmly established by the legends concerning Gautama Buddha's mother, Queen Maya, and indeed the mothers of all previous Buddhas. In order to maintain complete purity, it seemed essential that the mother of an enlightened-one-to-be was chosen not only for her good *karma*, but also because she would only have one week to live after his birth. This ensured that the vehicle of his entry into the world could not herself be further contaminated in any way by sexual contact. The mythology of this legend has been retained by the Tibetans whose lay people frequently allude to it as evidence for claiming the particular holiness of a lama whose mother has died following his birth. Nonetheless the mother's humanity is often emphasised and juxtaposed against the divinity of her son. Regarding Queen Maya, 'This mother may have been of noble birth but she was otherwise a normal mortal woman'.[9]

In the literature pertaining to the birth of tulkus, references are usually made, however, to the *pre*-natal experiences of the mother, particularly the conception of the child, and his activities whilst still in the womb. Unusual dreams or occurrences are documented as evidence of the forthcoming child's spiritual powers. A common theme is that the mother dreams of being entered by a deity or mystical animal during pregnancy, signifying the child as being the product not of human sexual union, but of divine beings. Often he has the power of language on birth and can quickly define himself and his allegiance to the sacred male lineage.

> During her pregnancy his mother dreamed that Guru Padmasambhava came towards her and entered into her. There were many auspicious omens. When the baby was born he took one step in each of the four directions, sat cross-legged in the centre and said 'Om Mani Padme Hum Hri! I pity the sufferings of humanity, for I am the Karmapa!'[10]

The child's super-human qualities are also emphasised through the documentation of his state of difference in relation to his parents, who frequently have humble origins, but are religiously devout.

> When he was born he sat cross-legged, wiped his face and said, 'I am the Karmapa!' He remained sitting in that position for three days and his father was so overawed that he started prostrating before him. At this the child stood up, said 'Om-Ah-Hum!', and started to laugh. His mother untied her apron strings and tried to wrap up the child in it, but he threw it off saying 'Oh No No!' Then he was wrapped up in a sheepskin which he accepted.[11]

In these extraordinary accounts of the births of two children destined to become, at different historical moments, the head of the Karma Kagyu sect, it is possible to discern the different elements which make up the key aspects of the tulku system. The child must have divine origins. He needs to be super-precocious. He needs to demonstrate power and knowledge, and he must reject the secular and particularly that of the female and enter the world of male exclusivity, in order to prove his divinity.

Following the death of a tulku-lama, the reincarnate successor to him would be chosen, usually from a selection of candidates, by an élite body of men in whose hands lay the power and responsibility of choice. The visions and dreams of different mothers, and the omens surrounding their claims might well be considered, but in the end the ability to 'recognise' the divine child was in the hands of men. In this way a rebirth controlled by and within the paternal lineage was ensured. With the usual mundane needs and wishes of the mother obliterated in a system where divinity preceded human relationships, the male lineage was able take over the maternal role and relegate the mother to the background. Unlike Christianity, where the mother's divinity was recognised alongside that of the son, in the Tibetan Buddhist tradition only the tulku was divine, whilst the mother was a useful vessel for his apparently self-chosen rebirth.

As an integral part of the system, the texts required to confirm the divinity of the tulkus not only through the written statements made by lamas before their own deaths, but also through the dreams and omens of the mother of the new incarnation. Most frequently, as I have shown, she dreamt of a divine being, creature or symbolic object entering her body at the moment of conception. In the numerous accounts of such miraculous births, however, there appear to be no instances in which the mother dreamt of *herself* as divine. Even in the autobiographical account of the birth of Yeshe Tsogyal, the female consort of the founder of Tibetan Buddhism, her mother dreams of a golden bee which 'vanished into her husband's fontanelle'.[12] After the birth, Yeshe Tsogyal reminds us that as a baby her first words were to praise her future husband, and that her body 'was free of the womb's impurities'.[13] This kind of language, whilst reflecting the contrast between the 'divine' child and the 'worldly' mother, appears frequently in philosophical texts. For example, the Mahayana Uttara Tantra on the 'Changeless Continuity of the True Nature', describes Buddha nature in a series of metaphors concerning perfection situated within polluted images. Buddha nature is 'a king . . . a future ruler of men in the womb of an unfortunate, ugly woman', and its emergence, the 'birth of the royal child' who escapes the 'impurities of the womb'.[14] With the metaphor of enlightenment encoded in this way in gendered terms, the female body represents the imperfect or dangerous containment of the (male) Buddha nature, along with other polluted metaphors such as the 'decaying lotus', 'the bee-swarm, the husk, the filth, the ground, the fruitskin, the tattered rags . . . and the clay mould'.[15]

In Yeshe Tsogyal's case, the non-divine nature of her mother is also emphasised by her observation that the first food offered by her mother to her is 'coarse', and that she eats it only to 'complete my mother's happiness'.[16] These kinds of images hardly portray the female gender as significant, or as sacred in its own right, despite the fact that the text itself clearly views Yeshe Tsogyal's life as important and *her* status as divine. In Tibetan literature, little is written of the role of the mother after the birth of the child, apart from her compliance in giving him up to the monastery and distancing herself from him physically and emotionally. Trungpa Tulku, one of the first Tibetan lamas to settle and teach in the west, after the Chinese annexation of 1959, gives some clues as to the process which took place for him. In his autobiography Trungpa states that his mother left him when he was five years old. Initially, after his enthronement, she visited him every day, but Trungpa writes, 'her visits became more spaced out, until after a fortnight without seeing her, she came to tell me that she was going back to Dekyil; *I missed her as only a small boy can*' (italics mine).[17] As to the status and image of the mothers of *tulku*s he alludes only fleetingly in one of his many books to his own relationship with his mother, and how it affected him. He recalls that his mother was shy, and as a child he had once asked her about his family name, 'Then I remember asking her whether I was her son who came out of her body . . . . . . "Well", she replied, "maybe I'm an inhuman being, a subhuman being. I have a woman's body; I had an inferior birth."'[18] Trungpa writes of this exchange, 'We had an intense moment of relationship with one another.'[19] He also adds, '*I learned a great deal about the principles of human society from the wisdom of my mother*' (italics mine).[20]

Forced into the all-male society of the monastery at such a young age, perhaps it is not surprising that Trungpa did recall this particular exchange, out of all possible exchanges with his mother, for it seems to encapsulate everything which the tulku system represents. That his mother's pathetic statement about herself should be associated in Trungpa's mind with wisdom, underlines his own conditioning into a system in which men can achieve the status of divine, whilst women are viewed as inferior vessels. Furthermore that Trungpa should also associate this event with his understanding of 'the principles of human society' is highly significant, given that it does indeed essentialise the elements of the Tibetan patriarchal system, the only 'human society' of which he was aware. One can only imagine the heart-breaking sorrow of a child such as this, subjected suddenly to the rigours of the monastic life and a new identity, and betrayed by the terrible rejection which he experienced at the hands of his mother. Is it any wonder that, once grown, these men would have little difficulty in promoting the ambiguous teachings concerning the female? Is it unsurprising that future relationships with women might be characterised by a disdainful distancing, or by the desire to become involved in secret relationships which carried no responsibilities, were completely in the control of the lama, and which were conducted in such a way as to enable the lama to maintain his position within the all-male hierarchy?

One only has to read Trungpa's evocative poem, 'Nameless Child', to begin to understand how easy it would be, for someone with his childhood experiences, to elevate to the realms of the spiritual and divine, the phenomenon of so-called 'self-birth'. Given his unique circumstances, perhaps only a spiritual context could be sufficient to explain what it meant to be a tulku.

> Suddenly, a luminous child without a name comes into being. . . . In the place where metal birds croak the instantaneously born child can find no name. . . . Because *he has no father*, the child has no family line. He has never tasted milk because *he has no mother*. He has no one to play with because *he has no brother or sister*. Having no house to live in, he has no crib. Since *he has no nanny*, he has never cried. There is no civilization, so he has no toys. . . . Since there is no point of reference, *he has never found a self*. (Italics mine)[21]

This poem, which expresses the sentiments of the so-called 'self-born' child, comes very close to an articulation of the literal meaning of the word tulku (Tibetan *sprul.sku*), which is 'illusory body'. There seems no doubt, given the present understanding of child development, that the tulku system was indeed apposite in its organisational format, for it provided the conditions in which a child could grow up feeling abandoned by family, cut off from the 'real' world, and perhaps even 'illusory'. Denied at a very young age the usual social contacts which establish a sense of self in the mundane world, the young boy with his new identity would have had to suppress his 'old self', relegating it to the realms of the insignificant. In Trungpa's case, his original identity later became a source of fascination, as well as some confusion, as illustrated by his conversation about it with his mother, and the fact that he obviously stored this memory, only to recollect it later and introduce it into his writings as one of great significance. Living in the kind of ambiguous position which the tulku system created would certainly have given him an unusual perspective on the world. Whilst relinquishing one identity in order to take on that of a dead person, the young boy must have felt neither one nor the other. From this unique position one can understand how he could come to view with equanimity the inconsistencies and dualities which characterise reality. The alternative would surely have been despair. As Trungpa says of his 'nameless child', 'The child's world has no beginning or end. To him colors are neither beautiful nor ugly. He has no preconceived notion of birth and death. . . . The child exists without preconceptions.'[22] In the language of the Madhyamika school of Buddhist thought, these sentiments have meaning, and can easily be accommodated, whilst in the language of psychoanalysis they describe a time, before entry into language, when his body and that of the mother were experienced as indistinguishable. It would be to this time that the growing tulku would yearn in later life – a deeply embedded memory of relationship with the mother from whom he was forcibly separated.

For believers, naturally, the rationalisation of the events surrounding 'recognition' meant that the child was viewed as divine and therefore had no reliance on ordinary human relationships. Belief that the tulku lived outwith the bounds of conditioned existence meant that he was not subject to the emotional responses and limited vision of the ordinary being. From a psychoanalytic perspective, however, the trauma which surrounded the early lives of these boys, albeit with societal support, can only be seen as of great importance to the development of their sense of self, and to the nature of the relationships into which they subsequently entered.[23] It seems not without significance that, as grown men, both the Dalai Lama and Chogyam Trungpa spoke of the loss of their mothers as though the events had human rather than spiritual meaning. In Trungpa's case, as a severe alcoholic in later life, and as someone who lived on the edge of danger in his personal relationships and actions (as has been documented), his behaviour could easily have been interpreted during his lifetime, by believers, as typical of the 'mad yogi' tradition.[24] Those viewing his life from a humane perspective would surely connect his early traumas with his later actions.

The tulku system relied on the body of the mother, not as a participant in the power structures, but as a subsidiary element to the process. Understandably, the mother's collusion in both ascertaining divine events during conception and pregnancy, and her co-operation in giving up her son, were crucial to the maintenance of the whole system. In order to partake of the *kudos* surrounding his recognition, and gain some kind of sense of identity *vis-à-vis* the lineage system, mothers of tulkus invariably endorsed their child's sanctity by making statements about divine visions, omens and signs associated with the birth. Immersed as they were in the rich and dramatic culture of their society, it is not unsurprising that they, like any other humans of a particular culture, would dream and fantasise in the signs and symbols which that culture had evolved as an expression of its psycho-social organisation.

However, through the use of the mother as 'a mere receptacle',[25] and her subsequent exclusion, the Tibetan system promoted a patrilineal ideology which in essence privileged the son over the mother. Not only that, but the implication that a lama was actually 'self-born'[26] by virtue of his miraculous powers, and could control the means and manner of his own rebirth, established a belief in the male lineage of succession as one which simply *made use* of the female, rather than *depended* on her. This deception, in turn, reduced the value of the female in the system, and attributed to the patriarchal system an ability for a symbolic male motherhood, through enlightened males who could choose the time and place of their birth. As one commentator has noted, 'The aim of a rebirth from the father is to undo or overcome the mortality implicit in the female, phenomenal world and achieve a timelessness or unchanging absolute quality, associated with maleness.'[27]

This statement is interesting because it clearly spells out that, for men, the disassociation from the female is motivated by a desire to overcome the profane, and the worldly, already defined in many texts as akin to the female. This is why Tsogyal, herself female, also rejects the womb as 'impure' and views her mother as profane in her act of giving food, because to do otherwise would be to go outwith the bounds of the sacred, and thus the position of the male lineage, and the imperatives of society itself. While profane motherhood had to be scorned, symbolic male reproductivity in the form of the tulku lineage became the cornerstone of the conceptualisation of the sacred *as* masculine. It is my belief that this deeply unconscious mechanism did indeed arise through the psychopathologies of the men involved, so that the distancing of women and the metaphorical process of 'male motherhood' which the monastics embraced, came to replace female intimacy as an institutional structure. As Mary Daly argues, the disassociation of the female from the male is in fact the very substance of *all* patriarchal myths and religions, which derive their meaning through symbols which elevate the male and exclude the female. Fatherhood, or 'male motherhood', she maintains, takes on immense significance in the maintenance of the whole system, and is central therefore to the myths, religions and social structures of all patriarchal societies. Seen in this way, the mother of the divine lama-king becomes synonymous with other mythical mothers, such as Semele, the mother of Dionysus, whom Mary Daly describes as 'epitomizing the *patriarchal ideal* of mother as mere vessel' (italics mine).[28]

The mystical association of the redundant mother and the divine son is revealed in yet another form in the account of the life story of Tibet's most famous ascetics, and eleventh-century member of the Kagyu lineage, Milarepa. His autobiography tells of his search for truth, beginning with his leaving home to study under different lamas. Eventually Milarepa returns to his village after many years to find that his mother has died in the mean time. Overcome with grief he visits his old home and finds a heap of bones which he intuitively recognises as those of his mother. Gathering them up, he makes a cushion of them, on which he sits in order to meditate, and after seven days reaches the realisation that all worldly life is meaningless. The anguish he experiences over his mother's death finally gives him the determination to renounce everything for the sake of the spiritual life. His recollection of these events move him to write later, 'Henceforth, the world had nothing to tempt me or to bind me to it.'[29]

The imagery projected by such words and deeds strongly suggests that it is through the ossification of the life energy of the mother imago that the son progresses spiritually. In other words, it is only when the female is rendered lifeless, as an absent force, that the conditions are right for the male to overcome his fear of mortality. When the mother dies the son is free to become enlightened, when she is absented through the power of the lineage, his path is cleared for the monastic, spiritual life. Either way, the tulku's relationship with the paternal becomes prioritised. When Milarepa becomes the 'spiritual son' of Marpa, through the transmission of Buddhist teachings and the endurance of terrible hardships which are only given meaning in the context of their relationship, the lineage of lamas is continued, and maleness, associated with asexual reproduction, becomes the means through which this is achieved. Even Trungpa Tulku, in his poem 'Letter to Marpa', cannot help but convey the idea of male motherhood and its importance,

> solid Marpa
> our father
> . . . .
> we sympathize with you for your son's death
> . . . .
> yet you produced more sons
> eagle-like Milarepa, who dwells in the rocks
> snow-lion-like Gampopa, whose lair is in the Gampo hills
> elephant-like Karmapas, who majestically care for their young
> tiger-like Chögyam roaming in foreign jungles
> as your lineage says, 'the grandchildren are more accomplished
> than the parents'
> your garuda-egg hatches, as the contagious energy of mahamudra
> conquers the world.[30]

Here Trungpa names the various members of the Kagyu lineage, including himself, depicting them as offspring, miraculously born, like the garuda, 'the celestial hawk of Indian mythology which hatches from its egg fully developed'.[31] The theme of the 'self-born', complete son, whose existence is owed to the father-line alone, is emphasised by these words. No expression of the significance of the lineage would be complete, however, without reference to that crucial other aspect of its success – the absence of the female. Trungpa makes one reference to Damema, the wife of Marpa, and the woman responsible for supporting both Marpa and Milarepa in their quests for enlightenment. Adulating Marpa for his earthy qualities, he describes his person as being characterised by his 'stout body sun-burnt face *ordering* Damema to serve beer for a break' (italics mine).[32] Having defined the place of the female in Marpa's life in terms of man as master, woman as servant, the elucidation of 'the message of the lineage'[33] is complete.

The story of Milarepa and his relationship with Marpa is only one of a host of such tales in which the ideal of a perfect identification with the master provides the key to enlightenment. Complete identification, achieved through meditation, permits the 'son' to be born of the 'father', without a female presence, thereby replicating the cloning process. This represents a 'perfect identity between the prototype and the copy, which is impossible in sexual reproduction'.[34] This kind of practice ensures that the tulku system is beneficial to the male psyche, not only because it offers an outlet from the base, physical world of sex and reproduction with real women, but it also satisfies men's desires for creativity by providing a model by which symbolic cloning may take place. In addition, the phenomenon of perfect identification with the 'master', as the key to the symbolic transmission of teachings between 'father' and 'son', is something which women could not achieve. Robert Paul calls it 'the right to reproduction through the transmission of a symbolically encoded teaching.'[35]

It is interesting that Luce Irigaray in her work, *Sexes and Genealogies*, should identify this process so clearly when she writes,

> when the father refuses to allow the mother her power of giving birth and seeks to be the sole creator . . . he superimposes upon our ancient world of flesh and blood a universe of language and symbols that has no roots in the flesh and *drills a hole through the*

female womb and through the place of female identity. A stake, an axis
is thus driven into the earth in order to mark out the boundaries
of the sacred space in many patriarchal traditions. It defines
a meeting place for men that is based upon an immolation.
Women will in the end be allowed to enter that space, provided
they do so as *nonparticipants*. (Italics mine)[36]

This is precisely what I maintain takes place within the Tibetan
tulku system, with power over the birth process in the hands
of men, the negation of the mother as the prerequisite for
male sanctity, and the inclusion of women in the system as
non-participants.

Tsultrim Allione in her book, *Women of Wisdom*, addresses the
issue of female sanctity within the Tibetan system through her
examination of the lives of some female yogis. She implies that
their biographies are important to women because they contain
certain elements of difference from the stories of men.

The differences between individuals must be appreciated and
even celebrated . . . In order for women to find viable paths
to liberation, we need the inspiration of other women who
have succeeded in remaining true to their own energies *without
becoming fixated on their sexual gender* and have, with this integrity,
reached complete liberation. (Italics mine)[37]

Allione agrees that *difference* is central to the process of finding
a female genealogy, but seems less convinced that it should be
expressed in sexual terms. The kinds of differences she articulates
as relevant to women are concerned with events such as the
restrictions of marriage on women, childbearing, wife-beating, and
depression over family life, all closely related to the issue of woman
as mother, and mother as woman. Given that the male genealogy
depends on the male *fixation* on its own sexuality, it is difficult to
see how women could do otherwise than become *fixated* on theirs.
What may be implied by Allione's assertion is that women are less
likely to be fixated on *gender* than men, and therefore may more
easily attain success in practice. If *difference* is to be fully expressed in
women's stories, it has to include three specific factors – women's
right to subjectivity, by and for herself; the establishment of real
female genealogies; and the essentialism of a female divinity. The

denial of this right to women, whether whole or partial, has been fundamental in the maintenance of the tulku ideology, even up to the present day, when boys of western origin are being selected to inherit the thrones of deceased Tibetan lamas. There is no doubt that as long as women are contained within the confines of the staked-out sacred space, as paradoxically *absent* presences, whose differences are subsumed by the dictates of patriarchal imperatives, then their unique contribution to human civilisation will go unheard or ignored, with the direst of consequences.

Allione is right to identify motherhood as a crucial ground in the battle for female subjectivity, for it is the *imaginary and symbolic relationship* to the mother which is very often denied in patriarchal societies, not least in the Tibetan tulku system. In the biographies of women practitioners, one would certainly expect the different facets of women's mundane lives to emerge as significant in the way in which women achieve a sense of autonomy in their spiritual lives. This is illustrated by the various stories which describe the struggles pertaining to marriage and childcare. Keith Dowman, in his commentary on female energy, is keen to point out that difference in this sphere is indeed significant, and as a man he is quick to overplay the power this gives women. Talking of Yeshe Tsogyal's life he states

> The status of women in the society into which Tsogyel was born, practically, could be said to be one of equality with men. *True it was a patriarchal society*, but besides *the basic power that resides in woman as mother and mistress*, a power that unmarried feminists invariably underestimate in their evaluation of the status of woman, in every sphere of human activity women were active. (Italics mine)[38]

The power which Dowman so elequently pleads to be recognised, however, is the very one which is denied by the lineage system, and one which every patriarchal society conspires to hide, through fear of the maternal imago. Perhaps Dowman could not bring himself to consider that it is not the work of 'unmarried feminists' which devalues motherhood or dismisses the role of the 'mistress', but rather the evolution of the suppression of the female by *all* participants in patriarchal societies, and their institutions, which privilege the rule of men. Luce Irigaray argues that the lack of recognition of the power of the female is linked to the denial of her participation in the 'sacred space'. 'Forbidden to celebrate ritual or to participate in social institutions, women are reduced to the polemics and rules of the private sphere.'[39] This means that it is precisely the hidden nature of the mother (Tibetan *yum*) and the lover (Tibetan *gsangs.yum*)[40] which is the foundation of the tulku system, something which, far from being chosen, is imposed upon women, as a means to incorporate them into the sacred space on the terms laid down by men.

Chapter 6
At One with the Secret Other

Alongside the absent mother, whose gender-specific role of giving birth and mothering became symbolically usurped by the system, there existed also in the sacred space the secret consort or *songyum*, whose female sexuality was essential for those lamas wishing to practise Tantric sex secretly. Whilst the word *songyum* is an honorific title meaning 'wife' which is applied to the actual wives of those lamas belonging to the lay tradition, it is also used to mean the 'sexual partner', and means literally in Tibetan, 'secret mother'. The fact that in the Tibetan language the words for 'wife' and 'mother' are synonymous, is not, as I hope to prove, insignificant. The purpose of the secret *songyum* was, in the context of the monastic establishment, to provide for male practitioners the opportunities for sexual activity, without the disruption of the structures of the system. So while a lama would, to all intents and purposes, be viewed publicly as a celibate monk, in reality he was frequently sexually active, but his activities were highly secret. Even highly prestigious lamas of the status of the fourteenth-century scholar, Longchenpa, resorted to this method. 'Outwardly wearing the habit, but inwardly a yogin of the Mantrayāna, he took that nun as his secret consort so that nobody knew about it'.[1] These actions were only achieved, however, with the collusion of the women involved, and also of those monks who were particularly close to the tulku or lama, and who would protect him so that his activities would not be subject to public disclosure.

This shroud of secrecy extended also into the literature where most references to actual women in biographical accounts of lamas' lives were omitted, or given metaphorical status. Even in contemporary works by Tibetans or their followers, the *songyum* is often described as the visualised deity of the monk's imagination, the female consort to a male deity, whose presence had to be conjured in order for the meditator to realise certain insights pertaining to the symbolic union of so-called *opposites*, the male and female. However, this aspect of the practice was only part of the whole story, for in the actual social world of the monastery, the lama often acquired the secret services of a real woman in order, allegedly, to achieve these insights. In my own experience, as the *songyum* of a tulku-lama of the monastic Kagyu order, Kalu Rinpoche, only one other person had knowledge of the relationship, which lasted for several years, and which took place within the strictest bounds of secrecy. When the biography of this high lama was written it included periods of time during which I acted as his *songyum*, yet there was no mention whatsoever of my name in the text, or even references to a metaphorical 'consort'.

The Tibetan system was to all intents and purposes a 'secret society', as confirmed by the synonym for its religion, *Songwa Dorje Tegpa* (Tibetan *gsang.wa.rdo.rje.theg.pa.*), which means the Secret Vajrayana, or Secret Diamond Vehicle. There is no doubt that secrecy played a large part in the religious practices of Tibetan Buddhism, and that this secrecy extended not only to the requirement that only initiates could attend certain rituals, but also to the fact that certain activities took place which even other initiates did not know about. That these activities concentrated on sexual acts is hardly surprising, because the institution, with its outward appearance of monasticism, could hardly have survived in the form it did, had the importance of the woman's position and status *within it* been openly acknowledged. The two elements which I believe helped to sustain the secret society of Tibetan Buddhism were the downgrading of the mother to a 'receptacle' for holy tulkus ; and the hidden status of the *songyum* in the monastic system which made use of her. As Mircea Eliade observes in a study of secret societies, whilst they always 'emphasize the sexual element' they also 'constitute an attempt by men to establish life independent of women, a rejection of feminine power and influence'.[2]

Miranda Shaw, in her book *Passionate Enlightenment*, sets out to rationalise historically the status and the role of women within Tantra, by providing examples from ancient texts, many more than a thousand years old, in which details are given about Tantric women teachers, and the emphasis on the importance of viewing the female as an equal partner in sexual rituals. Shaw points out at the beginning that the secrets of the Tantric tradition in which she was most interested, i.e. the sexual aspect, 'are counted among its most esoteric and closely guarded features',[3] yet she describes them in great detail in her book. This is done in order to support her case that the women involved in Tantra, a thousand years ago at least, had equal status with the men, and were at least as responsible as the men for the propagation and continuation of the tradition. She believes that her research counteracts the work of many other commentators who have 'attempt(ed) to project a mood of male domination onto this movement'.[4] Shaw further criticises 'Western scholarship and feminism for their emphasis upon domination and exploitation'[5] in their reading of the Tantric tradition, suggesting instead that culturally they could not appreciate the 'highly nuanced balances of interdependence and autonomy that can characterize gender relations in other societies'.[6]

Certainly there is much to be said for her observations, because it is apparent that the importance of the female within this tradition in ancient times implies a very different cultural ambience, in which it is possible that the relationships between the sexes were not the same as they are now, either in the west *or the east*. One can only conclude that the female prominence has either been suppressed throughout the last five hundred years or more, in the Tibetan tradition at least, or that there has been a degeneration of the teachings in general, which has resulted in women losing touch with their own powers and knowledge as Tantric lineage-holders. In her own search for a teacher who would transmit the details of the practices to her, and help with the translation of the texts, Shaw names the lama who agreed to co-operate with her, but fails to name any woman who could substantiate the teachings from a practice viewpoint, despite saying that 'it is necessary to obtain access to an oral commentarial tradition that is secreted in the minds and hearts of living masters (both male and *female*)' (italics mine).[7] Clearly it begs the question, in the absence of actual commentaries by live women on their practices with actual men within the tradition, where are the living female masters of the Tantra in the Tibetan tradition, and if they exist, why must the woman's position, name and commentary be kept secret? It is obvious from Shaw's work, and the work of many others, that the actual details of the so-called 'secret' practices are in fact known and have been published many times. If, therefore, the secrecy is not in the details of the acts themselves, where is it? My contention is that the secrecy is in the 'hidden' subjectivity of the female, either as a participant in the acts, or as a symbolic figure whose mystical presence, though necessary for the continuation of the lineage, was gradually eased out of the picture, so that live women would not be seen to accede openly in the human form to the status of 'Buddha'. Shaw herself puts forward this same view in a way which implies the *necessity* of the woman's hidden nature, as if a kind of *essential* female nature was to be found in her suppressed or hidden status.

> The women of Tantric Buddhism and their divine counterparts are often called *ḍākinīs*, translatable as women who dance in space, or women who revel in the freedom of emptiness. As their name suggests these are not ladies who leave a heavily beaten path. At times their trail disappears into thin air where they took flight on their enlightenment adventures, but sometimes the trail resumes in the dense underbrush of ancient texts, amidst the tangled vines of Tibetan lineage histories . . . *The traces of women of Tantric Buddhism are sometimes obscure, enigmatic, even hidden and disguised*, but they are accessible to anyone who discovers where to look for them. (Italics mine)[8]

However, it is not just the organisational context of the system which is of relevance in the diminishment of the prominent role and purpose of women's spiritual lives. The power of that particular system lay in the hands of men who themselves had often been traumatised by unfortunate childhood experiences which separated them from their families, and in particular their mothers. Obliged as they were to be later locked into their role as monks or tulkus, with very little freedom of will until adulthood, the effect of their removal at an early age from the maternal environment into the harsh reality of the masculine world of discipline in the monastery must have produced conditions wherein many of them may have harboured secret longings for their mothers and for the intimacy of the female world. Even in Lacan's account of the socialisation of any young child, he believes that, 'With the entry of the named subject into language and the social order, the unnamed, repressed desires of the subject are driven underground'.[9] The kinds of yearnings which these young boys must have felt would have been doubly taboo in the environment of the monastery, especially where the monks of a lower status than the tulku dealt with their passions by viewing women as inferior and unclean. Despite this, there is some anecdotal evidence to suggest that often secret meetings and liaisons with their mothers or sisters took place during childhood and adolescence, with the knowledge of only the closest disciples.

These kinds of experiences, in which feelings for women were habitually channelled underground in an openly masculine environment, meant that the tulku became accustomed to associating women with secrecy, and later, when opportunites for sexual liaisons arose, whether in the context of Tantric practices, or quite simply as an expression of their own longings, they already perceived this kind of liaison as a norm. It is interesting that Irigaray categorises all patriarchal cultures in this way, by pointing out that 'Such traditions as these do not encourage love between women and men. Lovers fall back into a mother–son relationship, and the man secretly continues to feed off the woman who is still fertile earth for him'.[10]

From the patriarchal point of view, however, it is easy to see why this degree of secrecy developed, and why men colluded, in the name of the lineage and its power, to protect one another. But what of the women involved? In the absence of a female lineage of knowledge about Tantra and woman's role in it, and the difficulty of gaining access to texts which the monastic institutions often guarded jealously, how was their loyalty bought and what was in it for them, to bind them to the secrecy of a sexual relationship with a man of power? Was it simply profound faith in the lama-as-Buddha which helped them remain silent about their role, as they went unheeded and unrecognised as the '*dakinis*' of high lamas? Or were the conditions surrounding the liaison, created by the powerful men at the heart of the system, such that women found it difficult to do anything other than acquiesce?

In my own experience, despite the absence of a Tibetan cultural upbringing, there were quite specific motivating factors which helped to keep me silent over many years. These factors were probably similar to those which influenced Tibetan women over the centuries, and which would have provided for them the personal sense of participation in societal rites which normally excluded

women altogether. Firstly, there is no doubt that the secret role
into which an unsuspecting woman was drawn bestowed a certain
amount of personal prestige, in spite of the fact that there was no
public acknowledgement of the woman's position. Secondly, by
participating in intimate activities with someone considered in her
own and the Buddhist community's eyes to be extremely holy,
the woman was able to develop a belief that she too was in some
way 'holy' and that the events surrounding her were karmically
predisposed. Finally, despite the restrictions imposed on her, most
women must have viewed their collusion as 'a test of faith', and an
appropriate opportunity perhaps for deepening their knowledge of
the dharma, and for entering 'the sacred space'.

For Tibetan women, raised and conditioned in a culture whose
whole centre was the Buddhist dharma and the elaborate tulku
system of rule by lamas, the acceptance of these factors and the
idea that such an involvement would create 'good karma' for future
lives must have been utterly compelling. For a western woman
like myself, however, as a convert to Buddhism in adulthood, the
motivation and conditions which supported secrecy could never
have been as strong as theirs. Without such a background, it was
difficult not to question the purpose of secrecy which affected
the role of the woman in the whole affair, and also not to
doubt the contemporary value of such practices, outwith archaic
Tibetan society. At the outset, it was abundantly clear that any
secret activities, whether they were to do with initiation rituals,
or personal relationships with lamas, were always bound by vows
of secrecy (*damtsik*, Tibetan *dam.tshig.*). These vows were often
formally spoken as part of a ritual, whilst at other times became
an unspoken agreement to secrecy. In my own case it was only
when I became involved with a lama of very high status who
was openly living as a monk, that it was plainly emphasised that
any indiscretion in maintaining silence over our affair might lead
to madness, trouble, *or even death*.

As an example of what might happen, I was told that, in a
previous life, the lama I was involved with had had a mistress who
caused him some trouble, and in order to get rid of her he cast a
spell which caused an illness, later resulting in her death. I was also
told that this woman must have been a powerful demon, and that
the lama had only invited her to participate in sexual acts through

compassion, but her trouble-making had become impossible to bear and *posed a threat to the lama's position*. This kind of information was compounded by a more concrete example of what might befall me. Some time into my own relationship with this high lama, a young Tibetan woman in her late teens, who had been taken as a second *songyum*, unexpectedly died suddenly from – it was said – a heart attack. The fears engendered by such events ensured that my own view of the situation into which I had entered became similar to that of someone living under a taboo. For outsiders to traditions such as this, these fears may seem unbelievable, but in the claustrophobic atmosphere of a closed group such as many of these religious sects become, the culture of the 'insider' can quickly predominate. It seemed that within the protecting environment of secrecy and esoteric ritual, safety would be guaranteed, whilst any step outwith these boundaries would be tantamount to breaking a taboo, with all its subsequent ramifications. In her account of the workings of taboos, Mary Daly astutely points out that,

> Women are terrified by phallocentric Taboo and thus are kept back from Touching the 'object' – our Selves – in which the *demonic* powers (our own Elemental powers which are disguised by the Possessors) lie hidden. Women are paralyzed by this injected fear that our powers, if we Touch them or use them 'unlawfully', that is in ways contrary to the Lecherous State, will take vengeance by casting a spell over us as 'wrong-doers'. (Italics mine)[11]

The imposition of secrecy therefore, in the Tibetan system, when it occurred solely as a means to protect status, and where it was reinforced by threats, was a powerful weapon in keeping women from achieving any kind of integrity in themselves, for it seems clear that the fundamental and ancient principles of Tantric sex – the meeting together of two autonomous individuals as partners for sexual relations to promote spirituality – was tainted by the power wielded by one partner over the other. So whilst the lineage system viewed these activities as promoting the enlightened state of the lineage-holders, the fate of one of the two main protagonists, the female consort, remained unrecognised, unspoken and unnamed. Shaw's implication that this very state of being *encapsulates* the female experience, and is a necessary part of a woman practitioner's path to the subjugation of ego, nonetheless does not take into account the fact that this imposed hidden role meant that, within the Tibetan monastic system which dominated the *Vajrayana*, for other women practitioners, there were no overt role models and no open system of exchange between women.

The extent of the bounds of secrecy concerning not the nature, but the context of these kinds of practices, meant that often women were more knowledgeable about the 'underside' of the system, and of the nature of the men involved, than most of the men who constituted the establishment itself. It is only since the death of the lama with whom I was involved that I have been able to see the elaborate mechanisms which lay behind his secret relationships, and can now question them in the light of their transposition to the west, where, I am sure, many western men would happily adopt such practices, as part of their 'dreams of power'.[12] It is certainly intriguing to know that despite Kalu Rinpoche's activities with women, and even quite some time after his death, several Tibetan scholars in the west continued to show complete ignorance of the hidden life existing within the lama system. In his study of the history of Tibetan Buddhism, and in particular the difference between married lamas and celibate monks, Geoffrey Samuel wrote in 1993, 'Kalu Rinpoch'e was a monk, however, not a lay yogin, and most of his career took place in the celibate *gompa* setting of Pelpung'.[13] Whilst it is true that Kalu Rinpoche spent many of his early years in the monastery of Pelpung in Tibet, it is also true that, after escaping Tibet in 1959 when the Chinese annexed the country, he spent many more as the abbot of a monastery in India, and during many of these years was not a monk, yet was afraid of the consequences of revealing his secret life.

My aim in naming him here arises out of a wish to clarify the extent to which this kind of practice was endemic within the system, and in order to de-mythologise the harmful forces which prevail to the disadvantage of both the women who were involved and the men who were excluded from the knowledge of what their gurus actually required of the women students around them. At issue is not the question of what particular individuals may have done in the belief that they were pursuing their religious practice, but rather the context and implications of these beliefs and practices, once mythologised and used to the detriment of others. It is patently clear, through examples in the past, that the potent combination of religion, sex, power and secrecy can have potentially disastrous effects on individuals and groups, and that any system which bases itself on these forces may be open to abuse.

The revelations pertaining to the sexual activities of lamas once dead, are, however, nothing new, for it has always been the case that stories concerning the prowess of lamas, particularly their use of so-called dakinis to further their enlightenment, have been told after their death. Certainly, with the passage of time, it may be easy to mythologise the real women who participated in these events, and, by romanticising what happened, the stories quickly take on mythological proportions. In retrospect, it may also be easier to view their sexual activities (in the absence of *real knowledge* as to what actually took place, that being in the ken of the women only) as a Tantric method used by divine beings, rather than ordinary humans. In the case of the most famous of Tibet's yogis, e.g. Padmasambhava, Milarepa and Drugpa Kunley, details of their liaisons with dakinis appear in their biographies, and are accepted because people believe that their spiritual realisation was so great that any activities which they undertook, including sexual, would be for the benefit of all beings. The extraordinary stories which are written about their miraculous exploits certainly portray these individuals not as humans, but as being of divine form.

So what made the imposition of secrecy – not just about the *content* of the sexual practice, which is one issue, but also about the actual non-celibacy of a lama – take on such importance in the Tibetan Buddhist world? The clue is in the most common explanation given by lamas about their secret lives. When asked why details of sexual encounters often emerge after a lama's death, I have often been told that it is because ordinary people might misconstrue events, and lose faith in their lama, thus breaking their own personal vow of faith in him, and also helping to bring about the lama's downfall. Naturally any fall in the status of a lama *who outwardly maintained a position of celibacy* would threaten the whole hierarchical system of theocratic rule, itself dominated since the 1500s by monasticism, and as a consequence the heart of the society itself.

As I have already discussed, the tulku system lay at the centre of the monastic way of life, and symbolically depended not only on the exclusion of women, but also on the metaphorical idea of male motherhood and divine succession. Seen in this way, any lamas outwardly transgressing the rules of the system threatened the very life of the system itself. For those close to the power bases, who had privileged knowledge of anomalies in the system, their method of dealing with such information was simply to employ a mechanism of denial, or adjust their view in order to accommodate what could not be acknowledged. Most lay people preferred to believe in their lamas as celibate and therefore superior beings, and the practices as symbolic, to be undertaken as meditational visualisations rather than actual physical actions. Only one school of Tibetan Buddhism, the Nyingma, openly acknowledged throughout its structures the importance of women *within* the system, and for this reason the lama lineage-holders are usually married. Despite this fact, however, it is known that many of the tulkus within its school do conduct 'secret' affairs before or after marriage, and that promiscuity in the name of Tantric teachings is not unknown. This either means that many lamas use sex as a justifiable method of religious practice, or that it becomes the excuse for undertaking illicit relationships which are usually brief, non-committed and keep the woman hidden from public view.

It is my contention that the secrecy factor in *any* of these relationships has little to do with the Tantric rites as such, which, in any case, are well documented in other schools of Tantrism, such as in India or Nepal.[14] My view is that the secrecy was invoked, not just for protection of the lineage, but in order to allow the lamas to maintain *control over the women* who became involved, so that any decision-making which should concern both of them regarding the duration of the relationship, and the conditions under which it was perpetuated, were all made by the lama himself. The consort, as a non-person, was restricted by the authority of the lineage and the teachings, which decreed her role as secondary. Clearly the dangers of such a system operating in the west, where religious and therapeutic relationships carry the imperative of ethical behaviour in sexual matters, are obvious. There would certainly be questions about a situation in which a lama engaged in secret sexual liaisons with his female students (or male, as has been known) using deception which implied that ordinary sex with him would naturally constitute Tantra, or even that a secret relationship with him would automatically be spiritually beneficial (i.e. make good karma) because of his alleged spiritual status. All of these approaches would deny the integrity of the woman as an autonomous individual wholly capable of relationships in which mutuality and interdependence are the key factors, and not as one constrained to the passivity and submission demanded of her in the secret arena. A final point which is just as crucial to this debate is the fact that many women in their longing for closeness to the father figure who is the lama, often actively desire (either consciously or unconsciously) physical intimacy with their teacher. Depending on the nature of their own previous life experience, and their own ability to deal with the break in the fiduciary relationship, the outcome of fulfilling such a fantasy as having secret sex with an idealised father figure, then being replaced by another woman, could, in certain cases, be traumatic. Additionally, where the woman concerned already had a sexual partner or husband, the stress involved in splitting off a part of her life from her partner could have significant consequences, especially if the man involved became aware of his wife's obligation to the guru.

But what of the actual nature of the sexual practices themselves? In Tibetan society, the representation of the sexual encounter signified the union of opposites, and the possibility of enlightenment through transcending duality and all its manifestations. But in addition to this symbolism it was widely recognised that actual sexual relations afforded the opportunity, through the Tantric teachings, of attaining special realisation, provided the lama had undergone a yogic training. So, given that a lama *could* be trained in the yoga of breath control, and therefore retention of semen, (the prerequisite for Tantric yoga),[15] and that the fear of losing power, and his desire to maintain control, motivated him to insist on secrecy, were the subsequent secret activities in which he engaged with his consort of any benefit to the woman concerned? In order to consider this, I will firstly discuss the importance placed on Tantra in the Tibetan Buddhist system, then examine in some detail the actual nature of the practices which were kept so secret, and speculate on what relevance they had for women.

It is known that in Tibetan society there existed Tantric texts which contained teachings pertaining to the philosophy and methodology of sexual ritual, and that there was also a plethora of colourful paintings and statues which depicted adequately the importance of sexuality in the teachings of Tibetan Buddhism. Despite this, monasticism was viewed as the most appropriate vehicle for the transmission of power by three of the four main schools. As far as the Vajrayana was concerned, the sexual images portrayed the highest facet of the religion, for it is the case that each deity, in its *secret* aspect, is represented in *yab-yum* with its counterpart in sexual union. Even deities such as the benign and compassionate Chenrezig have a secret aspect, *Pema Garchi Wongchuk* (Tibetan *padma.gar.gyi.dbang.phyug.*), who is represented, red in colour, with his Tantric partner. In the visual representations of the Tantric act, the overwhelming number of images show a male deity, standing or sitting, face towards the viewer, with a female deity, back to the viewer, united with him in sexual union. This image, known as *yab-yum*, literally 'father-mother', is used in visualisation by many celibate monks in their practice of meditation. As part of the enormous range of practices available in the *Vajrayana*, the essentiality of sexual practice was confirmed by all the great scholars and yogis throughout history.

Milarepa, who determined to renounce all worldly things after sleeping on his mother's bones, later resorted to the practice of the *karma mudra*[16] or secret consort. His biography provides us with details of his sexual encounters, as does that of the so-called 'mad yogi' Drugpa Kunley, who is said to have used sexuality almost exclusively as a means of raising spiritual awareness. In Milarepa's biography, he reiterates the necessity of sexual relations for the practising yogi, 'It is said in the Supreme Tantra, [That the qualified yogi] should attract the maids of heaven. . . . It also says that of all services the best is Karma Mudrā.'[17] Elsewhere, the fourteenth-century philosopher Longchenpa states, 'Since enlightened understanding does not come without resorting to a *mudrā*, we are fettered to the triple world without such understanding.'[18] Similarly, the Indian mystic Naropa writes, 'Without Karma Mudrā, no Mahāmudrā',[19] thus confirming the concept that, for the male practitioner, complete enlightenment is impossible without sexual relations with an actual woman, as opposed to a visualised, imaginary sexual relationship in meditation practice.

It is well known that these kinds of practices had their origins in the ancient Hindu Tantra, which proposed that female energy was primary, active and symbolised in the dance. The early Indian system, however, allowed for a transmission of its teachings through female priests. Pupul Jayakar, who researched worship of the Great Mother in India, wrote of bone images of the Mother Goddess which were found in caves in Utter Pradesh and carbon-dated to 20,000 BC. She concluded from her work that the transmission of myth and initiation in very early Indian society was actually from mother to daughter. There seems little evidence to support a theory that this mode of transmission ever existed in Tibet in Buddhist times. Accounts of the lives of female practitioners of great fame like Yeshe Tsogyal, Machig Labdron and Drenchen Rema show that their achievements were incorporated into the male lineage system, and functioned as part of it. They were never depicted as members of an all-female lineage exclusively. In spite of this, the ancient diagrams, iconography and symbolism pertaining to a more ancient philosophy survived to a certain extent, giving a degree of autonomy to women and the potential for positive identification.

However, it is my contention that the onset of the particular kind of patriarchal power which evolved through the tulku system promoted male subjectivity as primary, and this was ultimately responsible for eroding images of female subjectivity, excluding the possibility of such an all-female lineage, and reducing women's role in the system to a secondary (and inferior) position. Clearly the imposition of secrecy by the one party in the relationship who perceived himself to have much to lose if his sexual activity became public, and the kinds of real and textual evidence which support the view that women were actually threatened with dire consequences in order to retain silence, meant that the Tantric relationship was not one of equals, and that women were rarely in a position to take the initiative. The consequences of this one-sided aspect to the relationship was, in my view, the degeneration of the principles of the Tantric practices, and therefore of the potential benefits of two individuals participating in ritualistic rites on a basis of true mutuality.

Historically, the evolution of the Tibetan Tantra, from the

archaic emphasis on female subjectivity and the power of maternity, to the centrality of the male as divine and the holder of power, meant that the actual purpose of the female involvement became more and more obscure. According to the male view, women were the necessary 'ingredients'[20] in the process of birthing and sexual activity, but, in the context of autonomy within the societal structures, women became co-opted solely on male terms. The encouragement of women's passivity, the discouragement of their voices of difference, and the seductive ambience of the Tantra with its promises of enlightenment for all, have led to a critical situation for women who feel attracted to follow Tantric teachings in western society at this time. Whilst the male side of the institution is readily accepted by men as they aspire to enter into it, many women may be confused about their place and role in a system which does not 'recognise' them. As Julia Kristeva writes, 'He and all his avatars would be possible but not the other'.[21] Even the question of female tulkus, which some feminist Buddhists see as a step towards 'equality', opens up a whole new debate on the nature of 'reincarnation' and its meaning, something which has barely begun to be discussed in Buddhist circles.

In general, very few women have been publicly recognised to have high spiritual qualities, and none holds a position of power within the hierarchy. Those who achieve acknowledgement are either married to lamas, are the mothers or sisters of lamas, or (and these are extremely rare) have achieved some kind of status through an extraordinary practice of meditation. Although many lamas do encourage women students by saying that women practitioners are some of their most devoted and skilful practitioners, no women are truly acknowledged as teachers, or take their place within the hierarchy. If so many lamas have had so many consorts over the years, why is it that there is no lineage of women as teachers in this area of knowledge? And why have so few women written about their actual lives and roles within the system, if they had truly participated as mutually co-operative partners with equal status in the rituals of sex?

These questions are fundamental to Shaw's argument that the mutual respect between men and women in the Tantra clearly gave them the authority to teach and write about such interdependence within their society. This seems to indicate that societal and personal interdependence between the sexes would be connected. While Shaw states that, '*Buddhism* can coexist with oppressive social conditions' (italics mine),[22] I wonder if an overt Tantric tradition which was widespread in a society could possibly exist openly in 'oppressive social conditions', given that the whole purpose of the Tantra is, as Shaw remarks, 'to deconstruct . . . an armored, boundaried, or selfishly motivated "self"'.[23] Were many individuals to undertake and teach this kind of co-operation, it would surely have an impact on society in general, and gender relations in particular.

To argue, therefore, that it is simply woman's role to remain 'hidden' is plainly detrimental to the cause of improved relations between the sexes, for, as Shaw's work uncovers, there existed at a different time women in Tantra who were at least as powerful, as active and as vocal as men, a fact which substantiates her claim that her 'study has "discovered" a different gender pattern'.[24] My own view is that the area of knowledge itself has largely disappeared, and that women no longer know how to use the symbolic means of representation which would allow them proper subjectivity in contemporary western society. It is also my view that if anything had to remain 'secret' it was the truth of the fact that the patriarchal system had repressed the female in many covert ways, in order to maintain its male power, both on a personal and on a societal level. In Tibet the rights of transmission were held by the male lineage, so that rarely did women act as initiators to other women. It may have been the case that in the lay traditions one or two famous female yoginis were incorporated into the lineage, but in the last five hundred years there are no women included as lineage holders in any of the major schools. This meant that even though the images which symbolised female subjectivity and sexuality were retained, but classified largely as 'secret', their control was in the hands of men, as were the sexual consorts who, once initiators of sexual rituals to men, now became participants whose role was dictated by the male lineage. As Irigaray so aptly remarks on the effect of women's purpose being defined by men, women are amputated of the purpose of their action, forced to be disinterested, self-sacrificing, without ever having chosen or wanted this. *The path of renunciation described by certain mystics is women's daily lot.* But it is not possible to ask one people to be saintly in the name of a purpose espoused by another people. In fact – as Hegel understood very well – neither the people nor the gender are one. But one part lays claim to the right of ethical consciousness and leaves the other no purpose, no effectiveness, except as double, shadow, complement. (Italics mine)[25]

Padmasambhava, as the earliest example of a holder of Tibetan Buddhist patriarchal rule, happily declared to his followers that the realm of female energy was under his control, 'I Pema Jungne, this Great Being, miraculously appeared, [S]pontaneously manifest, unborn and undying, [W]ith dominion over the hosts of Ḍākinīs'.[26] Concerning the objective role of the female, he also said, 'woman is a sacred *ingredient* of the Tantra, [A] qualified Awareness Ḍākinī is necessary. . . . [W]ithout her the factors of maturity and release are incomplete' (italics mine),[27] a statement obviously addressed by a man to men.

The loss of a potential female lineage, which since ancient times could have protected Tantric information of benefit to women, and created representations of female sexuality, meant that the purpose and goals of sexual activity became more and more concerned with the needs of the male participant. It has long been known, for example, that the male Tantric practitioner has as his aim the achievement of the retention of semen during intercourse, a practice which in many cultures is thought to be extremely beneficial for the man's health. Milarepa extolled the virtues of such practice, not only from the point of view of meditational and breath control, but also of pleasure, and described in his teachings both the characteristics required in a good *karma mudra*, and the various techniques which had to be employed by the man in order to achieve semen retention, and thus great bliss. He called this method 'a path of bliss – of voidness, of no thoughts, and of two-in-one, A path of quick assistance by a goddess'.[28]

The instructions which appear in the so-called 'secret' texts spelled out the methods which enabled the man to control the flow of semen, particularly through practices of breath control.

This kind of practice, known to many ancient cultures, determined that the semen had to be driven upwards along the spine to the head. In the Hindu tradition the semen was called 'ojas' – 'the more ojas is in a man's head the more powerful he is, the more intellectual, the more spiritually strong'.[29] Like the cults of ancient times, the semen was equated with the substance of the brain, and was valued as a commodity to be retained by the body, in order to promote bliss, intelligence, good health and long life. This practice was one of the two aspects of masculinity which coloured the meaning conveyed in Tantric texts and commentaries. The other was the subjective experience of the male as privileged, which, as I have already shown, was firmly established through the societal theocratic system, and through the incorporation of the human 'divine king' into the iconography of the religion.

Retention of semen, however, formed the central part of an ideology of the 'opposite', which was intricately woven into the philosophy of the religion, both through the iconography, and through yogic practices which aimed for control over, or union with, an aspect of the *opposite*, whether that was as a person, or as a function pertaining to life in the ordinary sense. For example, breath control interferes with normal bodily functions, sitting absolutely still for extreme periods of time goes against physical norms, stopping thoughts defies the brain's normal activity, and holding back ejaculation goes against the physiology of sexuality in the male. In Tantric sexual practices the aim of uniting the male and female aspects (however they are defined) into a whole, unitary experience is attempted (by the male) through the use of a female partner. Eliade calls this 'the symbolism of the "opposite"'[30] and claims that practices which involve it re-enact an experience similar to death, and also to divinity, two experiences which, by definition, are impossible to achieve in the live human form.

In shamanism, death is the prelude to rebirth, and forms a central theme in the practices which aim to take the shaman beyond mundane life. This goal is also that of the Tantric yogi. In Tibetan Buddhism, the supreme goal is for the practitioner to become enlightened in one lifetime, by overcoming the restrictions of death and becoming divine whilst still alive. The meaning of this extraordinary goal is that the yogi *steps outside of ordinary time*, the boundaries of which are only ultimately clear to humans through the phenomenon of death. By controlling both breath and semen, he enters a different conceptual reality in which he recognises his own divinity and is not bound by linear time. 'The yogin repeats and, as it were, relives the cosmic Great Time'.[31] This attempt to master physicality in order to experience extraordinary time dimensions is reflected in one of the epithets for highly realised lamas – *Dusum Chenpa* (Tibetan *du.gsum.kyhen.pa.*), which means 'the knower of the three times'.

But what is the importance of the symbolic break with linear time and why is it so closely associated with the male quest for enlightenment? Linear time is, after all, the time which is seen to 'pass', which is historical, measured, and is conceptualised in the logical systems of all societies. It is recognised through our perception of beginnings and endings, which colours our notion of entering into time, or even of controlling it. Death is always a part of our definition of linear time, perceiving as we do that time 'runs out' at the boundary point which ends life. In his work *Being and Time* Martin Heidegger proposes that awareness of one's own death is the ground for authentic existence. This kind of view is also to be found in Freud's works, when he associates the male experience of authenticity (phallic existence and sexuality) with linear time. He theorises that, for men, castration and death are often synonomous in the unconscious, and relate quite specifically to their experience of orgasm. Indeed in several languages the post–coital state for men is referred to as 'the little death'. In her essay on women and time, Julia Kristeva maintains that linear time 'is readily labelled masculine and . . . is at once both civilizational and obsessional'.[32]

In a similar vein, the Tibetan tulku, Tarthang, describes linear time as having 'the effect of appearing to cover all the possibilities for expression',[33] with its relentless emphasis on sequential moments, through which it seems impossible to break. He also suggests that we tend to believe, 'that ordinary lived time is actually a hidden, autonomous force that pushes us about'.[34] Until the advent of relativity theory and sub-atomic physics, when the whole space–time paradigm was articulated, this perception of an omnipresent paternalistic Father Time, who watched over our march through life, would have seemed an apt metaphor, but we now know space and time are interconnected, so that body-space, which is dependent on gender, must be significant in the appreciation of time, its limits and qualities. The male yogi, in his attempt to experience a state beyond linear time is compelled to use his body-space, and thus his sexuality, as a means to experience what Tarthang calls 'Great Time'.

This kind of concept of time is present in most world civilisations, particularly those whose art and literature are religiously inspired, like those of Tibet. It has been called both cyclical and monumental time. Cyclical time is a deeper current in human experience than linear time, and seems to lie at the boundary between linear and monumental time. For women, the physiological experience of cyclical time binds her to corporeality through menstruation and gestation, placing her at the boundary of space-time. Not only that, but the experience of cycles within the body which so closely mirror extraneous forces in nature which seem eternal (the moon's phases, the tides) suggest an affinity with monumental time, something which men lack in this specific way. Monumental time, which is impossible to articulate, has been described as having a 'massive presence . . . without cleavage or escape'.[35] It is often conceived as all-pervading, mystical and beyond language, and, as a consequence of these associations, described by philosophers as within the female domain and therefore semiotic. Even Tarthang Tulku describes it as, '*the muse* that all artists seek, the feature which allows us to perceive and celebrate the otherwise hidden dimensions of all the presentations that constitute life' (italics mine).[36] For the male practitioner, that muse is always female. By reversing ordinary trends, and metaphorically stepping outwith the boundaries of ordinary time as it is perceived, going beyond language, and entering the sacred realm of the symbolic female, construed as Great Time and Space, the Tantric yogi seeks to achieve the transcendental aim of transcending his own body and its natural limits.

In sexual ritual, where the aim is to experience this different dimension of space-time through reversal and control, the male practitioner attempts to negate the subject–object dichotomy to be *at one* with the *other*. This enables him to experience a mythical state of being which is characterised by his ability to feel at one with all phenomena, a state in which no separation between himself and the 'other' is felt, a state not unlike that of his first relationship with his mother, before the idea of *difference* and separation arose.

The witholding of semen is a crucial aspect of the practice which enables the yogi to unite with his so-called 'opposite'. In Tibetan semen is called *tigle* (Tibetan *thig.le.*), meaning literally 'dot' or 'essence'. Metaphorically, semen becomes *changchubsem* (Tibetan *byang.chub.sems.*, Sanskrit *bodhicitta*), meaning literally 'mind of enlightenment', but subject in the texts to a variety of interpretative meanings, one of which is 'semen'. 'In Tantra the word *bodhicitta* also denotes sperm and female juices, and the injunction to retain the *bodhicitta* for the sake of others therefore possesses a powerful dual meaning.'[37] Of the different translations of *tigle* and *changchubsem* (which incidentally are frequently used interchangeably to indicate an essence equated with male life-force), 'seed-essence', 'white *bodhicitta*' and 'psychic energy' are the most common. One commentator translates *tigle* as 'bioenergetic flow-input' and quotes the fourteenth-century Longchen Rabjampa's definition, '"*thig*" means "unchanging" ("unalterable") and *le* "all-encompassing by virtue of its spreading far and wide", . . . *thig-le* is similar to what we call the "genetic code" and its presence in every single cell'.[38] Taking this definition into consideration, it is apparent that the word *tigle*, which is the specific word used in texts which describe the physical witholding of semen, could also be used generically to mean DNA.

In spite of the wide-ranging applications of the term, there does exist a counterpart to describe the female 'essence', which is known as 'red *bodhicitta*'. Referred to as *trag* (Tibetan *khrag*) which means 'blood', it is also known as *dazen* (Tibetan *zla.mtsan.*), which means 'monthly sign' and clearly refers to menstrual blood. It is also clear that the male and female essences, when described in physiological terms, i.e. semen and menstrual blood, are hardly synonymous, as one is of significance during the act the sexual orgasm and the other is not. It seems unlikely that the crude equation of menstrual blood with semen in Tibetan texts was due to an ignorance of the facts of male and female physiology and sexuality, but in the medical texts which describe human physiology it is written that 'Refined marrow forms semen or menstrual blood (conceived as female creative seed)',[39] thus linking the two substances as parallel. Why the female creative seed should be equated with red menstrual blood, rather than the yellow *corpus luteum* of the ovum, which, as the carrier of the life-force, would be the true equivalent of the semen, can only be supposed, but it is evident that the symbolism associated with the colours red and white, to represent the female and male respectively, are conveniently found in these two fluids. It is also apparent that the function of menstrual blood is confused by its association with procreativity and the sexual act, for, as modern scientific investigation has shown, the ovum, if not fertilised, is destroyed long before the onset of menstruation, and therefore menstrual blood contains no 'seed essence' in the way semen can be said to. Indeed the most recent research points to the purpose of menstrual blood as being related to a protective mechanism in female physiology, to prevent infection by rogue sperm, rather than being simply the aftermath of ovulation and unsuccessful fertilisation, as has long been thought.

The confusion between the equating of semen with menstrual blood is further demonstrated by Keith Dowman in his explanation of Tantric practices, when he proposes that 'refined semen is stored in the heart centre as "radiance", which produces long-life and gives a shine to the complexion'.[40] He goes on, 'loss of semen, by any means, causes life-span to be shortened and causes a pallid complexion'.[41] It is clear from this latter statement that in this case the word 'semen' literally means *semen*, and not the generic term 'seed-essence' which would encompass menstrual blood, a substance impossible to 'withhold' and unrelated to the sexual act. Yet in other statements the word 'semen' is used interchangeably for seed-essence, or *bodhicitta*, which females are also said to produce.

In many cases the use of male gender identified terminology to cover both male and female reality or experience, may be, if not theoretically inappropriate, at least partially transferable, but in this particular case the equations do not balance. If it were simply the fact that the word 'semen' were used metaphorically, to describe a symbolic energy which had to be controlled through use of breathing techniques, during a visualised meditation, there might be no need for men to aim to withhold ejaculation, but clearly this is not so because the texts and the practice link breath control with this actual physiological achievement. Miranda Shaw agrees that menstrual fluid and semen are not the same, but further confuses the issue in her discussion of the sexual fluids. She recognises two

types of Tantric sex, one which features the 'mingling' of the sexual
fluids (and here she describes the woman's sexual fluid, whose flow
the man has to stimulate, as *'the female equivalent of the man's seminal
fluid'*) (italics mine),[42] thereby implying ejaculation on the part of
the man. In the other type of Tantric sex the man withholds
ejaculation but absorbs the woman's fluids, in a reversal of ordinary
sex. According to Shaw, 'the *tantras* (both Hindu and Buddhist)
place somewhat more emphasis upon the man's absorption of
female fluids',[43] and this is certainly borne out in the texts which
declare that not one drop of *bodhicitta* should be spilled in the quest
for enlightenment.

What is interesting, however, about Shaw's comments on this
kind of sexual practice is that its origins, in the Hindu Tantra,
stipulate the passivity of the male, and the active nature of the
female, as was the original designation in the Hindu Tantras. This
allocation of qualities to the male and female, as I have already
shown, is the opposite of the one adhered to in the Tibetan sexual
iconography, where the female represents passivity. This almost
seems substantiated by her other comment that, 'The gathering
of the female fluids by the man . . . expresses the relative status of
male and female within the ritual, for it signals *the power flowing from
the female to the male*' (italics mine).[44] This reversal of the roles and
processes involved in physiological sexual activity, again reinscribes
the shamanistic imperative to undertake an ideology of the 'opposite' which may well have been thought physically possible by the
ancients who developed these practices. It is my view, however,
that the emphasis on this particular practice of Tantrism has
reinforced in the Tibetan system the notion of imbalance between
male and female, and that power has not flowed to the female,
either metaphorically or literally for quite some time. Shaw herself
concedes that 'Tantric Buddhism displays the conviction that all the
powers of the universe flow through and from women'.[45]

It seems likely, as Shaw herself states, that any degeneration in
the way in which the rituals and practices of the Tantra were
enacted, were surely due, as I have argued here, to 'cultural
forces, institutional factors, and social patterns that have eclipsed
the original vision'.[46] Nonetheless, there are several problematic
areas in attempting a reconstruction of Tantra in the west, under
the terms of the philosophical goals which are stipulated by Shaw,

and which she describes as consisting of the 'merging of identities
. . . loss of ego boundaries, forgetfulness of self, and absence of
subject–object dualism'.[47] Whilst I argue later for the recognition
of *all* identities and ego boundaries as ultimately fluid and unstable,
the idea that the bodies of the male and female, *already inscribed as
male-subject/female-object through their gender allocation* in the philosophy, could be merged into a unitary whole, is something which
clearly requires to be debated. From the western psychoanalytical
perspective on the relationship between subjects, the importance of
autonomous difference is seen as a key factor in the development
of healthy female subjectivity. The dangers therefore that the
female would easily be subsumed by the male into a phallocentric
arena of meaning, where 'unity' meant 'man', are very real, and
require to be considered if male and female are ever to become
autonomous yet different individuals with the capability of relating
to one another harmoniously.

When Yeshe Tsogyal instructs a female disciple by saying,
'Practise to perfection the skill of retaining your seed-essence',[48]
she clearly does not mean semen, but rather some form of
autonomous energy which *requires to be held on to*. If the ancient
Tantras are to be interpreted now, it is my contention that the
secret area of practice which is alluded to in many texts and whose
aim is to establish female subjectivity should be read as the practice
of retention of *difference*, as encoded in an essential aspect of being
female (i.e. seed-essence). It is this *difference* which requires to be
sustained through meditational visualisation, or breath control, and
which helps to create open bodily awareness during any form of
physical activity, including sexual intimacy. So while both men
and women can potentially control breathing and orgasm through
certain practices, which in turn increase pleasure, it is only men
who require to control the unique physiological functions which
pertain to *their* orgasm during sexual acts.

The different nature of female physiology is addressed to some
extent in the Tantric texts of other traditions, by taking the focus
of attention from the genital area in women to other parts of the
body, in accordance with the contemporary view that women's
sexual pleasure is not as specifically genitally located as men have
described their own to be. The ancient Chinese texts are quite clear
about the difference in physiology,

In his *Secret of Feminine Alchemy*, Liu I-Ming says, 'There is a true secret about starting practice. The operation is *as different for men and women as sky from sea*. The principle for men is refinement of energy, *the expedient for women is refinement of the body*.' Men begin practice with the attention in the lower abdomen, just below the navel. *Women start work with the attention between the breasts*. (Italics mine)[49]

Whilst the Chinese promoted the breasts as the centre of energy control for women, the Tibetans, by default, allowed the Tantric texts and images to prioritise the male side of the practice. The unfortunate generic application of the term for energy which is put forward in certain texts as representative of the life-force in both sexes, simply privileges male over female, by the linking together of a *specific* male biological reality with something which is said to be universal. The symbolism of *tigle*, for example, is described by one commentator as having, 'clear connotations of the ultimate ground of the universe, conceived *both as semen* and as pure spirit or thought' (italics mine).[50] This kind of statement clearly places the male-essence as fundamental in nature, yet another misconception which prioritises the male, for, as we now know, the essential building block of all nature, *if it must be gendered*, is female. It is this tendency in the male-biased texts to privilege one gender over the other that also leads to the need to reflect a token presence of the female, often by attributing to her qualities and aspects which are defined as 'opposite' or 'mirror-image' to the male. Whilst *bodhicitta* may be used metaphorically to refer to particular states of mind, or indeed energies which flow in the body, there can be no justification for linking male physiology to enlightenment, in the absence of *a different physiological model which is in tune with the reality of being a woman*. As most linguistic analysts would now maintain, the sexism inherent in the use of a word with exclusive male associations, *semen*, to stand in for a general concept of universal relevence, does little more than to encode the superiority of the male in language itself.

This, together with the notable absence of an equivalent term for *songyum*, which would be *songyab*, establishes the male as the only viable *subject* in the sexual rituals of Tantra, in whose power rests the conditions and the meaning which pertain to the act of sexual union. Seen in this way, Andrea Nye's statement about masculinity in language can be paraphrased by substituting Tibetan words for her English examples. 'Masculinity' she claims, 'is the positive presence around which the meaning of words like 'father', 'mother' and 'child', is structured, and around which, by extension, all meaning must be structured'.[51] I would paraphrase this to 'masculinity is the positive presence around which the meaning of words like '*tulku*', '*songyum*' and '*tigle*', is structured, and around which, by extension, all meaning in the context of Tibetan Buddhism must be structured'.

The one-sided perspective on reality which I have shown is one with which western thought is beginning to come to grips, by recognising that philosophy, language and gender are interrelated, and as such have provided a blueprint for our way of living which has lasted for thousands of years. That the blueprint of many different cultures is now being subjected to scrutiny by thinking women and men is shown by the fact that it is no longer acceptable for the female experience to be either peripheral to that of the male, or to be defined as 'opposite' to the alleged centrality of the male experience. Even Yeshe Tsogyal, as an early 'female practitioner said, 'Unite (male) solar and (female) lunar energies . . . Female assisting male and male assisting female, *the principles of each being separately practised*' (italics mine).[52] This statement is interesting because the analogies of the sun and moon are very appropriate. Usually thought of as representing opposite forces, the sun and moon are clearly two separate, unique and *different* entities. Just because they are associated with the creation of conditions which are *categorised* as polarised opposites – day and night, or dark and light – does not mean that they themselves are in opposition to one another. Yeshe Tsogyal's acknowledgement therefore of sexual difference, and the presence of different principles, points out the need for *separate* practices. By so doing, the view that maleness and femaleness are somehow interchangeable, as absolutes, or simply mirror-images of one another, is undermined. Not only that, but any acknowledgement of *difference* as a crucial variable in human experience, like that articulated by Tsogyal, sets the scene for the establishment of a viable female subjective.

Interestingly, the view that is taken by Janice Willis in her article on the dakini is in stark contrast to that of Tsogyal. Willis strives to maintain the classic Buddhist position, so often adopted by gender-conscious commentators, which rationalises the absence of female experience and perspective by maintaining that the dualisms of gender are ultimately the illusions of unenlightened minds. Milarepa expresses this position when he states, 'Though . . . born in a female form, which is considered to be inferior, nevertheless, so far as the Ālaya [Store] Consciousness is concerned, there is no discrimination between man and woman.'[53] Willis ties herself in semantic tangles when she attempts to neutralise the female-oriented implication of the term 'dakini' by placing the words referring to her in inverted commas. By this means she can show that dakini is of relevance to both men and women, as 'she' is simply an energy form which, whilst always represented in Tantric symbolism as female, is, in reality, according to her, a '*feminine* principle' (italics original).[54]

The differentiation implied by labelling the *dakini* as 'feminine' rather than 'female' means that gender classification is seen as an arbitrary facet of being, of irrelevance to the practitioner, who must view her qualities as energies rather than as arising out of *female* being. This is the same argument in reverse, of the significance of *tigle* to both men and women. Whereas *tigle* must be read as having universal relevance, while it is clearly only of relevance to men, *dakini* must be seen as beyond gender, when she is clearly female. Of this paradox Willis says, '"she" is *not* "female"' (italics original),[55] but goes on to point out that the dakini is 'the *necessary complement* to render us (whether male or female) whole beings. To put it another way, "she" is what is lacking, the lacking of which prevents our complete Enlightenment' (italics original).[56]

As noble as this sentiment might be in philosophical terms, Willis fails to explain why it is that the dakini is first and foremost the *sexual consort* of the male lama, in all Tantric mythology. The unlikelihood of the texts implying that the dakini, as female, could also be the sexual consort to a woman, leads one to suppose that this kind of dualistic labelling of concepts is ultimately male-centred, and somehow adapts itself, somewhat clumsily, to 'fit' the notion of 'woman as practitioner'. Just as woman can have no connection to teachings which relate specifically to male physiology, so woman can have no access to the concepts of wholeness, developed erroneously in her name. Whilst the recovery of the historical facts about the Tantra and women's position in it by writers like Shaw represents a crucial factor in the development of understanding women's place in Buddhist history, there seems little doubt that any uncritical adaptation of ancient customs to the contemporary situation in which gender relations are under a different kind of philosophical scrutiny might oversimplify the issues which we face as humans *now*.

Chapter 7

A 'Traveller in Space': The Significance of the Dakini and her Sacred Domain

In Tibetan texts there is some evidence of the recognition of divine beings in female human form, but of the tiny minority of cases where a woman tulku was recognised (Dolma and Dorje Phagmo are among the very few documented), little importance was given to their position in the hierarchy, apart from the required acknowledgement by the monastic order that such female incarnations existed. In addition, some biographies make reference to female practitioners and teachers, but it is clear that the transmission of teachings and the authority of the lineage, which are said to be at the heart of Tibetan Buddhism, are now, and have been for quite some time, in the hands of men. The importance of the guru-lama to the maintenance of the Tantric lineage, which incorporates the female/feminine as an essential component, is elucidated by several commentators,

> On the Bodhisattva path no Guru is needed, but as soon as the complex but enriching elements of *enigma, paradox and twilight language (sandhyābhāṣā)* enter into the expression of the *dharma*, the aspirant needs a Guru preceptor, a Lama, to make the appropriate meaning quite clear and to convey the empowering oral transmission and authorisations (*lung*). (Italics mine)[1]

It is clear from this statement that certain teachings which are associated with the dakinis (particularly the twilight language, which is said to originate from them) can only be understood with the help of a lama, and although it is not specified that the guru or lama should be male, it is always implied. 'The Lama's pronouncements and precepts *are* the *dharma*, and his word assumes the sanctity of absolute truth . . . Obedience to the Father-preceptor remains of primary importance even after the Guru's parinirvāṇa' (italics original).[2]

In general, there are very few exceptions to the rule of guru as father-preceptor, and these tend to appear only in lineages where marriage is permitted amongst the clergy, and of them very few examples in the last five hundred years. The interesting proposition therefore, that only *'father*-preceptors' are essential to the tradition in which the so-called 'twilight language'[3] of the dakinis is employed, gives credence to the belief that only qualified men are in possession of the knowledge which is 'written on the female body', and which relies on a particular philosophy of femininity. This means in effect that the male lineage, in whose power lie the teachings transmitted by the Buddha, and subsequent enlightened men, also claim the right to the holding of knowledge related to the female. In the absence of an all-female lineage, whose sexuality and historical gender difference might have endowed them with different and unique ways of expressing their insights on reality, the all-male lineage acknowledges the importance of the female body in the expression and practice of the teachings, yet does so from the peculiar perspective of the male yogi.

While other schools of Buddhist thought are happy to exclude the female and sexual relations with her as a legitimate means of practice, the *Vajrayana* school at least recognises the presence of the female, and has constructed philosophies around her body. Their assertion that a father-guru is essential when dealing with teachings which pertain to the female body, and which are characterised by concepts to do with 'paradox', 'enigma' and a language which is undecipherable to ordinary mortals, signals a recognition of philosophical complexity. The transmission of teachings which incorporate this kind of complexity has traditionally been restricted to those who have the capacity for unwavering devotion, and a reasonable intellect. These teachings are in turn incorporated into the lama-system, where they form part of the canon concerning sexual practice, largely addressed to men. As I have already shown, there are very few available and equivalent sets of structures (either lineages or texts) which address women as practitioners in this respect.

Notwithstanding this anomaly, most commentators might argue that the very fact that Tibet's religion has female deities, a so-called 'female language', and a female paradise, is reason enough to claim the egalitarianism of Tibetan Buddhism. But it is my contention that the mere existence of such symbols in no way guarantees either a living female tradition, or positive and beneficial symbolism for women practitioners. I have already shown that the Tibetan tulku system succeeded in assimilating and appropriating women both as symbols and as participants, so much so that not even their role as *essential* participants in the system was ever properly acknowledged. Even the supposed existence of a '*Dakini* Lineage' (a misnomer, because the lineage is only associated with the dakinis, and is not held by them), does not ensure that women understand their position in the philosophy or iconography. Kelsang Gyatso in his work on the practices of the dakini lineage, even places the primary source of insight into what might be called 'the female mysteries' in the realm of a male deity, 'The first Guru in the lineage of these instructions is Buddha Vajradharma [male], and the *second* is Buddha Vajrayogini' [female], he writes (italics mine).[4] Even at the level of Buddhahood, it seems, the male gender is privileged as guru.

On the symbolic level, it is worth considering what the textual references to dakinis, their teachings, lineage, Pure Land, 'twilight language' and significance might represent in the context of the whole system. In order to facilitate an understanding of my thesis concerning the dakini, I have divided the remainder of the chapter into five sections, each of which deals with a particular facet of the dakini. I begin with the nature of the teachings which are associated with her, and their modes of transmission. I then describe the significance of her sacred domain and language. Next I consider the essential femaleness of the dakini, and I then go on to discuss the meaning of female subjectivity which can be extrapolated from her representation. Finally, in the last section, I examine the etymological roots of the Tibetan word for dakini in order to substantiate some of my arguments about her essential nature historically.

THE SECRET TEACHINGS OF THE DAKINI
There seems little doubt that the authors of the Tibetan Buddhist Tantras were almost exclusively male, despite the fact that the Indian Tantras from which they were derived involved the participation of women at every level in very early times, and that evidence of female lineages with transmission of myth and initiation from mother to daughter is to be found in ancient Indian

writings. Even the later *bhakti* movement,[5] which began in South India in the fifth century, retained into modern times important aspects of female involvement and female autonomy, which were characterised by poetry in the 'mother tongue'. These are the kinds of lineages and traditions which, had they reached Tibet, might have survived in some form, but there is no evidence that they ever existed. Luce Irigaray remarks of this kind of absence, 'Through incredible neglect and disregard, patriarchal traditions have wiped out traces of mother–daughter genealogies'.[6]

The largely male authorship of the Tibetan Buddhist Tantras ensured therefore that the practices were geared towards men, and the imagery slanted towards an understanding by the male reader. This meant that for ordinary men, not schooled in the intricacies of the philosophical tradition, the gender polarities and dualities which existed in everyday life could be used to convey a meaning which they might understand. Certainly, for those involved in the monastic tradition, stereotypical images of women as temptresses and so on were used in order to help them maintain celibacy, and for those using the iconography in their meditation practice the female came to represent something which was transcendental in her form as an idealised mother or sexual consort.

The particular scriptures that were said to emanate from the dakinis were guarded with great secrecy, and written warnings on the texts ensured that access to these kinds of teachings should be limited only to those able to understand their meaning and to maintain the required degree of discretion concerning their contents. In particular, texts which were reputed to have been hidden by dakinis (or revealed by them to practitioners who then hid them), to be found at a later time, and said to be written in the dakini script, a kind of secret language, were highly prized for their esoteric nature. Historically, the discovery and interpretation of such sacred hidden texts written in the so-called 'twilight language' and known as *terma* (Tibetan *gter.ma.* literally 'mother treasure') were made by yogic practitioners called *tertons*. The role of the *terton* was to reveal the truths of the text at an appropriate time. 'The Ḍākinī cypher, says the Lama, can be understood only by initiated tertons'[7] and 'Treasure-finders are invariably emanations (*sprul-pa*) of Guru Pema or emanations of his emanations'.[8] In other words the vast majority of *tertons* were men, and since the time of Yeshe Tsogyal, in the eighth to ninth centuries, when it was at least acknowledged that women had powers concerning truths pertaining to 'the feminine', the men of the lineages have proclaimed their right to hold that power, although in many texts it is made clear that they require the help of a female partner in order to do so.

> The *terton* seem to represent the 'wildest' and most shamanic end of Tibetan Buddhist practice. Most of them are male but very few are monks. According to Tulku Thondup, most *terton* do Tantric practice with a female consort and the presence of the right consort is part of the circumstances . . . which enable the discovery of the *terma*.[9]

It seems very clear therefore, that the tradition of hidden texts is associated with the female, not only through the language of the dakinis, and Yeshe Tsogyal, the initiator of the system, but also (if the *terton* herself were not a woman), through the necessity for a woman to be sexually involved with a male *terton* in the revelation of such a text. Furthermore, the use of such language as 'hidden', 'secret' and 'mystical', which pertains to those components of a patriarchal tradition which are represented in the female body, has similar resonance in the writings of other cultures, at other times, when woman has been associated with the unknown or with nature, and her body perceived as a metaphor for the mysteries of the world which require to be revealed or 'penetrated'[10] by men. In the Tibetan case, these dakini texts were often buried in 'mother earth' or revealed through a *terton*'s esoteric power to 'read' from an aspect of 'mother nature', such as clouds, rocks or a body of water, the mystical hieroglyph which contained a treasure of enlightened knowledge. The practitioners of Bön thought that there were nine oceans of treasures associated with female symbols such as pearls and lotuses. The proviso for such acts of discovery was of course that the *terton* had received the initiation of the dakinis, symbolised most commonly in his sexual relations with an actual woman. '[W]ithout the Ḍākinī's initiation into her mystic language (*mkha'-gro gsang-brda'-i dbang*) we fumble in the dark', writes Dowman.[11]

For those practitioners who pursued perfection on the Tantric path, therefore, it was no wonder that the dakini, *par excellence*, came to represent the secret, hidden and mystical quality of absolute insight required by men, and that her name became an epithet for a sexual partner. Her presence was characterised in texts by her ability not only to enable practitioners to overcome obstructions on the path, but also as a required element in their practice, whether symbolic (in meditation) or real, as a sexual consort. Of the four major schools, the Nyingma in particular appear to have maintained closest links with this latter tradition through their lay lamas, who openly married, and through some of their practices which were and still are nearest to the shamanistic roots of Tibet itself. Of their key teachings the Nyingma sect places particular importance on the *terma* known as the *khandro nying thig*, sometimes known as the 'dakini's heart drop', but which I translate as the 'the mark of the dakini's mind'. However, even within their liberal system, it is the lama who, with his essential dakini as a partner, retains the power of the teachings, and it is the lama who transmits meaning in such a way as to preserve and encode the view of the dakini as *a required complement* to the centrality and subjectivity of the lama. She rarely enters the frame as the mistress of her own domain, a state to which women could aspire, but rather takes her identity from her role as a *complementary* force, in situations where her intervention or participation enables practitioners not to become *like her*, but to become more like the Buddha. Clearly this perspective on the role of the dakini makes sense for men, but is more problematic for women, for whom the symbolism casts them always into the role of helper, whether as human consorts, or as divine beings such as dakinis, or the goddesses of Amitabha's Pure Land.

However, the interesting aspect of the debate on the understanding of the dakini and the 'female domain' is not who controls or articulates it, or who gives it meaning, because that is apparent, but what that meaning is perceived to be, especially in the context of a male-dominated religious institution. Logically, one might expect that such a symbolic domain as is represented by the dakini's Pure Land would be the antithesis, or counterpart, of the Buddha Amitabha's homo-exclusive Pure Land of untainted men, into which no woman can achieve entry in a female body. Here, the fortunate being is miraculously reborn from a lotus flower, in male form, to enjoy the pleasures of a paradise where the only female forms are beautiful goddesses, whose role is to attend to the needs and wishes of the 'self-born' and 'enlightened' males.

If a similar kind of paradise existed where beings might take rebirth only in female form, then access, one might conclude, would be limited to those in female form. Similarly, if such a female domain were to be given the same symbolic status as those of the male Buddhas, then the power of transmission of the teachings of that realm would lie in the hands, for the most part, of a female lineage. According to Diana Paul, the only reference to an equivalent 'land of women' appears in a Chinese Buddhist Sutra, where the option of a female achieving enlightenment in a female body, in a land peopled by women, is only one of four options for achieving enlightenment which relates to gender.[12] This domain is not featured in the mythologies of the Tibetan spiritual quest. Instead, the Dakini Pure Land offers some notion of the worth of the female body in the context of the Vajrayana, albeit without the possibility of the unique and subjective gender exclusivity for the female. Initiation into the teachings of the dakini land appears to take place through transmission of teachings by women in the guise of sexual partners, or as facilitators on the spiritual path, and *not* as direct teachers within their own female lineage. The boundaries of subjectivity, therefore, which protect the male symbolic, in his representation as Buddha and lineage, fail to withstand the intrusions of the male psyche when they pertain to the female. This dichotomy of significance, in which the male body resists encroachment by that of the female, further strengthens its own subjectivity by depriving the female body of hers.

HER SACRED DOMAIN AND LANGUAGE

Descriptions of the dakini Pure Land, known in Tibetan as *Ngayab Khandro Ling*, do suggest a more egalitarian representation of the gender question, than appears in some of the symbolic representations of male-gendered icons. Unlike the strictures of exclusivity which seem to surround issues regarding the male gender, no equivalent gender boundaries apply on the female side. Textual references show that male practitioners have access to the dakini Pure Land for the purposes of obtaining initiation, and even, as in the case of Padmasmbhava, to give initiation to the dakinis themselves. Furthermore, whilst the dakini Pure Land is the acknowledged destination of enlightened females such as Machig Labdron or Yeshe Tsogyal on their death, it is also the destination of certain male yogis such as Milarepa, who appear, from textual evidence, to retain their male form once they have entered that Pure Land. In the context of 'the enlightened state', this kind of disregard for the importance of gender or sexed categories seems much more in the spirit of the Buddhist teaching than the disenabling emphasis which is placed on gender in other areas of Tibetan Buddhist thought. But the problems of representation still pertain, because, for women, the issue is not about gender and its limitations, but about the ways in which the 'truth' is written on the female body.

Given that there are no mirror-like comparisons between the male and female domains, the symbolic female, whilst carefully not resting in the control of women, is incorporated completely into the patriarchal system. This enables the men of the lineage to speak not only for themselves, the symbolic male Buddha, and his descendents in the lineage, but also on behalf of the divine female, in a way which is quite plainly denied to women. The implications of this gender bias are not just that, at a simplistic level, male power is equated with dominance, but that the complex philosophy which appears to offer models of symbolism to both men and women actually fails to achieve egalitarianism at the everyday level. This failure is encoded again and again in the commentaries concerning the dakini, whose symbolic presence is interpreted from a point of view which consistently defers to the position of the guru *as male* and the female as *complementary*.

Clearly it is important to state that there is no reason why the feminine, as a fluid gender concept, could not be interpreted and experienced by men, for this is not only possible because it is a socially constructed concept, but also because men have just as much access as women do, to the feminine, and also to the female body, in the first place, through symbiotic uterine experience, and later through physical relationship with her or other women. However, at issue are two distinct questions in this debate. Firstly, one has to consider the importance of the interpretation of meaning which is specifically related to the female body, but given by one gender (i.e. the male) on behalf of the other. This act inevitably reflects the personal experience and bias of the interpreter, and *in the absence of a corollary*, or of an acknowledged 'difference' by the male speaking subject, appears to take on universal significance. Secondly, the use of the female body as a vehicle of symbolism *for women* remains problematic for them, because of the ways in which her representations are often less than validating of her subjectivity. It is very apparent that the relevance of these factors inevitably tilts the system towards an understanding by men, and reinforces the negation of women as subjects.

Other features of the interpretation of the characteristics of the dakini and her domain, reveal similar problematic areas for women. The significance of the 'twilight language', for example, reveals the reasons *why* the dakini is represented as female, and elucidates the connection between women's status and language itself. In the history of Tibetan Buddhism, those texts which were said to be written in the 'twilight language' of the dakinis often consisted of a single syllable, or were discovered written in a mysterious language which required to be deciphered by an able exponent of the spiritual path, such as a *terton*. Essentially, the notion was of a symbolic language, whose musical sounds could not only be heard mystically by advanced meditators, but whose elaborate meaning could be condensed into a single and mystical hieroglyph. Sound seems to have played an important part in the mythology of the teachings, for even in straightforward lineages where ordinary language was used, the texts were often said to have been received by the lama through a whispered communication by the divine voices of the dakinis.

Standing outwith the limits of ordinary understanding, and outwith the boundaries of language as we know it, the dakini 'twilight language' was a metaphor for divine transcendence, a state of 'otherness' which was transmitted through the female body, and in particular, the female *voice* of the dakini. Allione defines it as a language which is translated 'through "another way of knowing" which comes from a space which is far from the sunlit rational world dominated by the logos, and at the same time it is not from the dark abyss of the unconscious but rather a twilight world'.[13] She makes reference particularly to 'The Song of the Vajra', a chant used by certain schools, which is said to be in the dakini language, and whose sounds 'vibrate in the body of the individual and . . . bring(s) forth waves which massage the vibration of the being, bringing an integration with the spherical sounds of the universe'.[14]

The whole concept of a kind of language which is associated in this way with the female body, and which is both symbolic and indecipherable in conventional terms, is nonetheless interesting for the female voice is often absent in discourse, marginalised, or seen as hysterical. Also, as Julia Kristeva has pointed out, the expression of meaning through symbol, which is the subject of study in semiotics, is always associated with the feminine. She maintains that the expression of meaning which takes form in human existence in all artistic endeavours including the 'languages' of music, dance, poetry and art, has its roots in the early experience of pre-linguistic relationship with 'the other', who in most cases is the child's mother. Even if a child is removed from the mother at birth, it has still been subject to the mother's body for nine months, and contemporary research has shown that sound, and especially the mother's voice, plays a very important part in the baby's development. There is a link too between the experience of sound which the baby has, not only *in utero*, but also in its first year of life, through the closeness to the mother's actual heart, where the sound of the heartbeat is reminiscent of the sound of the drum, an instrument closely associated with the dakini, and one which may give its name to her Pure Land, *Nyayab Khandro Ling*, which could be translated as 'Dakini Land of Drumbeat'. It is no coincidence that a drum, struck in such a way as to excite the listener, clearly replicates the sound of the human heart beating faster in times of peril, or excitement.

Because this pre-linguistic state, which is characterised by the intensity of the senses, particularly hearing, touch, smell and taste, occurs before entry into the world of what Kristeva calls the 'law of the father',[15] and to the development of language, it is deemed 'feminine'. But, as Kristeva points out, the pre-linguistic stage of development actually knows no sexual difference, because infants have not yet developed an awareness of their own identity or gender, so whilst it may be related to *the body of the mother* it is a state in which paradox and enigma *do* exist side by side, without the presence of limiting polarities, amongst the first of which to arise is the difference in sexual identity. These are the very polarities which artistic endeavour attempts to reveal and elucidate, by crossing the boundaries of logic and reason to uncover expressions of ambiguity and paradox which are understood without suspension of belief.

THE DAKINI AS ESSENTIALLY FEMALE

In western discourse, it has been the divine intervention in the form of the female muse which has been credited with the inspiration of artists and writers, in addressing the paradoxes of everyday life. In the Tibetan system, the female body serves a similar purpose, as in the case of the dakini, who is clearly perceived as a form which transcends gender boundaries, like an early mother-figure to a pre-linguistic child, and has a strong connection to the primal sounds which lie outwith language as we know it in societal terms. In a sense this kind of association of art, the 'semiotic', or the 'symbolic female' as being 'beyond gender', 'other' or 'transcendental', is close to what Janice Willis expresses when she maintains that the dakini is 'not female',[16] all the while acknowledging that she is represented by the body of a woman. Paradoxical as this statement itself is, it nonetheless provides a degree of truth, but is, I maintain, only useful as an insight into how the categorisation of the female as a vehicle of meaning for men has been developed, much in the way the muse has become a symbol of the creativity arising from the psyches of western male artists. On the other hand, it is also my view that Willis's statement is extremely problematic for women themselves. In her study of the dakini, Janice Willis glosses over any explanation as to *why* the dakini is represented in female physical form, and is always used as an epithet for a female sexual partner, by claiming that the dakini is not female, but *feminine*, and as a representation goes beyond gender categorisation.

Related as the dakini language is in texts and in the iconography to the female body, this cypher is not, as Willis suggests, merely a *gender form*, as *feminine*, but is, I propose, more closely linked with female sexuality. This crucial difference of emphasis is important in the understanding of the symbolism and philosophy of Tibetan Buddhism as it pertains to women, for while it may be easy to abstract gender from either the male or the female body, it is impossible to abstract the human body from its sexuality. This means that whilst men and women may all be variations of a prescribed gender ideal, which in Buddhist terms is ultimately a manifestation of illusion, they are nonetheless restricted as different individuals to the experiences of their different physical bodies in relation to sexuality. It is this sexuality which is represented so vividly in the art of Tibet, not least in the images of the female form, with her nakedness, her swinging breasts, detailed vagina, and often wrathful appearance, which suggest something more than the simple gender category of 'femininity', as it has traditionally been defined.

For Willis, however, the dilemma of the dakini's gender and sexuality is summed up, when she acknowledges that it would 'require at least a book'[17] to explain *why* the predominant form of the dakini is female. My concern here, none the less, is to ensure that any discussion of the philosophy surrounding the dakini (and therefore her representation in a female body) *has* to be undertaken, *before* the dakini can be abstracted from the female body, and classified in some esoteric way as being 'not female' but 'feminine', as Willis suggests. If this is the case, there would be no reason for the dakini not to be portrayed in male form, having 'feminine' qualities (as Chenrezig does) and, if gender categories can be so easily swapped, there would also be no reason why male and female *yab-yum* representations could not be read as reversing the wisdom–means polarity embodied in them. Wrathful female deities such as Ekajati, for example, could be visualised in meditation as embodying 'masculine' (means) as a Tantric partner, or the Buddha himself, the 'feminine' (wisdom) partner. These kinds of shifts in perspective offer the possibility of opening the debate on what 'feminine' and 'masculine' really mean in respect of the deities in the pantheon, but the arguments about gender still seem to centre on how the female is perceived, whilst the resistance to de-gendering the male in the same way is very apparent. In particular, there is very strong resistance amongst Buddhist lamas to acknowledging the possibility that one of the historical Buddhas born into this world could take human form as a woman. By abstracting the 'feminine' from the female body of the dakini the place of the male as subject is unconsciously protected, whilst creating a notion of fluidity around the concept of the female body. This construct throws into question women's carnality, rather than the concept of femininity, which is certainly a potentially unstable social construct. Advocating a position which claims the irrelevance of gender is certainly a justified stance, but the consequences of such an argument when it relates to the sexed body is somewhat more complex. We must embrace the dakini, Willis says, 'regardless of whether we are "male" or "female" beings'.[18] Here the idea of gender as a fluid concept is expanded to encompass the more concrete reality of one's physical and sexual identity, proclaiming a kind of absolute Buddhist truth which, when applied to life as it exists, simply does not transfer. If 'male' and 'female' were as interchangeable in reality as Willis implies are 'masculinity' and 'femininity', then the patriarchal system would clearly have collapsed long ago.

Willis also maintains that whilst the dakini goes beyond gender 'she' may, however, take a myriad of forms, and includes as examples a stone statue, and a dog, but does not give the example of the dakini as male. Willis goes so far as to refer to the dakini as 'it' which she characterises as 'highest wisdom . . . direct, unmediated, non-conceptual understanding of Voidness',[19] a characteristic which, she says, is a necessary facet of Buddhist spiritual practice. Her Lacanian assertion that the dakini is not female but is '*all* that we lack!' (italics original)[20] firmly places the dakini in the role of complementary presence, where symbolically she becomes not what we are, but what we are *not*. This reading of the dakini is obviously more in tune with the psyches of men than those of women. Willis does go further, however, by acknowledging that '"she" is often the sexual partner or "mystic consort" (Tibetan, *rig ma*) of the *siddha*',[21] where the *siddha* (yogic master) she refers to is implicitly male. She writes, 'According to Katz's count, "fully fifty six of the eighty-four [Indian *mahasiddha-s*] are depicted in the company of a woman".'[22] The fifty-six must be read as men, so the "she" who is the sexual partner is patently female, for according to her statement, 'the aid of an actual flesh and blood partner is useful and/or required'.

Willis provides no textual example to show that a male dakini could be represented as a sexual consort to a woman practitioner, although the masculinised term *daka* is sometimes used, but with none of the connotations of the dakini. Male consorts to renowned female practitioners are usually considered to be emanations either of the Buddha, or of some other deity or mythological being. Perhaps if scholars were able to abstract the Buddha from his male gender, and all the lamas of the lineage from theirs, there might be more possibility of reaching an understanding of the emptiness of all gender categories, not simply those which relate to women. In the Tibetan case, it is clear that the non-static figure of the dakini, has been manipulated as a transformational symbol in whom gender may be used as an expedient means of either fixing or refuting particular concepts.

By repeating the tendency to deprive the female of a subjectivity whilst allowing the male his, Willis perpetuates a one-sided perspective by reading the dakini as 'lack', 'void' or a 'complement', thus echoing the western psychoanalytical notion of Lacan that the phallus is the signifier, and the feminine merely an absence. Lacan's infamous statement, 'woman does not exist', can easily be seen to be valid *vis-à-vis* the Tibetan system and ideology, because while she clearly does *not* exist as an acknowledged force within the system, she clearly *does* if one considers her essentiality for men. What many commentators fail to articulate is that it is *because* woman has been defined by men and in men's terms, her gender can be exploited as a movable entity to be used to reflect men's sense of 'other' or to be abstracted to the transcendental, when the acknowledgement of her subjectivity by-and-for-herself, becomes problematic for them.

This is adequately demonstrated by the many male commentators whose blind spot regarding gender and sexuality is revealed when they make statements such as, 'The woman, or rather the Dakini, transforms the man who lusts after her into *her* Guru, *the man of her dreams*' (italics mine).[23] Furthermore, 'It is the Dakini's nature of complete receptivity, empty space, that assuages male aggression; and it is *the female organ's 'empty space' that is receptive to the symbol of his aggression*' (italics mine).[24] Whilst these kinds of sentiments may be meaningful to male readers, and even hint at a symbolic rape of the female, there is no doubt that the polarised categorisations which they reveal are extremely problematic for women. Women may indeed be reinscribed in history, philosophy and representation as 'lack', 'empty' or 'receptive', but, in the absence of the articulation in history, philosophy and representation of a *something* which is the female body, which is the female voice and which is its sexuality, women's subjectivity will always be difficult to achieve.

THE DAKINI, FEMALE SUBJECTIVITY AND MEANING

It is apparent from traditional texts that the dakini as a female helper and sexual consort fits well into the arena of male-centred fantasy and spiritual endeavour. Willis's attempt, however, as a contemporary commentator, to rationalise the meaning of the dakini to women relies on a further negation of the female body in which her essential sexuality, *and its meaning*, is abstracted to a concept of enlightened energy of *universal* significance. But it is clear that the female body has a different meaning for men than it does for women, so, while men may be reassured by this definition of the dakini, it does little to enable women to understand their own unique subjectivity. The de-stabilisation of a concept related to the female body at once hinders women in their quest, and simultaneously promotes the cause of men. It is this kind of interpretation of philosophical concepts concerning the physical body which, whilst claiming to be 'beyond duality' are, on the contrary, locked into it.

The word dakini, as has been illustrated, is widely used to represent a number of concepts, including a certain kind of esoteric and dynamic energy, a female deity, and a woman who has achieved status either as a practitioner, or through sexual involvement with a high lama. The human dakini, so often referred to in texts as an outstanding practitioner, is described most often in association with a male yogi, who attempts to further his own practice through sexual acts, or who requires the intervention of a wise woman in order to clear his spiritual path of obstacles, or awaken him out of a tendency to intellectualise. Whilst in the former role the dakini is represented as a very young and beautiful woman (16 years old seems to be the optimum age), in the latter role she frequently appears in the form of an old and ugly hag. These polarised representations associate the dakini, in turn, with virginal sexuality or with the figure of the crone, two of the three aspects of the ancient triple goddess, the third being the mother. Similarly, iconographic representations tend to show the dakini as a young, naked figure in a dancing posture, often holding a skull cup filled with menstrual blood or the elixir of life in one hand, and a curved knife or a drum in the other, sometimes wearing a garland of human skulls, with a trident staff leaning against her shoulder. Her hair is usually wild and hanging down her back, her face often wrathful in expression, as she dances on top of a corpse, to represent her complete mastery over ego and ignorance.[25] Dakinis may also be represented in different colours, to show their association with the five different

'Buddha Families' each of whom represent the purified wisdom of a certain aspect of emotional defilement.

In the sense that each individual iconographic figure represents, through its colour, stance, demeanour, and accoutrements, certain facets of the Buddhist teaching, the dakini is no different from other Buddhist deities. It is in the association of her body, however, with *essentialist* qualities which pertain to the meaning of the female that her representations of 'lack' or 'emptiness' become problematic. It is certainly the case that the original form of these philosophies, written as they were in ancient Sanskrit texts, did attempt to break the bounds of dualistic thinking by expressing paradoxical notions in language. One only has to read the text of the Heart Sutra to understand this, 'Form is emptiness, emptiness itself is form; emptiness is no other than form, form is no other than emptiness'.[26] But the transference of a written philosophy to visual representations within the iconography (which already favoured the male as subject, both as Buddha and as lama) meant that the religious concepts which were supposed to be 'beyond duality' were simply encoded in notions which perpetuated the superiority of the male, and represented the paradoxical or the unrepresentable in female form. The Heart Sutra, for example, was personified as the Prajnaparamita (in Tibetan *Yum Chenmo* or the Great Mother), and worshipped in deified form as a female deity who was associated with emptiness and transcendence. In the case of the dakini it was the particular aspect related to emptiness, or 'lack', as Willis calls it, which seemed to make her a suitable medium for man's enlightenment quest through sexuality. These kinds of concepts, which were related to certain deities, and which involved gendering notions such as 'enlightenment', 'means', 'wisdom' and 'emptiness', further complicated the issue of sexual being as it is understood in the context of Tibetan Buddhism.

Agehananda Bharati, in his study of Tantra, points out the discrepancy between the Buddhist Tantric assignation of the static principle to the female, and the dynamic principle to the male, while the Hindu Tantric assignation was the opposite. With the Indian tradition being older, he claims that the Tibetans made a choice to create their polarity symbolism in this way, but somehow retained the *shakti* element of the Hindu goddesses who were sexually dynamic. In this way, the Tibetans had representational

access both to the passive goddesses, whose iconography fitted
in with the philosophical notions of female/wisdom (*prajna* in
Sanskrit, *sherab* in Tibetan), and male/means (*upaya* in Sanskrit,
tab in Tibetan); *and* the dynamic, autonomous goddesses such as
Dorje Phagmo, who were often represented alone. Bharati suggests
that these dynamic goddesses emerged in Tibet during a period of
transition to a more orthodox Buddhism. That they survived at all
may be due in no small part to the fact that indigenous tradition was
very strong, and very little centralisation of power possible in the
vast expanses of hostile terrain, with a large itinerant population.
As a result, the Tibetan pantheon can be seen to offer images of
the female which have the possibility of disrupting the traditional
significance of male/active, female/passive, and thus offer for
women the kind of representations of the divine which might
bring about a different kind of subjectivity. My contention is that
the passive mother images, alongside the *yab-yum* representations
with their conservative aura, were allowed to predominate through
tradition and neglect, created by more powerful imperatives in the
social sphere, whilst the dynamic images were relegated to the
realms of secrecy, with their practices only in the hands of an élite,
who controlled access to them.

In the Tibetan system the focus on a particular paradigm of
sexuality expressed in the *yab-yum*, meant that the dakini formed
the concrete means through which men could unite with 'the
other' in order to achieve the mystical experience of unity, the
forerunner of supposed Buddhahood. The 'twilight language',
on the other hand, offered an esoteric cypher by which men
could gain access to the mystical world of the female, and by
so doing gain a sense of wholeness. Keith Dowman maintains
that, having reached this symbolic level, the male might then be
able to articulate the language (and therefore the feminine) in
an 'appropriate'[27] way to others. The difficulty with these kinds
of concepts for women, I would argue, is that any supposed
clarity which might be interpreted from the translation of a
female-centred symbolic into the patriarchal world of dualisms
would inevitably fall into the control of its (male) proponents.
This is the very reductionism, incorporation and assimilation of
the female into the male domain, which renders her as 'other',
a category in which she is defined by and through her relation

to the dominant force – the male. In other words she is unable to define herself, and must rely on the 'enlightened' men of the lineage to establish her position *vis-à-vis* their own. In terms of the evolution of the lineage system, therefore, the absence of a female-centred symbolic, articulated in the context of a *female* subjective, has given rise to an ambiguous presence within the institutions of Buddhism, and has created a situation of compromise for women practitioners.

The same is also true of the female role in the sexual practices of the Tantra. It should be apparent that women ought to have more of an affinity than men to the experiences and meaning of female sexuality. In the absence of opportunities for the legitimate expression of this crucial assertion of subjectivity, women easily fall victim to charges of passivity and exploitation, but in most societies the taboo against this very articulation has meant that women have failed to express the power of their own being in the same way as men have done. It is not just the expression of female sexuality which is missing from historical texts, but also its *symbolic* representations. In psychoanalytic terms, the female imaginary, which relates specifically to the female experience of early relationship with the mother, and to the development of the female-as-subject, has been suppressed under all forms of patriarchy. On the other hand, the male imaginary, and the establishment of male subjectivity centred on the male experience of relationship, have been well articulated throughout history, in myth, religion, literature, art, and more recently in psychoanalysis itself. In European philosophical traditions, for example, there is plenty of evidence to show the predominance in culture and thought of the Oedipal myth, which relates to the male experience of relationship to the parents and to power structures in society.

In Tibetan Buddhism it could be argued (as does Robert A. Paul) that this is not only present in the myths concerning the father–son relationship of the lineage, but is also expressed in terms of mother–son relationships through the valorised accounts of the mothers of tulkus, and through such analogies as the meeting of the mother–son, to represent the state of luminosity one may achieve in the *bardo*[28] after death. What is plainly missing in the symbolism of Tibetan Buddhism are representations of the father–daughter, and more importantly mother–daughter, relationship, which as

Irigaray has noted might provide the required kind of representation in culture through which women could create a viable sexual identity through the manifestation of female subjectivity. 'Woman must be valued as a daughter (a virgin for herself, and not so that her body has an exchange value amongst men), as a lover, and in her own line'.[29]

One could argue that the suppression of meaning *vis-à-vis* the position and subjectivity of the female has become an habitual tendency in different cultures throughout history, and that this has both preserved male power and neglected women. These powerful systems have, until modern times, either co-opted, cajoled or bullied women into colluding with the negation of representations of the female experience, and this has allowed men to dictate their world view at the expense of a balanced position. I have already shown how *yab-yum* symbolism is declared to be of benefit to men in their struggle for subjectivity, meaning and enlightenment, but what use is it to women, whose practice might require them to take account of their sexuality in forms which relate to *her* perspective? Perhaps one of the clues to the prospect of reversing the debasement of female subjectivity lies in the images of the female herself, and the meaning behind her gestures. It is certainly possible that the actual symbols used may not in themselves be detrimental, but the interpretation of their meaning has tended to be very one sided. As I have described, the word for the female sexual partner is *mudra*, or *chaja* (Tibetan *byags.gya*) which literally means (in both Sanskrit and Tibetan) 'seal', 'symbol'. The word is also commonly used to describe the ritualistic and symbolic hand gestures or body postures which are adopted by dieties within the iconography. From these meanings it can be seen that the female is clearly identified as the *signifier*. In Lacan's work, he theorises that 'the Other represents language, the site of the signifier' where 'the Other is the locus of constitution of the subject or the structure that produces the subject'.[30] In other words, the *mudra* is significant in the constitution of the male subject. However, in its usage as the female sexual partner, it is usually written as *karma mudra*, or *lae chi chaja* (Tibetan *las.kyi byags.gya*) where *karma* (Tibetan *las*) meaning 'action', clearly suggests *movement*. This kind of linguistic representation implies that woman is *not* sexually passive, but rather finds her expression in movement.

In the texts the *karma mudra*, in her form as a human dakini, classically appears to men at difficult moments, to clear away obstacles or to provide the sexual experience by which spiritual realisation could be achieved. The concept, however, of female *movement* embedded in this term, and also found in her iconographic representations which invariably show her as dancing or flying, is one which has been taken up by Irigaray, in a different context, in her analysis of the development of subjectivity in the female. She maintains that dance is one way in which the female 'can create a territory of her own in relation to the mother'.[31] Unlike the male, whose physical *difference* enables him to forge a differentiation from the mother in order to establish his identity as male, the female's relationship is more intimate and complex because the mother is of the *same* physical essence as the daughter, and thus the daughter can never be completely different. Irigaray suggests that whilst the boy may make use of objects, and ritual, which he manipulates in an attempt to achieve not only his own sense of subjectivity, but also mastery over the mother's absence at certain moments in his life, the girl uses dance or movement of *her own body*, in order to map out, by defining her own boundaries, her own special relationship with the mother. In an abstract sense, this is something which she points out is similar in composition to the Tibetan mandala, which, as a sacred territory, consists of highly symbolic boundaries which incorporate movement. Furthermore, her notion is that women need 'an axis of their own, which on the microcosmic level moves from between the feet in the standing position up through the head, and macrocosmically from the center of the earth to the center of the sky.'[32] She goes on, 'This axis can be seen represented in the iconographic traces of traditions in which women had some visible presence.'[33]

One only has to glance at the particular form of the dance position adopted by the ancient Tantric goddesses in paintings and sculptures, including the important Vajra Varahi or Dorje Phagmo,[34] as she was known in Tibetan, to see how viable a subjective presence she has. Furthermore, it is known from Hindu Tantric sources that the dancing posture of the female, especially when depicted as dancing on top of the male, suggested her *active* sexuality, something which was crucial to the early Tantric philosophy. Bharati declares that sexual advances intiated by the male were, in these times, construed as 'crude', and that the desired role of the *sakti* was active. The reversal of this role in Tibetan Tantrism therefore gave different meanings to the depictions of the dancing goddesses whose images were retained in the Tibetan iconography. The comparisons between contemporary western psychoanalytical thought and the images of Asian cultures may not be as far fetched as they might seem. If the Tantric teachings originated, as I have already suggested, at a time when female subjectivity was acknowledged and represented in societies which recognised the powers of female creativity and fertility, then the sacred rituals, diagrams and spaces created by such a philosophy would have had to reflect in some way a subjective essentialism of the female form. Also, if mundane subjectivity is achieved in different ways by men and women, then the symbolic representations of that subjectivity would have to take account of the different ways in which the two sexes express their subjective desire for union with the mother, or in metaphysical and historical terms, the Great Mother. This appears to have been done through the image of the dance.

It is certainly the case that the undertaking of gesture, dance, art and music in the ritualistic ceremonies of worship in many ancient traditions originated at a time when rational thought did not prevail, and when culture and nature were not posited as polarities. Whilst it could be argued that these symbols may still have the potential to be of value to both men and women, I sustain that their incorporation into an institutional system which has been predominantly patriarchal has meant that the reading of their meaning has been undertaken by and for men. Within this tradition, however, it is possible to see that for women the *potentiality* for positive identifiable representations is discernable in certain aspects of the symbolism, but very often it has been engulfed by the over-riding needs of the male, who has either objectified the female or incorporated her image for his own purposes. This has happened in relation to the imagery of the mother in her form as Yum Chenmo, or Kuntu Zangmo,[35] and in the imagery of the consort, in her forms as dakini. As a result, it has been difficult for women to achieve any degree of autonomy or subjectivity, equated with the symbolic representations of 'enlightenment', under the divine law of men. Much as the prospect of being a participant in male sacred rituals might be attractive, it in no way compensates for the lack of understanding which dictates the law which states that gender, or more specifically, sexuality, is ultimately insignificant in the quest for enlightenment. The iconography itself makes quite clear that this is not the case.

THE ETYMOLOGY OF DAKINI (TIBETAN 'KHANDRO')

In Tibetan the word *khandro* is everywhere interchangeable with the Sanskrit *dakini*, but its roots are entirely different in the two languages, and it is doubtful that the two words are synonymous. The roots of *khandro* are 'kha' (Tibetan *mkha.*) meaning sky or space; and 'dro' (Tibetan *'gro*) meaning goer or traveller. On the other hand, the Sanskrit word *dakini* is defined as a 'kind of female demon (in the retinue of Kali) that feeds on human flesh',[36] and has no roots in any meaning related to sky or space. The male equivalent of the dakini, the *daka*, appears in the Sanskrit language also defined as 'an attendent of Kali' and both words were clearly imported into the Tibetan language from India and adapted to Buddhist teachings to mean a variety of different goddesses. The other word which is sometimes used in Tibetan for *khandro* is *pamo*, which has both a male counterpart (*pawo*) and Sanskrit equivalents. Meaning 'hero', the words *pawo* and *pamo* are the same as the Sanskrit words *vira*, and *sura*, which both mean heroic. The word *khandro* therefore is quite a unique word, with no male equivalent, and would seem to have arisen not out of the Sanskrit background of Tantra, (as *pawo* and *pamo* do) but apparently from the shamanistic roots of Tibet itself. This is an important observation, because it does mean that as a term it is unusually confined to the female body, much in the same way that the term *Buddha* has generally been confined to that of the male.

On the one hand, the name 'sky-goer' obviously has connotations of the ancient goddesses associated with the heavens, and the notion of moving through the skies strongly suggests the supernatural, or magical attributes associated with such a deity. On the other hand, the philosophical notion of a 'traveller in space', which is an equally valid interpretation of the word, suggests a more esoteric meaning to do with the metaphysical attributes of the divine female in the context of space, and therefore time. As I have previously shown, it is the space–time dynamic as a crucial factor in the notion of the feminine, and in the female experience of cyclical rather than linear time, which places the dakini quite specifically in her own dimension of paradox. This is the dimension which Irigaray characterises as offering 'the features of the unconscious . . . its fluidity and mobility; its indifference to the laws of logic (identity and non-contradiction); its inability to speak *about* itself'.[37] As a movable symbol, the dakini occupies no ground, but rather, as her name suggests, simply moves in 'space'. This attribute is useful for the male practitioner who can make use of her non-position in any way which is expedient. Dowman himself confirms this view,

> The word Dakini, or Khandroma, has introduced a valuable new concept to the western world. The value of the concept is in its very *lack* of precise definition; it embraces a range of meaning – the female principle, a moment of spiritual integration, the Guru's Consort, a female sexual partner – that adds up to an enigma and paradox. (Italics mine)[38]

Of course Dowman is mistaken when he suggests that the Tibetan concept of the dakini as enigmatic and paradoxical introduces something new into western discourse, for it does not. However, the way in which these particular ideas concerning the female are transmitted through the language, philosophy and iconography of Tibetan Buddhism *is* certainly new to westerners, some of whom may be unfamiliar with the comparisons with certain strands in contemporary feminist philosophy and psychoanalytic thought. Furthermore, the implications of the association of the female with the concept of 'enigma' are made even more difficult to grasp in the context of Tibetan Buddhism, which, though structurally patriarchal, still makes use of very ancient symbols which carried a very different meaning, at a very different time and within a very different cultural milieu.

Chapter 8
The Question of 'Otherness' in Female Representation

The unique position occupied by the dakini, as a symbol of substantial meaning in Tibetan Buddhism, is augmented by other symbolic representations of the female, which tend to emphasise either her oppositional otherness, or her divine transcendence. As I have shown, in the Vajrayana Buddhist scriptures, 'otherness' is commonly represented as either demon or woman, or as both. In the spiritual realm, the Tibetan Buddhist's ultimate goal is to realise all phenomena (both external experience and the mind itself) as emptiness. As Longchenpa states of the appearances of the physical world, which he maintains are 'created by mind',[1]

> Although in their manifestation as errant appearance and in the mistaken belief in their reality they seem to be veridical for all practical purposes, actually they have no essence (of their own) and have never moved from the range of original awareness.[2]

Here mind and phenomena are brought within the same philosophical sphere, in which duality and otherness appear to collapse as concepts. However, as I will show, the promise of a non-dual philosophy, applicable to men and women, is not fulfilled, for in the allocation of symbolic femaleness to the concepts of both 'otherness' and 'emptiness', the application of the philosophy is rendered problematic for women. As I have demonstrated, women's 'otherness' is considered to be a real threat to the potential spirituality of the male. The monastic tradition emphasised the polluting aspect of women, and encouraged celibacy and physical distance from women. On the other hand, women were viewed as essential components to advanced Tantric practice, which addressed the understanding of man's being through his sexuality. In both respects, however, woman is 'other', either through her negative potential or through her female being and sexuality with which man had to associate in order to reach his full potential (Buddhahood). This state was sought, as illustrated previously, through the higher practices of the Tantra which involved meditation based on the utilisation of sexuality as a potent force for spiritual awareness, or realisation of emptiness.

As I have also shown, in the Tibetan case the symbolic male motherhood implied by the tulku system was a crucial part of its patrilineal ideology, for through it the male lineage was elevated to the realms of the sacred. In many examples in the iconography, Tibetan scroll paintings depict the lineage of lamas as divine beings alongside the Buddha, and various other deities, thereby signifying their centrality to the whole system. I have suggested that the definition of the mother as profane and the son as sacred in the social system, together with the abrogation of her role and its subsequent adoption by the male lineage, gave rise to a particular kind of religious philosophy which was reflected in the exclusion of women from positions of power within society. But how exactly did this philosophy express itself within the texts and iconography of Tibetan Buddhism?

One way was to make use of this particular philosophical concept in relation to the female, and to endow her, as mother, with the transcendental qualities which distinguish her from the mundane female who must be shunned. The most popular deity who represented the mother was Dolma, a variation, as I have already shown, of the Great Lotus Goddess of antiquity. We know also that the 'Great Mother' of the Mahayana tradition, the Prajnaparamita, was deemed to be the mother of the Buddhas, and a symbol of the absolute. Robert A. Paul has suggested that men construe the absolute *as* female, but taboo and untouchable in her form as Mother Buddha, or Prajnaparamita. From her realm, the *Dharmadhatu*, the Buddha is born, and she is viewed as unborn and uncreated, and therefore 'other' than the Buddha, who is viewed as male. The further association of a non-dualistic ideal, 'emptiness', with the specifically dualistic concept of the feminine, and subsequently of the female body, has succeeded in foreclosing the potential of a particular philosophy of relevance to women practitioners. Guenther's view that 'Male and female are only the adaptation to organic life of basic polarity pertaining to the very process of becoming'[3] certainly reflects the promise of a non-dualistic approach to the philosophy of gender, but his telling use of the term 'basic polarity' betrays his assumption of male and female as opposing categories, in which, if the evidence of textual reference is to be believed, the male is subject and the female 'other', either as an oppositional force, or as transcendent emptiness.

Whilst the symbolic allocation of woman's role as either harmful or expedient to the practice of the male can be understood as a straightforward example of the dualistic notions which concern religious practice, it is more difficult to understand the allocation of the female gender to the concept of the absolute, or 'emptiness', as being that which is *beyond duality*. Arguing that the understanding of 'emptiness' is the state to be achieved in order to become 'Buddha', i.e. a divine, transcendent being, Robert A. Paul maintains that because 'emptiness' is associated in the (male) practitioner's mind as being a state of 'otherness', it is therefore associated with the female, whose 'otherness' is already established in his mind. Guenther too points out the importance of the Tantric view of 'emptiness' and its association with the female,

> basic nothing is termed 'ancestress', which is a verbal symbol for pure transcendence. In the fine arts this *nothing* is represented as a female figure. . . . This conception of the ground of man's Being as female has important consequences for the whole attitude of Buddhism. It recognises the female principle in the nature of things as *valid in its own right* and attributes to it an inspiring and emotionally moving character of friendliness, tenderness and intimacy, the greatest one being the union of two lovers . . . its symbolic representation in the human female form lets the transcendent and the divine remain near man, who becomes the centre of this-worldliness and other-worldliness. (Italics mine)[4]

It is clear that Guenther's statement is not a general one in which the word 'man' could be read as either male or female, because for women, naturally, 'otherness' and the female human form would not be synonymous (except through belief in cultural norms, by which women often *do* experience their bodies/selves as 'other', a patently disfunctional state). Yet his view on what he calls the 'female principle' is interesting because Guenther's implication is that the male practitioner must accept the different and unique reality of the female, as a 'being-in-herself' (to para-phrase Guenther's terminology), whilst simultaneously objectifying actual women as the embodiment of 'other-worldliness'. His acknowledgement of the special Buddhist position which affirms the female not only as 'basic ground' but also as 'valid in its own right' is, however, undermined by his rationale for representing transcendence and emptiness as female. Guenther, in a blinkered view of the reality of the physical body and its relationship to the 'speaking subject', sees only the male side of the equation, ignoring completely the implications for women practitioners who might be involved in Tantric practices which already symbolised their bodies as transcendent or 'nothing'.

The question of the incorporation of 'otherness', as a pre-requisite for enlightenment, which Guenther implies must be experienced (by men) through sexual relations with a real woman, appears in many texts which try to show the relationship between external reality and the mind's understanding of emptiness. Often the concept of 'otherness' is associated with the subjugation of demons, for, as Paul has noted, 'In general it may be said that the demons, the passions and women are conceptually related, and thought of as opponents of Buddhism, and of patriarchal unity'.[5] Certainly this idea is not unique to Buddhist thought, but it does have implications for women practitioners, especially where diminished symbols of female subjectivity are the only ones which can be called upon to balance this one-sided view. In order to try and understand the way in which this philosophy of the incorporation of the 'other' works, it may be useful to turn again to one of the most popular pieces of literature in the Tibetan canon, the biography of Milarepa.

In 'The Tale of the Red Rock Jewel Valley', Milarepa is troubled during his meditation practice by demonic local deities,[6] who appear to him in a variety of physical forms. He realises that he must overcome their presence in order to advance his practice to the realms of perfect equanimity. His first thoughts concerning the demons reveal his acknowledgement of their reality as ghosts, 'These must be magical apparitions of the local deities who dislike me. Although I have been here a long time, I have never given them any offering or compliment.'[7] Deciding to try and pacify them, he sings a complimentary song, but when this does not work he begins a 'powerful incantation',[8] then preaches the Buddhist dharma to them out of compassion. Later, when they refuse to disappear, he realises, in accordance with Buddhist teaching, that 'all beings and phenomena are of one's own mind'[9] and ceases to fear them, *at which point they disappear.*

In another encounter with local deities who attempt to disrupt him with displays of aggression, he firstly prays for protection to his own guardian deities, and when this has no effect tries to quell their disturbing influences by offering them his own body. In the end he succeeds in taming and converting them by exposing them as simply 'creations of the delusory thoughts of the clinging (mind), which grasps forms and deems them to be real'.[10] This mysterious act of meditation which transforms perception so that fear vanishes, has, according to Milarepa, similar benefits for the demons themselves, 'The malignant male and female demons who create myriad troubles and obstructions seem real before one has Enlightenment; but when one realises their nature truly, they become Protectors of the Dharma.'[11]

There are several interesting features in these two accounts of the transformational aspects of a particular meditation practice, which parallel the Tibetan philosophy of the female. First of all, it is clear that there are three distinct ways of viewing the demons. They can either be seen as real, with substantial power, and therefore deserving of acknowledgement and pacification, or as inferior beings requiring compassionate help. A third alternative is to realise them as illusory forms which simply arise as projections out of the practitioner's mind due to its impure and unenlightened state. These three views, in turn, represent the different schools of Buddhist thought as viewed by the Tibetans. On the one hand, the Hinayana accepts reality as it is, with its polarised good and evil, and promotes a code of practice which adheres to rules and discipline in order to foster the former and avoid the latter. On the other hand, the Mahayana, which bases its view on the understanding of emptiness, nonetheless relies particularly on a doctrine of compassion for others as the essential path. The third interpretation corresponds to the Vajrayana perspective which anchors the transmutational quality of the mind in the very nature of dualism itself. The Vajrayana tackles the dilemmas surrounding duality by explicitly attempting to break the very boundaries which separate 'self' and 'other', 'good' and 'bad', 'inner' and 'outer'. Reality is often described as nothing more than a dream.

Kalu Rinpoche, in an explanation of the Vajrayana position to the French writer Arnaud Desjardins,[12] compared the practice of the three different Yanas to eating a bowl of poison. The Hinayana approach is to avoid eating it, the Mahayana approach is to eat it knowing the antidote, and the Vajrayana approach is to eat it deliberately, transmuting the poison to nectar through the realisation of the emptiness, *tongpanyi* (Tibetan *stong.pa.nyid*, Sanskrit *sunyata*)[13] of all phenomena. Milarepa's developing relationship with the demons appears to follow the view of the Yanas in consequential order, thereby inferring the superiority of the *Vajrayana*. Whichever way they are viewed, their presence *is* affirmed, however, as either definite entities, with an external individual existence, which can be perceived through the senses, or as manifestations of the deluded thought processes of the ordinary mind. Even the enlightened mind incorporates them into its perfect vision, not as the 'other' but as allies to the path of enlightenment. In this way the interdependence of mind and phenomena is established, with reality and illusion as terms or categories which cannot be fixed as opposing dualities, given the position and centrality of the mind itself, from which everything is said to arise.

This is the same process which occurs in the conceptualisation of the female. Firstly, she may be viewed as the very real physical enemy who causes obstructions for man on his spiritual quest, and therefore must be either rejected or denied so that he can proceed unproblematically. Secondly, she may be seen as deserving of compassion, because of her inferior birth, whilst being conceptualised, like man, as essentially empty by nature. The third view posits all phenomena as projections of the mind, and therefore sees woman in her manifestation of 'other-worldliness' as an embodiment of either emptiness or transcendence, which may be incorporated through sexual relations, so that man may achieve enlightenment. The Vajrayana view obliges man to confront deliberately the difference which woman presents, ideally bridging the gap between the view of woman as enemy and woman as nothing, by both recognising her mundane presence and conceptualising her as transcendent, through sexual activity. As man's archaic 'other', woman has been represented in Tibetan Buddhism in all of these ways.

Whilst providing a philosophical framework for men, however, these representations have deprived woman of the ability to define herself in terms of *her own* transcendence, because the iconography represents ultimate subjectivity in terms of the historically embodied male Buddha. Furthermore, a system which evolved to privilege the male cannot be simply transposed to produce concepts about the female which will mirror his experiences and perceptions of physical being, because the symbols which emerge in the iconography of a culture, ultimately relate to the social and cultural norms operative within the society which produces them. Logically any system which privileged the female, in the same way the system has privileged the male, would lead to radical social change. It is clear too that whilst woman is not the same as man, neither is she a polar opposite, for *all* humans (whether male or female) experience the 'other', in the first instance, in their relationship with the female as mother, which means that the earliest possible experiences, including those of being in the womb, do not always constitute for the female the obverse of the male.

It is not therefore appropriate to suggest that by simply reversing symbolism, significant meaning will be produced for female practitioners, for, as I have already shown, that symbolism is very much rooted in the bodies of the male and female. Textual evidence bears this out, because it is clear that gendered classifications and symbolic meanings are not seen to change depending on the gender of the practitioner. If they did, then logically, 'otherness' for women would be equated with maleness, and men seen as either embodiments of the transcendental, or a threat to women's good practice. Not only that but the image of Buddha, as the enlightened subject, would be female for women, and the significance of the female body, menstruation and the potential for motherhood as natural and fundamental facets of femaleness, would have to be reconsidered, and integrated into the female symbolic which would have to emerge.

If the symbols were truly read in this way, there is no doubt that societal norms, as well as theological perspectives, would change considerably. Perhaps this is the process to which Anne C. Klein alludes in her inconclusive critique of the status of Tibetan women. Klein proposes that there does exist within Tibetan Buddhism a seemingly positive female symbolism, and wonders whether an 'inappropriate reification'[14] displaces notions of spirituality which are potentially of value to women. 'In a Buddhist context this can happen' she writes, 'when the essential nature of things, emptiness or primordial purity, is treated as if it had a life of its own, apart from those persons and things whose nature it is. That sets the scene for women to be characterized in less exalted ways.'[15] Klein stops short of acknowledging that the actual association of such a primordial purity with the female, far from being liberating, creates an iconography which ultimately binds the female to her position in relation to the male, and not, as Guenther implies she should be, *valid in her own right*. That the non-dual should be characterised in dualistic terms, through the medium of gender, may reflect the ambiguities of language, but it does little for the cause of female spirituality which is stymied by the position in which women are obliged to be placed. Furthermore, in the context of the social and iconographical structures, the exclusion of the female in worldly terms, and the appropriation of the female in transcendental terms, can only be seen to be of benefit to the ruling class – the priesthood of incarnate lamas, and the lineage system.

Luce Irigaray is not as optimistic as Klein seems to be about woman's potential in the context of patriarchal power, for she writes, 'Woman, for her part, remains in unrealized potentiality – unrealized, at least, for/by herself. . . . Ontological status makes her incomplete and uncompletable. She can *never* achieve the *wholeness* of her form' (italics original).[16] This seems particularly true in the Tibetan system where the potential of wholeness in the female form, quite clearly represented in some of the more archaic Tantric images, is somehow never realised in the social sphere. I have argued that this is because the association of emptiness with the female links the female body to a concept of the transcendental, which means that the female body is exploited by the male in his quest for his own topology, while she herself has no adequate means to realise her own. The transcendental therefore becomes, as Irigaray understands it, 'the arena of the (philosophical) subject split off from its ground'.[17] This, she maintains, 'prevents women's accession to subjectivity'.[18] Furthermore, the creation and control of symbolic images of women by men also prevent 'woman from acceding to her own separate being; she must always be for-men, available for *their* transcendence' (italics mine).[19]

In the Tibetan Buddhist system and its iconography, the position/non-position allocated to the female helps to sustain a double-bind from which there is no escape. This is by no means unique to Tibetan society, for as Elizabeth Berg has stated, with reference to the dilemma for women in western culture,

> [I]f she is represented – this representation must necessarily take place within the context of a phallocentric system . . . in which the woman is reduced to mirroring the man. On the other hand, the presence of woman as a blank space – as refusal of representation – only serves to provide a backdrop or support for masculine projections.[20]

Apart from the blatantly negative representations of women which do appear in Tibetan texts, most other images fall into either of these two categories, so that, for example, the lives of saintly women tend to mirror those of men, i.e. within the lineage context, and therefore subject to the limitations of the system, whilst divine representations such as the dakini or the Yum Chenmo, embody the concept of emptiness or paradox. This latter 'refusal of representation' is, as Klein has noted, impossible to translate into egalitarianism within the social sphere.

In the Tibetan Buddhist hierarchical institution, the acquisition of power for women seems unlikely to go beyond tokenism for some time, because in their unique and complex social system (albeit in exile from their own land) the symbols of spiritual and temporal power have been so intertwined in the iconography and the philosophy, through the stress placed on the *lineage*, that any disruption of any part of that system would, I maintain, threaten to change the whole philosophical view. Because the image of the male-Buddha-lama predominates in the system, and the key to understanding that system remains locked in the secrecy of the practices, and the suppression of the female, it is my contention that its evolution within western culture will be signalled by the inevitable abandonment of the tulku system, as it presently stands, and the close examination of the principles of egalitarianism which are enshrined in the philosophy. This would be done through a reciprocity between the stated elements of dualism, notably the male and female, and an acceptance of *difference* as a determinant of culture, rather than *dualism* or *sameness*. Woman would then be viewed not as an *obstructor*, a *complement*, or as even as the *embodiment* of transcendence, but as a self-defining subject in her own right.

In order to reach that position as a speaking-subject, women would have to attain enough autonomy to speak and act outwith the approval, control or supervision of men. This would return them to a position of philosophical equality with men. However, it is often extremely difficult for women to extricate themselves from male-dominated systems of religious power, principally because the *ideals* of these systems are often akin to the kinds of experiences women have in day-to-day life. This means that their experiences are perceived to fit in with the ideals of the religion, *even though these experiences are the ones they wish to change.* As Irigaray states,

> If . . . the mystical experience is precisely an experience of the loss of subjecthood, of the disappearance of the subject/object opposition, it would seem to hold a particular appeal for women, whose very subjectivity is anyway being denied and repressed by patriarchal discourse.[21]

In the Tantric tradition many of the practices explicitly state the undesirability of an *attachment to self*, known in Tibetan as *dagzin*, (*bdag.'dzin*), encouraging instead a symbolic yet sacrificial approach to the human body and mind through meditation practices such as the *Chöd*[22] or the mandala[23] offering. Considering the sacrifical role which women are usually called upon to enact in the social sphere, it is tempting to agree with Irigaray's notion that women's affinity with certain religious practices mirrors everyday existential experiences, in particular those which tap into women's already weak sense of self (or female identity). In her analysis of the Buddhist teaching concerning the self, Rita Gross distinguishes between 'self' and 'ego' by explaining that 'ego' is what is required to be 'dismantled',[24] no matter what 'style' it has, because 'someone who is forceful doesn't have "more ego" than someone who is shy and retiring'.[25] Gross proposes that it is entirely possible to 'go directly from the unhealthy and often overly weak or co-dependent *ego styles that characterize women in patriarchy* to the health of egolessness' (italics mine),[26] and describes ego as that which 'names the defence mechanisms, projections, and other tactics habitually used to cope with and ward off direct experience'.[27] On the other hand, Gross maintains that 'a healthy, functioning sense of self or *identity* is necessary for . . . spiritual development' (italics mine),[28] and that, without it, it is not possible 'to pursue Buddhist spiritual disciplines, which, by themselves, may not be sufficient to heal the emotional deprivations'.[29] As emotional deprivations in everyone tend to manifest themselves in defence mechanisms and projections, it is not clear what that 'healthy sense of self' (which is required *in order* for someone to attempt dismantling the ego) would actually be.

I am therefore not as convinced as Gross that it is possible to separate self and ego in this way, nor to insinuate a third more stable factor which supposedly underlies the ego and the identity. In discussing what it is that must be destroyed, she says that ego is 'any style of habitual patterns and responses that clouds over the clarity and openness of *basic human nature*' (italics mine).[30] In the context of this search for female identity, the question of 'basic human nature' presupposes that there is, beyond individual experience *as men and women*, a unitary experience of humanity which does not take into account sexual difference. This notion fits very well with Gross's 'Androgynous Vision in Buddhism',[31] in which she sets out the mandating and institutionalising of gender equality through the adoption of androgynous institutions and 'androgynous thinking' which would recognise the dharma as 'both male and female', rather than the classic Buddhist position of 'neither male nor female'.[32] It is my view that an idealistic conception of androgyny which did not acknowledge difference and separateness as fundamental would ultimately be detrimental for women, because in the overall context of a debased female symbolic operative in Tibetan Buddhism, this kind of merging would reinscribe the loss of both male *and* female bodies to 'the phallic economy'.[33] Rita Gross, in her argument on egolessness as a Buddhist ideal, goes further by elevating the experience of the female 'ego' which she says is 'based on patriarchal projections',[34] to an advantageous virtue when she writes, women, by virtue of being 'the other', of being outsiders in patriarchal society, *are in a better position than men* to become aware of such oppositional duality and to think past it than are men, who, *not being the victims of duality*, frequently cannot imagine any other mode of being in the world. (Italics mine)[35]

The double-bind involved in this way of viewing women's task in throwing off the negative chains of 'ego' are obvious, for if women acquiesce within a religious system which seeks to encourage or exploit their 'better position', they remain fettered by it. Furthermore, Gross's extraordinary statement, that men are not victims of duality, somehow reinscribes women's position as inferior, by making *them* the only ones to be affected negatively by the manifestations of 'oppositional duality'. It is my opinion that the strange inverse privileging of women as 'fortunate to be unfortunate' can do no more than substantiate a particular way of thinking which does not challenge the inherent, yet very subtle, debasement of the female symbolic.

In considering women's actual experience of self, therefore, I believe it is important to recognise certain particular differences which *are* consequential, and which do not necessarily arise from the projections of the patriarchal world. Whilst not overlooking the fact, therefore, that women's bodies have often been abused and exploited by men, it is important also to consider those aspects of bodily function and those of experience which are uniquely female and can only relate to a female 'identity'. First of all, the actual physiology of women's bodies allows for a very real kind of invasion of her distinctive physical boundaries through vaginal intercourse, pregnancy and breastfeeding. These differences have been recognised in the social sphere as existing since the time of early humans. As one anthropologist writes, 'for millions of years the male has been taught to desire separateness and be wary of proximity and touching. *Maternity, by contrast, requires tolerance of continual invasion of one's space and body*' (italics mine).[36] Secondly, the female experience of being a daughter, *vis-à-vis* the mother, naturally carries different meaning to that of being a son. Kristeva goes as far as to say, 'sexual difference is the *result* of different relations to the mother' (italics mine).[37] Theories of psychoanalysis also point to a different process in the formation of ego between females and males, in which females, by virtue of being physically *the same* as their mothers, must find unitary identity not through physical difference, but through psychic separation from the other-of-the-same. Girls therefore are required to undertake the paradoxical step of both *identifying with* and *separating from* the other-of-the-same, in order to develop a sense of self. Boys, on the other hand, require to separate from *the other*, then identify with the other-of-the-same. This task, already complex for girls, leaves them with a different set of psychological features from boys, whose ego-formation is structured differently.

> As feminist theorists have shown in their accounts of the formation of the masculine self through differentiation from the mother and the feminine, such a self stresses sharply defined ego boundaries and emphasises its distinctness, autonomy and separation from others.[38]

If this statement is true, the central metaphor for the Tibetan Tantra in the *yab-yum* symbolic is more easily understood, because the male actively uniting with the passive female represents an attempt for unity which seeks to overcome *his* unique sense of dualism. In a book about Tantric representations, one western commentator notes, 'The male Buddha and his female counterpart are polar opposites in manifestation. . . . They are divided wholes . . . the opposites are united during the search for wholeness in Buddhism . . . the female part is his Prajna, his wisdom' (italics mine).[39] Unlike Gross, it is my belief that men are just as much victims of this dualism as women, because their maleness affords them the possibility of developing a more sharply defined ego or sense of self, and within the patriarchal system of Tibetan Buddhism, which emphasises the masculine and marginalises the feminine and the mother, they fall into a belief in their selves which reflects their subjective position *vis-à-vis* women.

In this way the female is established either as 'other' and to be completely avoided, or as 'other' and to be united with in order for him to feel whole. In the Tantric system, where union with the 'opposite' is considered essential, the male requires to seek a kind of union in which he is helped to destroy the very ego created in his *hyper*separation from his mother. Dowman associates the dakini with this process when he writes, 'from the beginning the Dākinīs were associated with the *meta-psychotherapeutic function* of ego destruction and the initiation of *yogins* into the *maṇḍala* of pure-being, consciousness and ecstasy' (italics mine).[40] According to Trungpa, however, this very destruction takes place as a result of a total surrendering of the ego to the guru, and brings about a state of being in which a 'sort of transparent experience of duality begins to develop in which things are really precise *without depending on each other*' (italics mine).[41]

The linking together of the dakini and the guru as important catalysts in the task of the destruction of ego suggests an unconscious association with the symbolic female, because the goal of the master–disciple relationship, or the *yab-yum* relationship, as interpreted contemporarily by Trungpa and Dowman, is to create (for the implied male) some kind of unitary state *in which dependence is negated*. It is my view that both these concepts relate specifically to a perception of ego development as seen from the male point of view, for in the Tibetan system, in the case of the tulku, or child-monk, the separation from the mother and the feminine sphere *was* often dramatic and significant in the development of a sense of self. Often it took place at such an early moment in the child's life that it is uncertain whether or not, as Trungpa's poems illustrate, the boy child had a chance to complete a process of individuation and develop a real sense of identity, ego, or separate self from the mother. Whilst the monastic system which took over the motherly function, *particularly that of dependence*, later established a new identity for the boy, and excluded the feminine from his sphere of influence (except through the female symbolic represented in the iconography), the sense of sacrificial indebtedness to the guru, as elaborated by Trungpa and others, does seem to reflect something of an unresolved denial of dependence. Indeed one might argue that the deeply repressed early feelings of dependency on the mother, all too often interrupted by removal from her, and the subsequent sense of loss in the face of what must have seemed like her omnipotence in banishing her son, could lead to a transference of dependence on, and sacrificial actions towards, that other great mother – the La–Ma, or guru.

It would be this La–Ma who, in all likelihood having experienced something similar, would, as an adult, subsequently take up the role of omnipotent mother, and demand, as befitted the tradition, that his spiritual children offer their bodies, emotions and minds without question as he inspired them 'to walk further into the desert of egolessness'.[42] Trungpa Tulku adequately explains the dangers of surrendering everything to the lama, as part of the spiritual process, yet his words carry a poignancy when read in the context of his own early removal from the secular world into the spiritual domain of the monastery.

> If we surrender our body to the guru we are surrendering our primal reference point. Our body becomes the possession of the lineage; it is not ours any more. I am not talking here of becoming *hysterical* and losing sense consciousness; I mean that surrendering our body, psychologically our dear life is turned over to someone else. We do not have our dear life to hold onto any more. (Italics mine)[43]

In a sense, Trungpa's aside about hysteria links this process, in his mind at least, with a condition primarily associated with women, and the male fear of it. Irigaray on the other hand reminds us that there is a 'revolutionary potential' in women who display it, for they 'exhibit(s) a potential for gestures and desires . . . .A Movement of revolt and refusal, a desire for/of *the living mother who would be more than a reproductive body in the pay of the polis, a living, loving woman*' (italics mine).[44] In the tulku system, it is this living, loving mother who is absent, because so often the mother *was* no more than a reproductive body, used by the lineage and metaphorically usurped by them. Trungpa's further elaboration of the process which begins with the body, proceeds to the surrendering of the emotions, and finally ends with the surrendering of the mind, could be seen, he agrees, as 'absolutely terrible', but argues that it is the only way to 'uproot this thing that we try so hard to hold onto',[45] in other words the ego or sense of self.

For women, the sacrificial role is one which has been tradition-ally expected in many societies, so that 'women in the traditional family are supposed to exhibit feminine qualities of altruism in the sense of self-abnegation, non-development or abandonment of their own projects, and putting others first'.[46] However, some psychoanalytical feminists have theorised that the sacrificial act demanded of women in western societies is of a more profound nature than simply being altruistic in both family and public spheres, and relates particularly to the development of a sense of self where that self is based on the sacrificial repression of the feminine through neglect of the mother–daughter relationship, female genealogies, and the body of the mother. Just as the infant tulkus are forced to adopt an identity which does not spring naturally from the mother–child bond, so women in the west enter the symbolic patriarchal order 'constituted from outside in relation to a social *function*, instead of to a female identity and autonomy' (italics original).[47] This frequently occurs because of the failure of many mothers to experience personal autonomy and individuation in their relationships with their daughters.

In the case of western women, then, the notion of sacrifice of ego within the religious context may mean an inappropriate understanding, which may further precipitate a denial of self, where that self has been constructed and defined within a western philosophical tradition which has put her on the side of 'the other'; object, not subject; and inferior, not *different*. In the case of the lamas, however, the complex psychology which must have come into play when very young tulkus were removed from their mothers, sometimes at such a young age as to have interfered with the process of the development of a sense of self, may well account for the readiness some lamas show in associating their identity with the *illusory body* (the literal meaning of the word *tulku*). Read in this way, Trungpa Tulku's poetry carries the poignant sense of abandonment and the uncertainty of identity in a situation where he was forced to create a new identity within the context of the monastic tradition. Interestingly, it is this very disruption of the young boy's life which leads to the establishment of a sense of self which can be moulded for the sake of the lineage, in a way reminiscent of the philosophy surrounding the dakini, whom I have shown can be represented in ways useful to male practitioners in particular.

Of course, these kinds of perspectives may be totally unacceptable to those who believe in the power of the tulku system as being, not a questionable phenomenon in a social system, but rather a divine manifestation of faith and belief. Be that as it may, there is no doubt that the association of the lama with ideas which pertain to the female experience, of lack, emptiness, or the absence of a sense of subjective identity *outwith that bestowed by patriarchal society* (in the lama's case the lineage) could be one reason why they are often idolised by westerners as embodying a deeply attractive persona which is difficult to articulate. Religion, after all, is described in psychoanalysis as, 'a system of internal objects constructed socially and over generations' which 'by its manifold repititions'[48] seeks to create and maintain the internal world. The outward ambience of the lama's spiritual cell, together with his appearance and an often covert, or suppressed, aura of sexuality do imply for some people a connection with female experience, in a way which has sometimes been viewed as idealistically androgynous. This kind of ambiguity, where there is a perceived merging together of male and female roles, may indeed hold its attractions for women not wishing to be compromised sexually by the 'guru' figure, but who find a dearth of women teachers to follow. In addition, for men, the often gentle, passive image of the all-caring lama in his attire of long skirts, and absence of stereotypical masculinity, create an ideal of androgynous sexuality with which to relate in the quest for the extinction of the subject/object dichotomy. Yet as I have already illustrated, the importance of sexuality *is* stressed in the Tantric teachings, but its manifestations largely hidden, through the requirements of the lineage system, which has an elaborate code of expressing sexuality in profoundly ambiguous ways. What is clear from the way in which the actual lives of the lamas intersect with the philosophical teachings, and in particular the expression of sexuality, is that there is an absence of a philosophy of female physicality which would translate into a radical enactment in the social sphere of the egalitarian principles enshrined in Buddhism in general. Additionally, the very complex and elaborate mechanisms which attempt to address the problematic areas of the inner lives of men (and which, perhaps, ought to be questioned in the contemporary context), fail to address the different experiences of women.

The assumption that the teachings are complete in themselves *for whoever practises them* may well be true as far as the basic doctrines, the moral questions and the articles of faith are concerned, but there is no doubt that there has been a decline in the consideration of women's difference, and no acknowledgement of what that would imply for spiritual practice, and for a deeper understanding of female identity. For example, the disappearance of the subject/object dichotomy, which is so revered by Tantrics as an ideal goal of practice, is complicated for women in western society because they already live within a philosophical tradition which has emphasised women's sense of being on the 'object' side of that dichotomy for some considerable time. Against this tendency, the ideas of the Enlightenment, the beginning of an era focused on rights, and the rise of feminist consciousness, have all contributed to a change in western society where a possible exploration and realignment of gender categories is at least now open to debate. The simple 'merging' of male and female identities which Miranda Shaw advocates as an ideal of Tantric practice, may in the end turn out not to be so simple.

On a more basic level, however, woman's very physical experience of pregnancy, childbirth and breastfeeding already give her a unique experience of the paradoxical relationship between subject and object, in which the boundaries are not always clear. Furthermore the complex relationship which women have with their mothers (who themselves may have failed to achieve existential autonomy) already prepares them for an experience of (sometimes problematic) 'merging' or 'sameness' which male children usually do not have. For these reasons, then, some of the Tantric practices (developed at a time when social and cultural norms had a very different flavour) may now be seen as positively unhelpful for contemporary women practitioners. These are the kinds of issues which emerge from a closer examination of Tantric systems, and which affect the way in which woman takes her place either as an 'oppositional' force, whether good or bad but certainly 'other', or as a transcendental force symbolising 'emptiness'.

With the evolution away from basic concepts around the Great Mother, the lotus deity and the Sky Goddess to the combined image of the divine lama-king and the Buddha, the subjectivity of the ancient symbolic female was lost, replaced instead by a symbolism which represented female deities as either mothers of Buddhas, or as consorts, but *not* as individual, active sexual females whose initiative emerges from subjective power, within *a self-defined sphere of action*. Given the huge range of deities in the pantheon (and it is not my aim here to analyse all of them or their meaning), many would argue that exceptions such as Dorje Phagmo[49] and Ekajati,[50] with their semi-wrathful and wrathful appearances respectively, give notice of an aspect of female nature which is not in the control of men. Not only that, but the textual and iconographical references to other aspects of essential femaleness, such as menstrual blood, do provide the powerful images required for identification and for the acquisition of supreme subjectivity. But given the rigid control which the lineage operates in providing access to, and understanding of, such symbols, the revolutionary qualities which can be read into them fail to materialise in the unequivocal acceptance of female practitioners and their role and status within the system. One of the few exceptional examples of a contemporary practice which reflects some of these issues is the Dakini Retreat as devised by Tsultrim Allione, an American woman teacher who makes different use of the dakini symbolism in her self-developed practices.[51]

The lack of prominence given to the exploration of potential symbols of use to women is often undermined, however, by writers like Willis, otherwise sympathetic to the idea of the value of the Vajrayana for women. Her caution to women that they should not think that any philosophically defined characteristics attributed to female aspects such as the dakini give women any special privileges over men in spiritual practice, leaves women wondering just what are the unique facets about being female which can be called upon to aid such practice. Clearly this is a complex issue, for if women were to accept the labels put on them by men and in the cause of men, they would be accused of collusion, whilst rejecting them could lead to a sense of being *nothing*, because subjective reality has traditionally been difficult for women to express. Irigaray, constantly accused of essentialism by attempting to describe 'woman', has reflected the paradoxical nature of this problem by saying, more or less, that although woman may be conceptualised as not *something*, she is also not *nothing*. What does this cryptic remark mean for women within the Buddhist context?

Whilst I have shown that the representation of the female as 'oppositional other' deprives women of status in the social sphere, I have also pointed out that the notion of 'mirroring' men in philosophical terms is a simplistic one, hardly worthy of consideration. In addition I have argued that emptiness as a concept associated with the female is equivalent to a 'refusal of representation', as Elizabeth Berg suggests, and has led in the Tibetan case to the transcendentalisation of the female in order to meet the needs, both social and psychological, of the male. Furthermore, I have attempted to describe the complexities involved in addressing the issue of the 'destruction of ego' as one of the central aims of Buddhism, and what this means for women within a system whose symbolic structure may disadvantage them enormously. Whilst it may be the case that the Tibetan Buddhist structures reflect to some extent the psychodynamic needs of the men who are a part of them, my contention is that there are no such structures, within the lineage system, which address the *different needs* of women. I have shown Rita Gross's idea, that the ideal of the destruction of ego is a process in which gender is irrelevant, to be doubtful, given that I have demonstrated that many of the practices of Tantric Buddhism are encoded with a privileging of the male position. Irigaray's question concerning an imagery for women, therefore, 'Where and how to dwell?'[52] seems relevant and timely, and, I suggest, could only be approached, in the context of woman's involvement with Tibetan Buddhism, by considering a reclamation of the meaning of the dakini, but only under terms laid down by women themselves.

Chapter 9
Perspectives on Culture and Gender

The search for female identity in Tibetan Buddhism has taken me from the historical roots of the religion, through its institutions, into its secret practices, and has culminated in an analysis of the way in which female identity is constructed within its philosophy. But an important aspect of this search has been my use of western theoretical approaches as a way of understanding Tibetan Buddhism, particularly in the context of its historical transposition to the west, and the implications of that phenomenon. The confluence of the traditions of Tibet with the rise in so-called 'New Age' philosophies, postmodernism and the general secularisation of western society has come about at a time when many people are actively seeking some form of spiritual practice which addresses the needs of contemporary society. In particular, there are those who seek some form of religious philosophy or secular wisdom which would not only take account of the destructive effects of industrialisation, consumerism and colonisation, but also put forward a framework for understanding relationships, especially those between the sexes.

There seems little doubt that Buddhism offers a kind of religious environment in which markedly different philosophies and practices from those of traditional western religions appear to predominate. The atheistic and humanistic aspects of Buddhism appear to place humanity within a seemingly greater space–time dimension than other religions, and appeal to those who fail to find meaning in some of the more rigid dogmas of the Judeo-Christian traditions. Furthermore, the emphasis which Buddhists place on non-violence, and the practice of meditation which focuses on the individual and the spirit within, has led to great interest in the powers of the mind and the possibilities of inner and communal peace through the use of particular meditation techniques. So, whilst it is important to recognise the potential value of certain aspects of the Tibetan Buddhist tradition as being helpful in creating a different understanding of human reality for westerners, it is also important, I believe, to examine what aspects of this tradition may prove to be problematic in their transposition to the west, and why.

It seems self-evident that any religious tradition from a different culture, in order to find relevance in the minds of new converts, would have to contain concepts or symbols which would be in some way recognisable, so that the meanings arising out of particular representations and texts would be different enough, but not so totally alien as to be dismissed out of hand. What is interesting about the Tibetan tradition for westerners is that it contains *both* features, as I shall show — the familiar philosophical base *and* the absolutely alien iconography. In the past, western travellers and academics were all too ready to analyse those aspects of the Tibetan tradition which they conceptualised as 'alien' and by so doing implied the 'inferior' nature of them. This categorisation prevented them from seeing the sameness of some of the approaches to the Tibetan world view, and as a result the culture and religion was consigned to the category of 'totally other'.

The Victorian orientalists, for example, expressed fascination for Tibet and its religion, but expressed their prejudicial view of its 'otherness' in a way which represented it as inferior, and therefore symbolically as the debased feminine. This was in line with the predominant societal view of women at that time, and simply reflected the association of man with science and culture, and woman with the passions and nature. Early explorers seemed inspired by the perceived mystery of Tibet's landscape and religion, and described its features in terms which reflected the rise of scientific exploration and the subsequent desire for mastery over nature. The use, for example, of sexual metaphors to describe man's 'penetration' of the mysteries, or exploration of landscape as a sexual chase, was frequent in all forms of literature. One writer describes the Tibetan explorer Marco Pallis's relationship with Tibet in a manner familiar to Victorian writers, 'Tibet is Pallis's Beatrice. It is his anima, a symbol of his soul'.[1] Tibet, anima, soul, unconscious, or woman — all these concepts were linked.

Since the Dalai Lama's exodus, however, and the spread of the Tibetan people all over the world, Tibet, as the primary landscape supporting the culture of Tibetan Buddhism and its institutions, no longer exists. The teachings, therefore, have been presented in refugee settings and in Dharma Centres created by lamas from all traditions in places where westerners have sought to establish new Buddhist institutions. The mysticism, therefore, has for many been conveyed purely through the teachings themselves, and not in the physical geography of the landscape which engendered them. The geographical and societal context in the west has also changed since that time, a hundred or more years ago, when the main influx of explorers to Tibet took place.

Many writers, including Tibetans themselves, have analysed the western and Tibetan traditions in order to find common ground, and have seen similarities between the teachings of Tibetan Buddhism and some western-based theories and philosophies of the moment, particularly in science, psychological theory, and in the peace and ecological movements. For example, much has been made of the interesting correlation between certain Tibetan and Chinese texts and the writings of contemporary physicists such as Fritzjof Capra. Many medical practitioners have also looked at the holistic approaches to medicine by the Tibetans, and found similarities with western scientific theories which explain the body–mind relationship. This has meant that, for some people, it appears that western science is only now catching up with eastern mysticism, rather than the other way around. The shift in the western perspective has also been made possible by the development of a more pluralistic western society, which to a certain extent now acknowledges that different religions offer relative truths to different peoples in different cultures at different times, and that the western cultural imperialism of the past is no longer acceptable. This, together with the transmission of the many sacred texts which were neither destroyed through political upheaval, nor lost through neglect, meant that the Tibetan tradition was recognised as containing many of the ancient and important philosophical teachings of the Indian sub-continent.

Many of these points are taken up very convincingly by Peter Bishop in his book *Dreams of Power*, in which he maintains that Tibet and its religion have found a place in the western imagination since early times, by fulfilling the western desire to place 'otherness' in an actual geographical setting. 'Tibet was a vital link in the West's imaginative connection with memoria, with the past, with the ancients', he writes.[2] Bishop argues that by sustaining the fantasy of a land, 'too white, too silent, too pure',[3] in which there is 'an avoidance of the shadow',[4] westerners provide for themselves the opportunity to believe in and long for, an idealised spiritual domain in which 'a reawakened appreciation of the Divine Father'[5] could take place. It is his belief that the lineage and tulku system embody, as I have also argued, potent archeytpes of the 'omnipotent and divine father' and he points to the iconographic representation of the lineage tree (which depicts the unbroken lineage of lamas who received teachings from divine sources and carried them forward through the tulku system), as the key to understanding the link between the social and the divine.

It is interesting, however, that in his analysis of the symbols and representations to be found around the tree he fails to mention the meaning which can be construed by the fact that *no women tulkus* are present in the representations of the lineages of lamas since the Middle Ages. So whilst the tree has a symbolic message pertaining to 'an idealized image of a cohesive hierarchical order, one which is unified around the principle of a direct kinship between the divine and the social hierarchies',[6] it also represents in the clearest terms the dependence of the existence of the idealised divine father on *the absence of women*. Bishop does argue, however, that the uncritical acceptance of Tibetan Buddhism through the '*partial* transportation to the West of a complex spiritual-cultural system' has 'resulted in a critical imbalance' (italics original)[7] and that this has led to a 'Western denial of Tibetan Buddhism's dark and messy aspects'.[8] What is surprising is that he does not associate the 'darkness', the 'underside' or the 'hidden' facets which he describes with the female, nor does he mention the possible link between the all-male lineage, and the quest for the divine father with the denial, subjugation and incorporation of the mother, as I have argued here.

Bishop's thesis is that Tibetan Buddhism can be seen as the focus of the west's desire to return to the infallible and omnipotent father at a time when he claims there has been 'a massive turning-away from orthodox patriarchal values'.[9] But by his own analysis he describes Tibetan Buddhism as 'a symbol of Otherness'[10] which, as I have clearly shown, is linked in western philosophy with the female. If his thesis is true, and Tibetan Buddhism has become the object of idealised projections by westerners, then the situation may be a great deal more complex than he suggests, for, as I have pointed out, a divine father who not only appears to incorporate 'the other', but whose existence also depends on the denial of the other, may not necessarily be a valuable symbol at this time, for either women or men.

Certainly the problem for all westerners, whether male or female, in adopting an orientalist stance, (i.e. viewing it as 'other') is that through idealisation, and denial of what Bishop calls the 'messy' aspects of Tibetan Buddhism, they themselves take on the position of (masculine) subject, and through their idealisation, objectify or 'feminise' Tibetan Buddhism as 'other'. This process masks the need to be realistic about what the Tibetan Buddhist system actually entails, so that many writers who seem ready to portray Tibet as magical, mystical or 'other', fail to acknowledge the patriarchal system which was the foundation of Tibet's socio-religious system, and thus to identify the aspects of sameness which are a part of it. This in turn allows western men the opportunity not only to idealise the *difference* of Tibetan Buddhism, but also to conceal their identification with the subjectivity and socio-religious power which men can achieve within it, and by implication *objectify* the female symbolic, which is repressed within it.

The result of such a view is that while Tibet's cultural system can be seen on an unconscious level to represent the female/feminine, thereby fulfilling the desire for union with 'the other', the hierarchical system offers opportunities for men to attain the real power of patriarchal rule. This interesting symbolic structure may then cause some men to confuse the blatant sexism of the institution with the rights and privileges which they would rationalise are a part of *cultural difference*, so that they no longer see a need to challenge a system which patently favours men on all levels. For western women, on the other hand, while the idealisation of cultural *difference* also reflects an orientalist position, their *dreams of power* within such a system are modified by the recognition that their place within it is limited to the roles and positions dictated by its patriarchal bias.

It is clear, therefore, that there is a tremendous difference between these two approaches. On the one hand is the idealising of

an alien system of socio–spiritual rule which *resembles* the symbolic
female because of its *cultural* difference (but is in practice denying
that female symbolic within a patriarchal structure). On the other
hand is the acknowledging, as an outsider, of the problematic
aspects of a patriarchal system within a culturally different context.
In the latter case it is always difficult for any outsider to comment
without appearing to imply cultural superiority, yet in the dynamic
created between cultures and genders, where Tibetan lamas have
engaged in unusual sexual relationships with western women
(which may be defined as being culturally constructed), western
women (if traumatised) *must have the right to speak of their experience,
and their view of it.* When confronted by western women who
expressed distress, confusion and concern over this issue, the Dalai
Lama himself affirmed, publically, in 1994, that this should be so.

The key to understanding the desires expressed by westerners
vis-à-vis the Tibetan Buddhist culture must however be understood
not just in terms of the gender of the scholar or student, but in
the reality of the desire and yearning which all humans have in
relation to the female/feminine, traditionally viewed as the dark
side, the mystical, or even the messy. The idea that only men
require reparation with the symbolic female, the Great Mother, or
at the very least require an understanding of the female/feminine,
is of course absurd, for women too are born of women, and often
require to pursue the symbolic mother in the same way as men,
in search of their unique subjectivity and autonomy *in relation to
her.* For western men who write about Tibet, its religion or other
facets, their position often reflects the dominant ideology which
posits the male as subject and the female as object.

Peter Bishop, however, in his contemporary analysis of the
western relationship with Tibetan Buddhism, does succeed in
undermining such a male/colonialist subjectivity by exposing
the unconscious determinants in the western psyche which drive
people to idealise Tibetan Buddhism. By so doing, Bishop thereby
'speaks the unconscious', exposing his own privileged subjectivity,
but subverting it by adopting the so-called 'feminine' position.
Despite this contribution to the debate, however, Bishop fails to
mention in *his* work the position of actual women in the system,
the female symbolic in representations, or the encounter of western
women with the lamas of the lineage. He proposes that what

westerners (*sic*) truly seek is 'the Divine *Father*', thereby succumbing to the notion that the mother has no status in the unconscious, neither of men *nor of women*. Although he does not state it, my view is that his analysis conceals the western male's desire for the *mother*, and that she is subsumed by the phallic presence of the divine father.

Peter Bishop acknowledges right from the start the masculine ambience surrounding the study of Tibet and its religion. In the early days when Tibet was used as an object of fantasy making, it was the exclusive domain of white European men, whilst other travellers, writers or scholars, whether women or from other cultures, were marginalised and excluded from describing their relationship with the culture. The travels and writing for example of Isabella Bird and Alexandra David-Neel were given prominence many years after their achievements, and there is much evidence in their writings to suppose that their motivation for travelling and exploration, whilst similar to those of colonial men, were to some extent different, and reflected their different sociological position as women in the society of their time.

Nowadays, the real and imaginary pursuit of idealised human realms on earth takes on a different meaning in a world reduced in size by mechanisation and technology. Furthermore, with a philosophical movement occurring in which gender is under scrutiny in the west, ancient categories of meaning like that of the omnipotent and divine father may well be falling apart, and a new discourse emerging about the nature of the 'divine'. This may mean that in the process of adapting and reinterpreting Tibetan Buddhism in the west, the subtext of many writings about its methodology and philosophy will be exposed, to uncover a relationship between the 'dreams of power', the nature of those dreams and the gender of the dreamer. Given that the systems of power in Tibet were excusively the domain of men, there is an unspoken assumption that men are the only ones to have 'dreams of power', and that these dreams necessarily relate in the first place to high status, and in the second place to spiritual power within patriarchal systems, whilst the question of women's desires regarding such power do not appear to be on the agenda. Clearly, in the past, Tibetan women achieved power through being mothers of tulkus, or wives of lay lamas, but few achieved social power and the right to be represented in the lineage trees.

The new fascination for Tibetan Buddhism which has come about due to the work of the Tibetan scholars and converts who have put Tibetan Buddhism into the public domain in the west since 1959 has meant that parts of the Tantric tradition now convey aspects of the symbolic meaning of the religion, outwith the major social structures in which it developed. This has happened at a time when the equal rights and women's movements of the 1960s and 1970s paved the way for major shifts in the perception of race and gender in the west, and challenged notions of certain kinds of institutional power and the domination of nature by science for the sake of the market. I would propose that the current fascination about Tibet is motivated more by a desire to *express* otherness and speak its existence as a reclaimed aspect of repression, rather than to *explore* otherness and objectify it, as was the aim of the Victorians and orientalists. For this reason I believe the ambiguous aspects of sameness and otherness which religious converts may discern in its teachings fit the contemporary desire for a reconciliation of the dualistic dichotomies between the rational and the mystical, the human and the divine, or in mundane terms, the male and the female. In a sense, it is only by reinscribing the paradoxes of existence on the 'other' that any form of patriarchal thought achieves its aim of understanding itself.

In terms of philosophical comparisons between western and Tibetan thought, I believe that there are several other deeply rooted points of contact which enable westerners to be attracted to Tibetan Buddhism, besides the need to believe in, and fantasise about, the idealised, omnipotent father/mother. These aspects relate to the underlying philosophical context of the tradition, particularly those parts from which the social system developed. As I argued earlier, the interconnection between the philosophy and the social structure in Tibet meant that only certain parts of the philosophy were translated into the power structures of the society, and that inevitably those other teachings which philosophically challenged the kind of dualism set up by the hierarchical system could not find expression in societal structures. Nonetheless, unlike many societies, there remained from the ancient influences traces of reference in the iconography to the essential subjectivity of the female. Furthermore, the radical presence in stories of so-called 'mad yogis' and wrathful goddesses meant that there was some acknowledgement of the disturbing influence of 'the feminine', or the dark chaotic side of the psyche. The society itself was, however, more profoundly influenced by hierarchical structures of a masculine order, and these came about through the application of a fundamental Tantric philosophy which polarised masculine and feminine as categories implying opposition, and setting up a philosophical framework which in western terms can be likened to that established originally by Plato and later elaborated by such philosophers as Descartes.

Val Plumwood has pointed out that 'Platonic philosophy is organised around the hierarchical dualism of the sphere of reason over the sphere of nature',[11] and that

> it is not only a masculine identity as such which underlies the Platonic conception of reason . . . but a master identity defined in terms of multiple exclusions, and in terms of domination not only of the feminine, but also of the slave . . ., of the animal, and of the natural.[12]

In her interesting anlaysis of man's relationship with nature, Plumwood maintains that the 'master' mentality, which originated in western thought with Plato, involved a denial of dependency by men on nature, women and all those others who were defined as 'inferior' by a kind of rationality which had at its heart a perception of the world in terms of dualisms. Amongst the pre-dominant pairings which made up this system of thought were of course male/female, mind/body, subject/object, reason/emotion, culture/nature, civilised/primitive. In western philosophy at least, the side on which woman was placed associated her with categories which were traditionally considered 'inferior', or to some extent 'alien' to man. Plumwood calls this kind of division, which leads to the objectification of beings and phenomena closely linked to the male-subject, 'hyperseparation', a process which is characterised by 'radical exclusion' of the other. It is her assertion that 'dualism . . . results from a certain kind of denied dependency on a subordinated other'.[13]

The Tibetan Tantric tradition very clearly maps out its philosophy in much the same way, particularly in its polarity symbolism which had its apotheosis in the *yab-yum* images of sexual acts in the iconography. Bharati confirms that the Tibetans were much more rigid than the Hindus about their assignments of male–female qualities. In his study of Tantra, he writes that,

> the Tibetans invariably assigned the dynamic function to the male, the static to the female metaphysical principle, and the essential homologies are: (1) *Buddha or Bodhisattva*: male (*yab*) = *upaya* (*thabs*); the method the manner, the way . . . = *karuṇa* (compassion). (2) *The Goddess* . . . = the female (*yum*, mother) = *prajñā* (*śesrab* supreme wisdom) = *śūnya* (*stoṅ pa ñid*, the Void).[14]

Although it may appear that no value judgements can be, or *should be* put upon these different categories (particularly in the light of the philosophy which states that all things are empty), it is interesting that the most fundamental concept on which Buddhism is based, i.e. the notion of the enlightened being, the Buddha, *is* associated specifically with the male body in historical terms. This in turn creates a powerful conceptual framework in which, as I argued earlier, the female is not only '*not*-Buddha' but she can also be objectified, particularly as dakini, mother, or void.

Concerning a similarity between Plumwood's other observations on the western tradition and my analysis of that of Tibet, I would argue that the 'radical exclusion' which she identifies in western culture takes place in the Tibetan system in the exclusion of certain categories of people, and of animals, from the philosophical sphere which predetermines the possibility for enlightenment. In the monastic way of life and in particular in the elaborate mechanisms of the tulku lineage, there is also an exclusion which operates through the failure to acknowledge the dependency which men have on women, especially the mother. This leaves them free to order their masculine world in such a way as to render women invisible, necessary though they are. Finally, it is through the exclusion enacted by the involvement of women in secret sexual acts with the masters of the tradition, together with their collusion and silence, which clearly place women in the Tibetan system on the side of passivity, where they can be both objectified and denied. Whilst in Tibetan Tantra the aim of the dynamic male is to unite with the passive female in order to go beyond duality, as I noted earlier, in the ancient *Indian* Tantras it was the female who always took the active role in sexual acts, and it was *her* activity which was thought to 'create unity from duality',[15] the opposite of what the Vajrayana proposes. In the Tibetan Tantras, the representations of the male as active symbolised *separation* through his activity, a philosophical position akin to what I have been suggesting formed the basis of the hierarchical social situation.

Alongside the fundamental polarisation of concepts, and the exclusion of and separation from the female, the fourth aspect of similarity between the Tibetan and western philosophical traditions, is the hierarchical concept of the 'master'. Naturally this category extends to both men and women who, in whatever way, adopt or abuse powerful and hierarchical positions. It has tended to dominate the western philosophical tradition in its promotion of reason and science, where 'man' dominates nature, develops culture, and distinguishes himself from the inferiority of the natural world. In the western world, it could be argued that the concept has moved away from the old meanings which were associated not only with the class system, and applied to the ruling class or landowners, but also to skilled craftsmen. Presently it seems to be associated with the masters of industry, commerce, the media and materialism, who appear to be the ones who control our lives through the promotion of capitalist ideals and a consumerist mentality.

It is perhaps unsurprising, then, that the notion of the '*spiritual master*' has been so enthusiastically taken up by western converts to Buddhism, who under patriarchal rule are familiar with the concept of the master-identity, but who have become aware of the destructive tendencies of western power structures which have systematically colonised other cultures, and used reason and science for selfish ends. These converts, whilst eager to escape the clutches of western materialistic masters, seem to seek the kind of authority which they might normally deny to other leaders within their own society, and show, particularly within the Tibetan system, a willingness to perform overt acts of obeisance to the master by, for example, making physical prostrations to him, or by placing his photograph on a shrine alongside images of the Buddha. Although these acts appear to take on a different significance in a religious context, nonetheless this kind of renunciation of basic principles of democracy and equality exaggerates the boundary line between master and disciple, and creates a relationship of submission akin to that of the master–slave or parent–baby, where autonomy is denied on the student's side, and obedience in the face of omnipotence is stressed. At its most extreme level, this kind of slavish devotion often leads to the creation of a cult, in which values and ideals may become reversed, resulting in the kinds of tragedies which involve murder, suicide, militarism or sexual abuse.

Peter Bishop discusses the uncritical devotion which so many westerners have shown towards Tibetan lamas since the arrival of Tibetan Buddhism in the west, and argues that the unquestioning nature of the student in this relationship is due to the wishful thinking of someone who longs to be in the presence of the divine father. He writes that, 'the claim of omniscience, inherent by definition in any reincarnated lama, plus the densely coded iconographical and ritualistic displays, create a myth of infallibility and omnipotence'.[16] Whilst I agree that the cultural factors which promote and sustain this kind of submission can be seen in the behaviour of the Tibetans themselves, it is my view that the relationship between lama and student bears more resemblance to the relationship between *mother* and child than to that between father and child. The infallible and omnipotent mother whom the lama represents is not only a symbol of the historical antiquity of the universal mother, the Great Goddess, but also of the mother who is present during the earliest of human developmental stages, when the baby has no individual autonomy and is *completely dependent* on her, due to its narcissistic needs. The lama fulfils therefore, for westerners, the role of what is called in psychoanalytical terms the 'phallic mother', or 'an idealised archaic mother' whose position is, according to Kristeva, 'a fantasy . . . of a lost territory'.[17] But, in addition, his own origins as a Tibetan reinscribe him, in the western psyche, as belonging to a land of mystery and of wild primordial nature, thereby accentuating the desires of those belonging to the 'melancholic western culture' to 'transfer . . . desire for the lost mother onto an "elsewhere".'[18]

Trungpa Tulku explains that 'to relate to the guru we need a tremendous amount of openness and surrendering' and that the process can have 'very deathly consequences',[19] for if disciples break their vow of promise to the master, they are destined to suffer the 'Vajra Hell',[20] a threat which goes beyond the bounds, surely, of a humane teacher. In many texts, the consequences of breaking with the guru are told in graphic terms, for it is believed that, once having left a guru, a disciple's spiritual progress 'comes to an absolute end' because 'he never again meets with a spiritual master', and he is subject to 'endless wandering in the lower realms'.[21] In the case of disrespect for the guru, it is said in the texts that if the disciple 'comes to despise his Guru, he encounters many problems in the same life and then experiences a violent death'.[22]

As Trungpa explains, the process of opening to the master involves trust, but may bring fear, for in the end the goal is the annhilation of the ego, and the process is as dangerous as 'riding on the edge of a razor'.[23] 'We have to give, to open up and display our egos, *to present our egos as a gift* to our spiritual friend' (italics mine).[24] This particular facet of the Tibetan tradition, which involves fierce devotion to the master, in which 'body, speech and mind'[25] must be offered up without question, is one which I dealt with to some extent in the previous chapter, when looking at the position of women. However, whilst I may have looked at the philosophical questions concerning the destruction of ego and the nature of gender difference, I did not consider the process of ego destruction in the context of guru devotion. What is striking in Trungpa's explanation of the consequences of failing to relinquish the ego to the guru, regardless of his behaviour, is the punitive aspect which threatens the student with different kinds of retribution, amongst them madness, illness or even death.

For western women practitioners (and in some instances men too), the extra dimension of secret sexual intimacy within a non-questioning relationship in which absolute trust is required of the student creates a powerful and complicated taboo, which taps into very deeply unconscious areas of the development of a person's sexual identity. With no cultural background to support this kind of liaison as a 'norm', westerners often fall into states of total confusion as to the meaning of having sex with the all powerful lama. Within Tibetan cultural boundaries, on the other hand, mechanisms of accepted 'secrecy' and the complete public adoration of the lamas did not allow for dissension by women. By all accounts, women either happily colluded with the lamas and

their requests for intimacy, believing that this was both beneficial
and within cultural norms, or if they did have doubts or distress
the supportive social ambience protected them from abandoning
their own cultural values, or expressing concern. According to
many folk tales, those women who did 'cause trouble' to lamas
were either badly affected karmically, or had to to be in some way
'subdued'.

Perhaps Bishop's notion of 'dreams of power' could be extended
to those western women who found disillusionment in the
aspect of Tibetan Buddhism which required *submission* (rather
than an open, autonomous relationship) to the guru through
sexual intimacy. It could be argued that their dream of power
was simply to achieve female subjectivity within a wholesome
and egalitarian relationship, or even to experience the *frisson* of
a kind of illicit relationship with a heroic figure. The fact that,
for many, these dreams were frustrated or complicated by the
power relations which became evident in the liaison meant that,
far from achieving the original aims of the Tantra (which were
unity through the merging of 'opposites'), the dissenting standpoint
of some women in the west ultimately challenged the institution
of Tibetan Buddhism and, as a result, its philosophical position on
issues of sexuality and gender.[26]

The potential risks involved therefore in the promotion of
certain philosophical ideals which depend on notions of sexuality
and *secrecy* for their fulfillment, in turn raise questions about the
symbiotic union with the guru-lama which is represented in the
iconography and in the meditational practices. In the context of
a changing world-view in the west, it may be that it is not only
the feduciary relationship which is under scrutiny, but also the
very basis of our own understanding of concepts such as 'unity'
and 'difference'. The scientist Donna Haraway has summed up
her opposition to the cause of 'unity' in philosophical or scientific
theory by viewing it as 'risky', and the forerunner not only of
dualism, but of a tendency to stabilise forces and concepts which
cannot and should not be stabilised. 'In difference' she writes, 'is
the irretrievable loss of the *illusion* of the one.' (Italics mine)[27]
It is this illusion, which often sustains those who undertake
'the spiritual search', that may also characterise an unhealthy
desire to avoid the reality of *individual identity*, with all its

contradictions, uncertainties and fragmented parts. These are the parts which, as non-substantial, and non-fixed, can be recognised in the Buddhist doctrine of self, but they are also the parts which must be valued as unique, separate and different in each and every being.

Conclusion

In this study of female identity in Tibetan Buddhism I have set out an historical context in which concepts concerning the female developed, and have shown how ideals of gender equality can fail to materialise when dominant groups in society selectively use (consciously or unconsciously) philosophical ideals to promote self-interest. Thus, despite the availability, for example, of the texts of the Yogacharyan epistemological school,[1] and later the Madhyamika tradition as propounded by Nagarjuna,[2] which provided theoretical frameworks for disclosing the dynamics of dualistic thinking, polarity became the central most important metaphor in the Tibetan iconography. This was most potently symbolised through the *yab-yum* representations of the Tantric tradition, which in Tibet reversed the ancient signification of the female as active and the male as passive, and was superimposed onto the already complex indigenous form of Buddhism (*Bön*) to form an even more elaborate system of thought. Eventually, the trend in monasticism and the widespread establishment of the tulku as the self-born enlightened male reinforced the denial of the possibility of female subjectivity within the system, and left many of the potential metaphors for her autonomous individuation largely redundant, for all save an élite within the hierarchical structure.

Now that its institutions have been firmly established in the west, the question remains, is it possible to adapt or change them (as proposed by some feminists) in order to accommodate what appear to be fundamental issues of egalitarianism and subjectivity, or is it simply impossible to tinker with a whole system of thought, intertwined as it was with a particular culture and way of life? Furthermore, is it enough to focus on the specific and *visible* signs of deficiency in a system operating to the potential disadvantage of women, or is it just as important to question the symbolic aspects which underpin some of the seemingly benign practices of meditation? In the history of Buddhism (and in accordance with its major philosophy of impermanence as the underlying force in all things) there have always been changes and upheavals related to doctrine and other issues, and these have taken place through debate and reformation of thought and institution. Since the early twentieth century, therefore, when, as Bishop states, the 'psychopathology of the west' has been in relationship with certain very specific cultural manifestations which encompass the simplicity of basic Buddhism, westerners have debated issues of interest. It is no coincidence that, at a time when cultural issues concerning sexuality and gender are prevalent in the west, female identity in Tibetan Buddhism should be examined critically from a woman's point of view.

In this work I have tried to highlight the fundamental importance of *not* separating the experience of individuals from either the social system in which they live, or the symbolic system which they create in order to sustain a sense of well-being. This psychoanalytical approach has, I hope, demonstrated the importance of considering individual pathologies as a crucial factor in the understanding of the institutions which emerge when individuals seek to pursue spiritual goals. As Kristeva has noted, 'Psychoanalysis calls on us to work toward this humanity whose solidarity is rounded on a consciousness of its unconsciousness'.[3] In an attempt therefore to search for facets of female identity in the symbolic arena as well as within human experience, I have also had to confront the complexities which arise when discussing relationships between the sexes, and also communication between different cultures. This endeavour has led me to surmise that evolutionary thought with regard to female identity has run on somewhat parallel tracks in both east and west. Contemporary expressions of the importance of sexual identity and difference, therefore, form part of the challenge to outdated modes of thinking in eastern and western philosophy, which have in the past denied the importance of the unconscious (and the female) in the social sphere. My study therefore has also attempted to create a context of common humanity very often missing in the accounts of the lives of religious teachers. It is my view that the emphasis on the 'divinity' aspect, in some writers' interpretations of the lives of lamas, for example, has not only created a problematic area for the lamas themselves, but has also reinforced the notion of cultural 'otherness' in the Tibetans, as if they were not essentially human like everyone else. As a result, outwith their own protective cultural environment which was capable of accepting their sometimes deviant behaviour *and* viewing them as 'divine', many eastern religious teachers in the west have paid the price of implying their own divinity but being unable to act within the restricting projections of many of their students, whose ideas of divinity clashed with their own different cultural view of divinity.

The emphasis I have placed on the link between the human and the symbolic, or divine, has enabled me to compare those elements in the culture of Tibetan Buddhism which manifest in human terms and which can be recognised in all cultures. These elements include attachment and loss, the development of identity, power and authority, and the desire to be free of suffering. By considering these aspects of human experience, I have tried to identify areas of common concern between peoples and cultures, and have attempted to create some understanding of the difficulties which ensue when any group is categorised to their detriment as 'other', or when 'divinity' is simply a masquerade for exploiting others through an abuse of power. These concerns have arisen out of the growing debate, in western society, on the nature of difference, on female identity, and on the changing nature of gender and cultural relations.

What is clear is that, in the western philosophical tradition, changes which have come about in the social sphere, through the promotion of reason and rights, have meant that access to knowledge, and the opportunities for expression, have become greater for women. This, together with Freud's legacy in the field of human understanding, has led to an upsurge in women's expression through writing in particular, so that in the philosophical arena the denial of the female body as an important denominator in the advancement of a way of thinking, may no longer be sustained because of the strength of challenge to it. As Jessica Benjamin has pointed out, there is a certain irony in the fact that the insights which psychoanalysis helped to release have allowed women to begin to speak from their own subjective position. '[T]he vulnerable core of male individuality' is, she writes, 'this inability to recognize the other, which the psychoanalytic focus on narcissism has finally brought to the surface'.[4]

In terms of what this means for women seeking to establish their own subjectivity, whether in religious institutions or in other projects, it seems clear that consideration of the specific nature of the female body and female experience has to take place, and find expression through symbolic representations in culture. In order for these expressions to find meaning in a contemporary context, they have to resist idealism in archaic images of the past so that the central metaphors of motherhood and female sexuality find resonance in the minds of women now. Furthermore, Irigaray's stress on the importance of a female genealogy has to emerge through a deeper understanding of the mother–daughter relationship, whilst the question of ensuing relationships between the sexes has to be addressed in an egalitarian framework. Given the distinct possibility of a multitude of variations of 'travel in space' in the future, aspects of human identity stand to be challenged, particularly if the prospect of *real* male motherhood, various forms of surrogacy, gender realignment, and sexual freedom begin to erode many of the fixed categories of meaning concerning gender identity.

By attempting to draw together so many different facets of culture and philosophical thought, I have tried, through a focus on female identity, to shed some light on the complexities involved in any culture when sexual relations are examined. I have shown that symbols which are created by people in an attempt to overcome worldly unhappiness *can and do change both their form and their meaning*, according to the time and the place in which they are significant. In the past, for example, the concept of the Buddha was certainly biased towards the male/masculine, not just because the predominant image of the Buddha was that of a man, but also because of the intertwining of concepts such as nirvana/samsara with the male/female polarities. If the female in Tibetan Buddhism was, as I have suggested, a symbol appropriated by practitioners to *achieve* wholeness, then perhaps she needs to be reclaimed to be *that which is whole in herself*, something which will serve women, the way the Buddha, to some extent, has served men. Additionally her role with regard to men could be seen not as a subsidiary force, but rather as a subject in herself, of equal status and right, with her own power and determination to be a separate and *different* entity, capable of relationship, but not reliant on union with him in order to find wholeness, nor the vehicle by which he necessarily finds his.

If this process evolves, it will mean that for most men their separation from 'the Great Mother' will no longer place them in the position of either denying her and their dependence on her, nor neurotically seeking her as reparation for their own abandoned selves. For most women it will mean they need not enter into the world of the father as a compromise, either mimicking their mother's deference, or attempting to be an equal to men, while suppressing their dependence, as the male does, on the mother. The world might consist of two subjects, and not one subject and one object. In ideological terms, the outcome of such a view and practice could be that each woman's singularity *and* multiplicity would be identified and valued; the dichotomy between men and women would become metaphysical, and the nature of identity itself would be questioned. In this way both the perceived solidity of male identity as represented by the Buddha, and the perceived insubstantiality of female identity as represented by the dakini would *both* be under scrutiny. Any new definitions or representations would have to take into account relativity, so that beings might be compared with a cell, or the cosmos, which as actual entities, we now know, are nonetheless free of *isolated* subjectivity, are fluid and unable to be fixed in time or space, much as I have shown the dakini representation is capable of being. Ideas like this would attempt to escape the paralysing discourse of dualities, and recognise the fundamental principle of interdependence of entities, in the context of a different perception of time. Barbara Adam describes this process as, 'Non-temporal time, . . . causality, truth and objectivity (having) to give way to temporality, fundamental uncertainty, the relevance of the future dimension, . . . the fusion of action, energy and time, and the mutual implication of observer and observed.'[5]

There is no doubt that most Buddhists themselves would argue that their teachings already enshrine such truths and paradoxes, and that their special position of promoting such visions outwith the sphere of western philosophy and science *per se* allows better and clearer access to anyone seeking meaning for the future. These philosophical links with occidental world views make Buddhism a most attractive alternative to the traditional religions of the west which have often been reluctant to admit secular truths to their belief systems over thousands of years. But to turn from the doctrinaire certainty of the traditional Tibetan view, which developed in tandem with its culture, however, to the uncertainties contained in any new view which *could* be promoted, would involve enormous changes in the structure of its institutions and would be unlikely to come about quickly because of the fear of chaos. This is the fear which naturally places chaos as an opposite force to order, and traditionally associates it in the western philosophical tradition since Plato, with the Void, and thus with the female.

Yet the awareness of the inadequacy of certain kinds of hierarchical systems of so-called 'order', which abuse power, colonise the other, and create suffering, is already in many minds, and as Barbara Adam has said in her discourse on the irreversibility of time, 'There can be no un-thinking, no un-knowing, no un-doing.'[6] Adam's view again links time and space, so that we cannot think of expedient change simply in terms of linear progression, but rather as a process of unfolding, which appears evolutionary, but in fact draws on all the known dimensions of space and time. Indeed scientific theories on chaos confirm a different view to the old one, namely, that it is *part* of the process of change in the cosmos, not in opposition to it. In the world of scientific theory a recognition of our relationship to space/time already exists, and is now evident in revolutionary technologies which are bound to threaten our entire perceptions of the delicate relationship between 'self' and 'other'.

In an essay on geometry and abjection, Victor Burgin maintains that 'Space has a history',[7] and is simply not unaffected, either in its being or its definition, by our perceptions of it. He suggests that many orthodox western theories have remained faithful to the now discredited Euclidian geometry, thereby fundamentally influencing all theories on boundaries, and the relationship between the subject and object. With an acknowledgement of woman as central to these theories, he proposes that 'Perhaps we are again at a moment in history when we need to define the changing geometries of our changing places.'[8] The implication of this statement is that if the boundaries between different disciplines were blurred, then it is quite possible for geometry to influence psychoanalysis and vice versa. As a result, who can say how long the present boundaries between gender categories of masculine and feminine could be sustained, and how long religion as we know it could be kept separate from science or psychoanalysis? Who can say how long the rigid, defensive boundaries between cultures could be kept and, if they were maintained, to what cost?

Within this changing philosophical context, the addition in the west of a new symbolism through the traditions and rituals of Tibet may offer, as some writers like to suggest, a vibrant alternative to the belief systems which have grown out of the western philosophical tradition. Within this new framework, ancient symbols of female identity might be reclaimed to fit the emerging debate on gender in the west and, more particularly, the needs and rights of women. In this respect I believe this could only be done by acknowledging the essential and different nature of the female body and its sexuality. This would have to take account of the many and varied aspects of the dakini, particularly the one which has the capacity to escape definition by men, through her power to be *out of control*, thus avoiding her inevitable positioning within any dualistic system of hierarchies. What would not be emphasised would be her 'emptiness' or her 'obscure, enigmatic, hidden or even disguised'[9] nature, given that insubstantiality is an essential quality of all entities, *not just the female*.

In this way woman, like dakini, could relate to her physical *presence* through a grounding in her bodily functions, which serve to create personal boundaries, *and* elude the ordinary gender constraints of linear/historical time/space in the way her name suggests, as a *traveller*. Furthermore, women would have to become more actively involved in self-identification, by recognising their own relationship with their mothers as significant, and their own specific dilemma of identity as crucial in their quest for self-acceptance and authentic relationship with others. It would also mean that women would no longer depend on male-biased texts and commentaries for a definition of themselves, and that women could not claim to be victims of the system which has dictated their position whilst they themselves remained silent and collusive. Furthermore, by viewing the dakini with her intrinsic nature of female sexuality, the position of the female could resist appropriation by the male, because the space in which she dwells could never be defined by 'the other', occupying as she does a space/time dimension whose definition, as quantum physics has demonstrated in relation to *all* entities, *is* paradoxical. There is little doubt that the dakini as a female-centred concept has the potential to move away from over-simplified notions of 'a helper for men', or the 'little something we all need' in order to get enlightened. The female body requires to be acknowledged and not abstracted as portraying *neither* this nor that. Then as a primordially *female* figure, and as a wrathful one, her symbolic anger must be grasped and understood not as retribution which inspires fear and submission, but for the powerful and constructive force which it is, a force for change, egalitarianism and understanding.

This process might then translate into the human realm, where women could express their real subjectivity, having realised their *difference* from men, then give voice to their experience, feelings and insights, not as a punishment for men, but as an act of concern in the process of developing mutual understanding. Men's role in the process would naturally have to be reciprocal, so that mutuality and interdependence, with a recognition of the pluralistic nature of human relationships, would both be acknowledged and valued. The possibility of all kinds of relationships between the genders would have to be acknowledged in a context of non-exclusion, and people and beings of all kinds respected within the sacred space.

It is clear that the female body both in Tibetan and western discourse has been the vehicle through which the body of the male has achieved its self-important and superior subjectivity. What is now required is that the male body, as the enlightened subject, be rejected as a fixed and universal constant, whilst the categories of male and female, masculinity and femininity, become deconstructed in such a way as to lose their opposition to one another. Without this very dualism, woman would have to be taken as seriously as man, and radical changes to the perception and understanding of religious teachings would have to take place. Furthermore, the interdependence of the institutional structures and the philosophy would have to be recognised, exposing the historical privileging of the male body which has been endowed with the capacity to incorporate masculinity and femininity, yet remain uncompromised in its own subjectivity.

This is the mechanism which I believe must be dismantled in order to abandon the curious dichotomy between the philosophy of the male and female bodies. This position would be neither 'both male and female' nor 'neither male nor female' but a third possibility which reinscribed 'male' and 'female' as individual but relating categories. This kind of perspective, whilst viewed derogatorily by some as 'feminist', could never be read as 'biased' in the way in which Dowman and others have seen it. The shifting of the historical positioning of 'woman' to ground which is self-defined, and to realms in which she refuses definition by and in relation to men only, means that as a consequence 'man' would also have to be reassessed. This dual process is long overdue because, as I have shown, the evolution of a system in which men are deified in society depends for its smooth running on the compliance of women at all levels.

Outwith the geographical isolation of Tibet, Vajrayana Buddhism is now subject to new and critical evaluation, in which the possibilities for mutual understanding between men and women and different cultures might be enhanced. At worst a new kind of cultural imperialism might arise in which some western men may choose to follow in the footsteps of the Victorian orientalists, by not only 'dreaming of power' within the institutions of Tibetan Buddhism, but also by marginalising and denying women's place in *their* sacred space. In their fantasy of eventually becoming what Bishop describes as 'the Divine Father' (but what I suggest can also be read as the Omnipotent Mother), many men might feel driven to re-enact the symbolic exclusion of the mother by attempting to become her, then replicating her omnipotence. The dangers in these kinds of activities (which often surround the evolution of 'new' religions in the west) have been well documented, and highlight the caution people must take when approaching any charismatic leader who makes use of esoteric practices and the imposition of rigid power structures in order to promote 'spiritual teachings'. Clearly many people are turning against such religious movements which can ultimately develop into closed and dangerous cults, and, with the rise of women's voices in all fields of literature, those women involved in religious traditions like Tibetan Buddhism may no longer choose to remain silent on difficult issues, nor rest as victims. The changes which could be brought about by such actions would inevitably involve the recognition of *difference* as a basis for understanding relationships, rather than the dualistic polarities which create unhelpful divisions and hierarchies, and on which so much human thought has already depended.

This task, 'to recognise the difference in ourselves as the condition of our being with others'[10] might bring forth a reality in which the supposed polarities of gender would collapse, and in which we would no longer be so bound by thoughts and actions which ultimately divided *detrimentally* one category of people from an 'other', or even one species from another. In this way the causes of oppression might be better understood. Furthermore, the dualism which stems from the patriarchal denial of dependency on the female and the categorisation of her as symbolically and socially 'oppositional other', or 'embodiment of emptiness', would come to an end. This could only be achieved through the mutual recognition of the unique subjectivity of each individual, and through mutual awareness of the interdependence which sustains each. This kind of recognition would truly open up the possibility of a *different* kind of spiritual insight, and a *different* future to the one we have imagined till now.

Notes and References

INTRODUCTION

1 'Taking refuge', *chamdro* (Tibetan *skyabs.'gro*), is the term used to describe the ceremony which takes place when a person officially becomes Buddhist. The objects of refuge in most Buddhist traditions are the Buddha, Dharma and Sangha (community of practitioners), whereas in Tibetan Buddhism there are three additional refuges – the lama, the *dakinis* and the *dharma* protectors. During the ceremony a piece of hair is cut from the person's head, reminiscent of the Buddha who shaved his head before setting out to gain his enlightenment, and to symbolise a renunciation of worldly ways. Usually the person is given a religious (*dharma*) name, taught the refuge prayer and urged never to kill any living being.

2 An article appeared in *Time Magazine* on 4 April 1994, reporting an open conflict between two sections of the Karma Kagyu sect over the choice of two rival claimants to the 900-year-old throne of the Karmapa Lama, the oldest line of incarnate lamas in Tibet. It was reported that the assets of the Kagyupa Buddhists amounted to $1.2 billion, and that the new lama would hold sway over 428 meditation centres throughout the world.

3 John Potter, in the introduction to *Officium* by Jan Garbarek and the Hilliard Ensemble, on ECM Records, 1994, when speaking of the degeneration of polyphonic music.

4 The *Guardian* newspaper of 10 January 1995 reported that Sogyal Rinpoche, a Tibetan lama living in England, would be sued for $10 million for sexual abuse of a female student who alleged he took advantage of her vulnerability to request sexual favours, and that 'according to the suit, Sogyal told her that "through devotion and his spiritual instruction, she could purify her family's karma"'.

5 Rita Gross, *Buddhism After Patriarchy* (State University of New York Press, 1993), p.3.

6. A *tulku* (Tibetan *sprul.sku*) is the name given to a lama who is considered to be a reincarantion of a lama who has died. The tulku system has operated in Tibet since 1204 when a successor to Tusum Khyenpa, the head of the Karma Kagyu sect was said to have reincarnated in a child who was then selected and installed as the first

reincarnate lama. Thereafter, other sects adopted the same practice, the head of the Gelugpa sect achieving greater fame and power in his position as secular head of state, with the new title, Dalai Lama. Trungpa Tulku writes of this phenomenon, 'The Tibetan Buddhist teaching concerning tulku declares that "although the moment of enlightenment releases one from the forces leading to rebirth, an enlightened intelligence which transcends the sense of 'I' or ego in the conventional sense may decide to continue to work on earth for the benefit of all sentient beings".' (Trungpa Tulku, *Empowerment* (Vajradhatu, 1976), p.14) In recent years western male children whose parents were Buddhist practitioners have been chosen as incarnate lamas and will in the future hold positions of great power in the Buddhist community. See Vicki Mackenzie's *Reincarnation: The Boy Lama* (Bloomsbury, 1988), which is an account of the death and subsequent 'rebirth' of Thubten Yeshe, a Tibetan lama, whose tulku was chosen (in 1985), with the approval of the Dalai Lama, to be Osel Hita Torres, a 14-month-old Spanish boy, the fifth child of Buddhist devotees, living in Spain. In July 1995, however, it was reported in the *Guardian* that the boy's Spanish mother was 'fighting to gain more control over his upbringing' (15 July), arguing that the monastic life was turning him into 'a little tyrant rather than a little Buddha', and that no matter 'how much of a lama he is, he still needs his mother'.

7 Gross, *Buddhism After Patriarchy*, p.89.

8 Tibetan Buddhism is known by many epithets – Lamaism, Tantric Buddhism or *Vajrayana*. In Tibetan the actual extended term for the religion is *Sang Nga Dorje Thegpa* (*gsang.sngags.rdo.rje.theg.pa.*), which translates literally as 'The Secret Mantra Diamond Vehicle'. The Sanskrit word *Vajrayana* also has the same meaning: 'thunderbolt' or 'diamond' vehicle. The other two vehicles of Buddhist practice are, according to them, the Hinayana 'small vehicle' (known in Thailand and Sri Lanka as Theravada) and the Mahayana 'great vehicle', which is practised now in Japan, and in some other areas of Asia. The scriptures of both Hinayana and Mahayana (the Sutras), as well as the monastic rules of discipline (the Vinaya), are all contained within the Tibetan tradition, in addition to the metaphysical branch of Buddhist study and the Tantric teachings.

9 Marion L. Matics (trans.), *Entering the Path of Enlightenment* (Macmillan, 1970), p.21.

10 Trungpa Tulku (ed.) *Garuda III* (Shambhala, 1973), p.47.

11 Beru Kyhentze Rinpoche, 'Guru-devotion' in Alex Berzin (trans,

and ed.) *The Mahamudra* (Library of Tibetan Works and Archives, 1978), p. 160.

12 Ibid.

13 Ibid., p.161.

14 Peter Bishop, *Dreams of Power* (Athlone, 1993), p.19.

15 Gross, *Buddhism After Patriarchy*, p.3.

16 Edward Said, *Orientalism* (Routledge & Kegan Paul, 1978), p.328.

17 Ibid.

18 Ibid., p.207.

19 Ibid.

20 Ibid.

21 Bishop, *Dreams of Power*, p.130.

22 Said, *Orientalism*, p.328.

23 See Kelly Oliver, *Reading Kristeva* (Indiana University Press, 1993), p.164 for a discussion and rebuttal of the term 'French feminists', which has been given to these three writers.

24 Toril Moi describes the symbolic order as, 'a patriarchal order, ruled by the Law of the Father, and any subject who tries to disrupt it, who lets unconscious forces slip through the symbolic repression, puts her or himself in a position of revolt against this regime' (*Sexual/Textual Politics*, Methuen, 1985, p.11).

25 Julia Kristeva, 'Women's time' in Toril Moi (ed.) *The Kristeva Reader* (Blackwell, 1990), p.201.

26 Ibid., p. 209.

27 Ibid.

28 Ibid., p. 200.

29 Ibid.

30 Margaret Whitford (ed.) *The Irigaray Reader* (Blackwell, 1991), p.126.

31 Ibid., p. 127.

32 Ibid.

33 Oliver, *Reading Kristeva*, p.174.

34 Significantly, 'songyum' (Tibetan *gsang.yum.*) literally translates as 'secret mother', and not 'secret wife', as might be supposed. See Chapter 6.

35 The 'democratic attitude' found in Scots literature and philosophy from the time of the sixteenth century reflects the 'Scottish love of arguing from purely individual points of view' (Kurt Wittig, *The Scottish Tradition in Literature*, Mercat, 1978, p.95). This found expression in the Presbyterian religious tradition, where not only was there no hierarchy, it was not thought improper to argue about religion, and there was no intermediary whatsoever between

a person and their 'God'.

36 Harry Guntrip, 'My experience of analysis with Fairbairn & Winnicott (How complete a result does psycho-analytic therapy achieve?)', *International Review of Psychoanalysis* 2 (1975), p.145.

37 Ibid.

CHAPTER 1: WHEN IRON BIRDS APPEAR

1 See Keith Dowman's account of the historical events of this time in *Sky Dancer* (Routledge & Kegan Paul, 1984), Chapter 4 of the Commentary.

2 See Garma C.C. Chang, 'The conversion of a dying bonist' and 'The miracle contest on Di Se Snow Mountain' in *The Hundred Thousand Songs of Milarepa*, 2 vols (Shambhala, 1977).

3 Ibid., vol. I, p.257.

4 Padmasambhava (Tibetan *Guru Rinpoche*), the mythical figure said to have taken Buddhism to Tibet in the eighth century AD.

5 Peter Bishop, *The Myth of Shangri-La* (Athlone, 1989), p.248.

6 W.Y. Evans Wentz (trans.), *The Tibetan Book of the Dead* (Oxford University Press, 1960), p.29.

7 One of the first Tibetan exponents of this approach was Trungpa Tulku, who set up the first Tibetan Buddhist Centre in the west, in Scotland in 1967, with Akong Tulku. His command of English, and his ability to translate Tibetan terms into the kind of language understandable by young westerners, gave him one of the largest followings in the west at that time. His early seminars on 'Buddhist Psychology' and the establishment of centres which actively promoted links between western thought and Buddhism were complemented by his teachings which made use of poetry and art, and which tried to relate specifically to the western experience of life (e.g. *Cutting Through Spiritual Materialism, The Myth of Freedom, Glimpses of Abidharma*.)

8 Evans-Wentz, *The Tibetan Book of the Dead*, p.xliv.

9 Indra Majupuria, *Tibetan Women* (M. Devi, 1990), p.118.

10 Ibid., p.42.

11 Anne C. Klein, 'Primordial purity and everyday life' in C. Atkinson *et al.* (eds), *Immaculate and Powerful* (Crucible, 1987), p.135.

12 By 'patriarchal' I mean in this context not only the rule of men, but also a system of rule which itself favours the rule of men over women and incorporates in its ideology ways and means by which this rule is perpetuated.

13 H.A. Jäschke, *A Tibetan-English Dictionary* (Routledge & Kegan Paul, 1978), p.iv.

14　Chandra Das, *Tibetan-English Dictionary* (Rinsen Book Company, 1979), p.872.

15　Ibid.

16　Ibid.

17　H.A. Jäschke, *A Tibetan–English Dictionary* (Routledge & Kegan Paul, 1978), p.393.

18　Chang, *The Hundred Thousand Songs of Milarepa*, vol. I, p.121.

19　Ibid., p.174.

20　Ibid., p.143.

21　Ibid., p.121.

22　Robert A. Paul, *The Tibetan Symbolic World* (University of Chicago Press, 1982), p.272.

23　Chang, *The Hundred Thousand Songs of Milarepa*, vol. I, p. 46.

24　Ibid., p.269.

25　Ibid., Vol. II, p.358.

26　H.V. Guenther, *Buddhist Philosophy in Theory and Practice* (Shambhala, 1976), p.194.

27　H.V. Guenther, *The Life and Teachings of Naropa* (Oxford University Press, 1963), p.182.

CHAPTER 2: ARCHAIC FEMALE IMAGES AND INDIGENOUS CULTURE

1　Garma C.C. Chang, *The Hundred Thousand Songs of Milarepa* (Shambhala, 1977), vol. I, p.329.

2　B. Kuznetsov, 'Who was the founder of the "Bön" religion?', *Tibet Journal*, 1975, p.113.

3　Chandra Das, *Tibetan–English Dictionary* (Rinsen Book Company, 1979), p.1347.

4　See Riane Eisler's *The Chalice and the Blade* (Pandora, 1990), which reconstructs prehistory and argues that there are two cultural models, partnership and dominator, the former being associated with goddess worship, and the latter with patriarchal religions and societal organisation.

5　The dakini, as the embodiment of female energy and wisdom, is, according to Trinley Norbu, a goddess figure who is both the mother of the Buddhas and their consort, in her different manifestations. Widely believed to be the energy which clears away obstacles on the spiritual path, the dakini is also believed to take human form, and can act as a sexual partner to practitioners of the Tantra. (Keith Dowman, *Sky Dancer*, Routledge & Kegan Paul, 1984).

6　Barbara Walker, *The Woman's Encyclopedia of Myths and Secrets* (Harper & Row, 1983), p. 70.

7 W.J. Pythian-Adams, *Mithraism* (Constable, 1915), p.82.

8 Walker, *Encyclopedia of Myths and Secrets*, p.663.

9 Mircea Eliade, *Shamanism* (Routledge & Kegan Paul, 1963), p.163.

10 Ibid., p.434.

11 René de Nebesky-Wojkowitz, *Oracles and Demons of Tibet* (Oxford University Press, 1956), p.540.

12 Mircea Eliade, *Birth and Rebirth* (Harvill, 1961), p.94. Eliade points out that this costume is the same as that of the Siberian shaman. It was thought that it protected the shaman from the escape of the life essence during ritual (believed as in Tibetan Buddhism to reside at the heart centre).

13 De Nebesky-Wojkowitz, *Oracles and Demons of Tibet*, p.538.

14 W.I. Thompson, *The Time Falling Bodies Take to Light* (Rider/Hutchinson, 1981), p.105.

15 G.R. Levy, *The Gate of Horn* (Faber, 1948), p.229.

16 M. Homayouni, *The Origins of Persian Gnosis* (Malvana Centre, 1989), p.35.

17 The word 'honeymoon' is of Mithraic origin, as it was believed that honey was produced by the moon after the bull's sacrifice.

18 Chang, *The Hundred Thousand Songs of Milrepa*, vol. I, p.121.

19 See R.B. Onians, *The Origins of European Thought* (Cambridge University Press, 1987).

20 See Chang, *The Hundred Thousand Songs of Milrepa*, vol. II, p.398, n.13.

21 Mircea Eliade, *Yoga* (Routledge, Kegan, Paul, 1958), p.300.

22 Ibid.

23 Janet Gyatso, 'Down with the demoness' in Janice D. Willis (ed.) *Feminine Ground* (Snow Lion, 1987), p.47.

24 Ibid., p.45.

25 Das, *Tibetan–English Dictionary*, p.318.

26 H. Hoffmann, *The Religions of Tibet* (Allen & Unwin, 1961), p.37.

27 N. Bhattacharyya, *History of the Tantric Religion* (Manohar, 1982), p.7.

28 Ibid., p.65.

29 Ibid., p.72.

30 Miranda Shaw, *Passionate Enlightenment* (Princeton University Press, 1994), p.45.

31 Ibid., p.70.

32 Ibid., p.58.

33 Ibid., p.71.

34 N. Bhattacharyya, *Ancient Indian Rituals* (Curzon, 1975), p.109.

35 Ibid., p. 111.

36   Agehananda Bharati, *The Tantric Tradition* (Rider, 1992), p.200.
37   Sanskrit *yoni*, meaning vulva or womb.
38   W.W. Rockhill, *The Land of the Lamas* (Longmans, Green, 1891), p.339.
39   Ibid.
40   Ibid, p.341.
41   The *Prajnaparamita* is one of the most important Mahayana Sutras, in which the Buddha preaches the essential emptiness of all phenomena.
42   *Mani* walls are structures made entirely of stones carved with the mantra *Om Mani Padme Hum*, and are to be found throughout the Tibetan Buddhist geographical region.
43   A.H. Francke, *Antiquities of Indian Tibet* (Calcutta, 1914), vol.I, p.21.
44   Ibid.
45   Bharati, *The Tantric Tradition*, p.61.
46   Ibid.
47   Ibid., p.22.
48   The *mantra* is the spoken invocation to a deity, made up of Sanskrit syllables which are said to encapsulate the essence of the powers of that deity, and whose recitation is said to bring spiritual benefit.

CHAPTER 3:   THE LOTUS DEITY – A LOST GODDESS

1   The word for image in Tibetan is *Ku* which literally means 'body'. The painted scroll or *thangka* (Tibetan *thang.ka*) is mounted on cloth and silk, with poles at each end, so that it can be rolled up for easy transportation.
 2   Diana Y. Paul, *Women in Buddhism* (University of California Press, 1985), p.249.
 3   Ibid., p.307.
 4   Ibid., p.308.
 5   Ibid., p.287.
 6   Ibid., p.247.
 7   Ibid., p.283.
 8   Ibid., p.176.
 9   Ibid., p.250.
10   Ibid.
11   Thomas Cleary, *Immortal Sisters* (Shambhala, 1989), p.2.
12   Mary Daly uses this specific term to mean 'actual participation in the Ultimate/Intimate Reality (*Webster's First New Intergalactic Wickedary of the English Language* (Women's Press, 1988), p.64).
13   Luce Irigaray, *Elemental Passions* (Athlone, 1992), p.1.

14　Joseph Campbell, *Myths and Symbols in Indian Art and Civilization* (Pantheon, 1947), p.96.

15　Richard Knight, *A Discourse on the Worship of Priapus* (Redway, 1883), p.50.

16　Barbara Walker, *The Woman's Encyclopedia of Myths and Secrets* (Harper & Row, 1983), p.102.

17　Ibid.

18　M. Edwardes, *A Life of the Buddha* (Folio, 1959), p.16.

19　Walker, *Encyclopedia of Myths and Secrets*, p.550.

20　D.Y. Paul, *Women in Buddhism*, p.249.

21　Joseph Campbell, *The Masks of God* (Secker & Warburg, 1962), p.157.

22　Alice Getty, *The Gods of Northern Buddhism* (Oxford, 1928), p.84.

23　E.J. Eitel, *Handbook of Chinese Buddhism* (Trübner, 1888), p.286.

24　Toril Moi (ed.) *The Kristeva Reader* (Blackwell, 1990), p.138.

25　Walker, *Encyclopedia of Myth and Secrets*, p.780.

26　Ibid.

27　Margaret Whitford, *Luce Irigaray* (Routledge, 1991), p.145.

28　John Blofeld, in his book *In Search of the Goddess of Compassion* (Mandala, 1990), states that the word *potala* has a Sanskrit origin, and means 'Kwan Yin's paradise', but the Sanskrit word, according to Jäsche, literally means a 'refuge for boats', or harbour, thus linking it again with images of the sea.

29　Getty, *The Gods of Northern Buddhism*, p.90.

30　Ibid., p.128.

31　Monier Monier-Williams, *A Sanskrit–English Dictionary* (Oxford, 1899), p. 774.

32　Agehananda Bharati, *The Tantric Tradition* (Rider, 1992), p.164.

33　A.H. Francke, 'The meaning of Om Mani Padme-Hum', *Journal of the Royal Asiatic Society*, 1915, p.397.

34　Ibid.

35　H.V. Guenther (trans.) *Kindly Bent To Ease Us* (Dharma, 1975), part I, p. 85.

36　Joseph Campbell, *Myths and Symbols in Indian Art and Civilization*, p.90.

37　Ibid.

38　Ibid., p.91.

39　Ibid.

40　Robert A. Paul, *The Tibetan Symbolic World* (University of Chicago Press, 1982), p.150. Paul suggests that the role played by such a male deity is one which embodies the mother imago, who is useful to the ascetic in his meditation practice, by having the qualities of a woman, but who is not too much like a woman. The youthful Chenrezig, with his qualities of compassion and symbolic associations with the mother, is, according to Paul, 'The ideal mother whom one seeks . . . an idealized version of oneself.' (p.150).

41 Ibid., p.148.

42 Mary Daly, *Pure Lust* (Women's Press, 1984), p.66.

43 Willy Fischle, *The Way to the Centre* (Robinson & Watkins, 1982), p.29.

44 Joseph Campbell, *Myths and Symbols in Indian Art & Civilization*, p.98.

45 Ibid.

CHAPTER 4: MONASTICISM AND THE EMERGENCE OF THE LINEAGE OF THE SELF-BORN

1 The Nyingma (Tibetan *rnying.ma.*) School or Old School remained unreformed, and still has the clearest links to the Bön tradition, with its lamas favouring the married tradition rather than the monastic. Its lineage goes back to the time of Padmasambhava, and it upholds the practices of the *terma*, or 'revealed truth'.

2 See Introduction, note 2. The practice, which survives to the present day, is that when a lama dies he is said to give written details of his future birthplace to his closest followers. These details are said to include such things as the time and place of birth, and the parents' names. After his death, the child is then sought and when found subjected to certain tests to ensure that he is the true incarnation. If there are several claims, as there often are, to positions of great power, all the children are subjected to tests, and the 'true' candidate acknowledged. It has not been unknown in Tibetan history for two or more rival claims to have established their own followers and for a lineage to have become divided. In modern times, the selection of the fourteenth Dalai Lama has been well documented, with a neutral candidate from a peasant family successfully selecting a rosary belonging to his predecessor, and being acknowledged as having the ability to recognise friends from his previous incarnation.

3 H.V. Guenther (trans.) *Kindly Bent to Ease Us* (Dharma, 1975), part II, p.100.

4 Chandra Das, *Tibetan–English Dictionary* (Rinsen, 1979), p.900.

5 Ibid.

6 See Riane Eisler's *The Chalice and The Blade* (Pandora, 1990).

7 Julia Kristeva associates the patriarchal system with the exclusion of women 'from the single true and legislating principle, namely the Word, as well as from the (always paternal) element that gives

procreation a social value: they are excluded from knowledge and power': *The Kristeva Reader*, p. 143.

8 Anne C. Klein, 'Primordial purity and everyday life', in C. Atkinson *et al.* (edsd), *Immaculate and Powerful* (Crucible, 1987), p.120.

9 Ibid.

10 The six realms are: The hells (hot and cold), made up of beings who have been particularly sinful and who have committed the most heinous crimes, such as murder; the hungry ghosts, condemned to wandering endlessly in search of sustenance; the animals, human beings; jealous gods; and gods. Rebirth in the latter three realms is achieved by the performance of virtuous acts in one's lifetime, but all six realms are nonetheless deemed to be within the cycle of existence, even the heavens in which the gods reside.

11 Kalu Rinpoche, *The Foundations of Buddhist Meditation* (Kagyu Kunkhyab, 1972), p. 7.

12 A Bodhisattva (Tibetan Changchub Sempa, *byangs.chub.sems.pa.*) is someone who postpones the achievement of nirvana for the sake of others, and is reborn again and again out of compassion until 'the last blade of grass is enlightened'.

13 Even in contemporary times the extraordinary coincidences of these so-called miracle rebirths stretch to the limit the belief of onlookers. The lama with whom I studied for many years, Kalu Rinpoche, and who subsequently died, was found to have reincarnated in the very same place as he died, as the son of his own nephew who had been his constant companion since he left Tibet in 1959. This of course ensured that the vast amount of wealth and property that had been gathered since his successful missionary activity in the west would remain in the family, and no outsiders could claim wealth or power in his monastery. The convenience of such a 'reincarnation' ensures that the system is held in the hands of a male élite who, as self-appointed guarantors of the veracity of the claims for reincarnation, can either place power and wealth in 'neutral' hands, if there seems a risk of political in-fighting, or confirm dynastic power as in this case.

14 Fosco Maraini, *Secret Tibet* (Hutchinson, 1952), p.124.

15 Robert A. Paul, *The Tibetan Symbolic World* (University of Chicago Press, 1982) p.7.

16 Joseph Campbell, *The Masks of God* (Secker & Warburg, 1962), p. 160.

17 Ibid.

18 Ibid.

19 R.A. Paul, *The Tibetan Symbolic World*, p.7.
20 Ibid., p.32.
21 Ibid., p.37.
22 Ibid., p.96.
23 Ibid.
24 Ibid., p.12.
25 Ibid.
26 See James Lovelock's *Gaia* (OUP, 1987) on the theory of the Earth as a living, self-regulating organism.
27 Luce Irigaray, *Sexes and Genealogies* (Columbia University Press, 1993), p.120.

CHAPTER 5: 'FREE OF THE WOMB'S IMPURITIES' – DIVINE BIRTH AND THE ABSENT MOTHER

1 Fosco Maraini, *Secret Tibet* (Hutchinson, 1952), p.128.
2 Ibid.
3 Ibid., p.129.
4 Dalai Lama, *Freedom in Exile* (Clio, 1991), p.17.
5 Michael Aris, *Hidden Treasures and Secret Lives* (Routledge & Kegan Paul, 1989), p.137.
6 Dalai Lama, *Freedom in Exile*, p.17.
7 Samten G. Karmay, *The Treasury of Good Sayings* (London University Press, 1972), p.xxi.
8 Marija Gimbutas, *The Language of the Goddess* (Thames & Hudson, 1989), p.321.
9 Willy Fischle, *The Way to the Centre* (Robinson & Watkins, 1982), p.29.
10 Nik Douglas and Meryl Whyte, *Karmapa, The Black Hat Lama of Tibet* (Luzac, 1976), p.83.
11 Ibid., p.79.
12 Keith Dowman, *Sky Dancer* (Routledge & Kegan Paul, 1984), p.10.
13 Ibid., p.12.
14 Arya and Asanga Maitreya, *The Changeless Nature* (Karma Kagyu, 1979), p.35.
15 Ibid., p.36.
16 Dowman, *Sky Dancer*, p.12.
17 Trungpa Tulku, *Born in Tibet* (Unwin, 1979), p.44.
18 Trungpa Tulku, *Shambhala, The Sacred Path of the Warrior* (Shambhala, 1984), p.94.
19 Ibid.
20 Ibid.
21 Trungpa Tulku (ed.) *Garuda III* (Shambhala, 1973), p.35.

22 Ibid.

23 See Introduction, note 6 on the response made by the mother of one of the first western tulkus to the manner of his upbringing by the monastic community.

24 These images are reminiscent of stories which form part of the canon of literature of the highest teaching of the Buddhist Tantra. In the so-called 'secret biography' of 'the divine madman' Drukpa Kunley, portrayals of sexuality and the abuse of power are described as potentially enlightening attributes. Keith Dowman, in attempting to explain Kunley's biography, which openly elaborates all his wild deeds, writes 'there is no distinction made between external events and the inner life . . . He works without any discrimination, inhibition or selfish motivation, to give meaning to other people's lives . . . Also it is secret, a mystery, because a Buddha's existence resolves the paradoxes and dualities of being' (Keith Dowman, *The Divine Madman*, Rider, 1980, p.9).

25 R.A.Paul, *The Tibetan Symbolic World* (University of Chicago Press, 1982), p.272.

26 Tibetan *rang.byung*. This is a common name given to tulkus of high status, e.g. Rangjung Rigpe Dorje, the 16th Karmapa Lama.

27 R.A.Paul, *The Tibetan Symbolic World*, p.279.

28 Mary Daly, *Pure Lust* (Women's Press, 1984), p. 66.

29 W.Y Evans-Wentz (trans. and ed.) *Tibet's Great Yogi Milarepa* (OUP, 1969), p.175.

30 Trungpa Tulku (ed.) *Garuda III*, p.23.

31 Ibid., frontispiece.

32 Ibid., p.23.

33 Ibid.

34 Paul, *The Tibetan Symbolic World*, p.59.

35 Ibid., p.233.

36 Luce Irigaray, *Sexes and Genealogies* (Columbia University Press, 1993), p.16.

37 Tsultrim Allione, *Women of Wisdom* (Routledge & Kegan Paul, 1984), p.20.

38 Dowman, *Sky Dancer*, p. 272.

39 Irigaray, *Sexes and Genealogies*, p.85.

40 See Chapter 6.

CHAPTER 6:   AT ONE WITH THE SECRET OTHER

1 Michael Aris, *Hidden Treasures and Secret Lives* (Routledge & Kegan Paul, 1989), p. 30.

2 Mircea Eliade, *Yoga* (Routledge & Kegan Paul, 1958), p.152.

3 Miranda Shaw, *Passionate Enlightenment* (Princeton University Press, 1994), p.15.

4 Ibid., p.201.

5 Ibid., p.257.

6 Ibid.

7 Ibid., p.14.

8 Ibid., p.19.

9 Lisa Lowe, 'Des Chinoises', in Kelly Oliver (ed.) *Ethics, Politics and Difference in Julia Kristeva's Writing* (Routledge, 1993), p.154.

10 Luce Irigaray, *Elemental Passions* (Athlone, 1992), p.2.

11 Mary Daly, *Pure Lust* (Women's Press, 1984), p.249.

12 See Peter Bishop's *Dreams of Power* (Athlone, 1993), in which he analyses the imaginary aspect of westerners' fascination with Tibetan Buddhism.

13 Geoffrey Samuel, *Civilized Shamans: Buddhism in Tibetan Societies* (Smithsonian Institution, 1993), p.351.

14 See David N. Gellner's *Monk, Householder and Tantric Priest* (CUP, 1992).

15 The Dalai Lama, quoted in an article (*Telegraph Magazine*, 25 February 1995) concerning the alleged sexual abuse of a student by Sogyal Rinpoche, when asked how many Tibetan teachers were qualified Tantric masters, replied, 'As far as I know – zero'.

16 Tibetan Lae Chi Chaja, *las.kgyi.phyag.gya.* has the same meaning as the Sanskrit, i.e. 'action seal'.

17 Garma C.C. Chang, *The Hundred Thousand Songs of Milarepa* (Shambhala, 1977), vol.II, p.358.

18 H.V. Guenther, *Buddhist Philosophy in Theory and Practice* (Shambhala, 1976), p.194.

19 H.V. Guenther, *The Life and Teachings of Naropa* (OUP, 1963), p.182.

20 Keith Dowman, *Sky Dancer* (Routledge & Kegan Paul, 1984), p.261.

21 Julia Kristeva, 'Women's time' in Toril Moi (ed.) *The Kristeva Reader* (Blackwell, 1990), p.193.

22 Shaw, *Passionate Enlightenment*, p. 203.

23 Ibid.

24 Ibid., p.197.

25 Luce Irigaray, *Sexes and Genealogies*, p.120.

26 Dowman, *Sky Dancer*, p.23.

27 Ibid., p.24.

28 Chang, *The Hundred Thousand Songs of Milarepa*, vol.II, p.360.

29 Ajit Mookerjee, *Kundalini* (Thames & Hudson, 1982), p.62.

30 Eliade, *Yoga*, p.362.
31 Ibid., p.271.
32 Kristeva, 'Women's time' in Toril Moi (ed.) *The Kristeva Reader*, p. 193.
33 Tarthang Tulku, *Time, Space and Knowledge* (Dharma, 1977), p. 125.
34 Ibid., p. 12.
35 Kristeva, 'Women's time' in Toril Moi (ed.) *The Kristeva Reader*, p. 191.
36 Tarthang Tulku, *Time, Space and Knowledge*, p. 142.
37 Dowman, *Sky Dancer*, p. 226.
38 H.V. Guenther (trans.) *Kindly Bent to Ease Us* (Dharma, 1975), vol. II, p. 94.
39 Dowman, *Sky Dancer*, p.248.
40 Ibid.
41 Ibid.
42 Shaw, *Passionate Enlightenment*, p.157.
43 Ibid., p.158.
44 Ibid.
45 Ibid., p.176.
46 Ibid., p.199.
47 Ibid., p.187.
48 Dowman, *Sky Dancer*, p. 156.
49 Thomas Cleary (trans. and ed.), *Immortal Sisters* (Shambhala, 1989), p.96.
50 R.A. Paul, *The Tibetan Symbolic World* (University of Chicago Press, 1982), p.116.
51 Andrea Nye, *Feminist Theories and the Philosophies of Man* (Croom Helm, 1988), p.183.
52 Dowman, *Sky Dancer*, p. 156.
53 Chang, *The Hundred Thousand Songs of Milarepa*, vol.I, p.121.
54 Janice D. Willis, 'Dakini: some comments on its nature and meaning' in *Feminine Ground* (Snow Lion, 1987), p.73.
55 Ibid., p.72.
56 Ibid., p.73.

CHAPTER 7:   A 'TRAVELLER IN SPACE': THE SIGNIFICANCE OF THE DAKINI AND HER SACRED DOMAIN

1 Keith Dowman, *Sky Dancer* (Routledge & Kegan Paul, 1984), p. 220.
2 Ibid., p.221.
3 As its name suggests, this esoteric language remains hidden from ordinary practitioners by virtue of their unenlightened state.

4 Kelsang Gyatso, *Guide to Dakini Land* (Tharpa, 1991), p.4.

5 The *bhakti* movements began about the sixth century in southern India, and attempted to act as a counter system to the Brahmanical traditions which had been prevalent for almost a thousand years. Their views were totally different to these patriarchal traditions on issues of gender, caste and theology, and re-established the notion of all-women lineages and sanctity within the Hindu tradition. Most importantly, they emphasised the possibility for women to achieve spiritual realisation *in the social sphere*, as part of their everyday lives, and made no distinction between the religious and social spheres.

6 Luce Irigaray, *Je, Tu, Nous* (Routledge, 1993), p.17.

7 Dowman, *Sky Dancer*, p.290.

8 Ibid., p.292.

9 Geoffrey Samuel, *Civilized Shamans* (Smithsonian Institution, 1993), p.196.

10 This is a motif which appears frequently in the language of nineteenth-century western writers who associated woman with nature, man with culture or science, and viewed nature's 'secrets' (inevitably female) as requiring probing by men, in terms of a sexual metaphor.

11 Dowman, *Sky Dancer*, p.291.

12 Diana Paul, *Women in Buddhism* (University of California Press, 1985), p.283.

13 Tsultrim Allione, *Women of Wisdom* (Routledge & Kegan Paul, 1984), p.44.

14 Ibid.

15 Kristeva proposes that the socio-symbolic contract which constitutes our external reality is defined and constructed by events which take place in the individual psyche, and which have their roots in sexual difference. Expanding the psychoanalytic/linguistic theories of Jacques Lacan, Kristeva suggests that each child has a relationship, pre-oedipally, with the maternal, which is characterised by its form as 'a wholly provisional articulation that is essentially mobile, and constituted of movements and their ephemeral stases' (Toril Moi, *Sexual/Textual Politics*, Methuen, 1985, p.161). This state, the semiotic, pre-dates language and is associated with the feminine. In order for signification to take place, a splitting must occur, whereby the child begins to recognise self and other, and subsequently acknowledge difference. It is from this process that language develops, the acquisition of which marks the child's entry into the symbolic order, which is dominated by the law

of the father. For the female, a position of lack (of phallus) is recognised during the oedipal phase, and she must choose either to identify with the mother, and therefore the semiotic feminine, and be marginalised in the symbolic order, or identify with the father and be thereafter accepted yet defined by that order, as feminine, and therefore as 'other'.

16 Janice D. Willis, 'Dakini: some comments on its nature and meaning' in *Feminine Ground* (Snow Lion, 1987), p. 73.

17 Ibid.

18 Ibid., p.75.

19 Ibid., p.74.

20 Ibid., p.73.

21 Ibid., p.68.

22 Ibid., p.69.

23 Dowman, *Sky Dancer*, p.250.

24 Willis, 'Dakini: some comments on its nature and meaning' in *Feminine Ground*, p.74.

25 See Tsultrim Allione's detailed analysis of the symbolism of the dakini, in *Women of Wisdom*.

26 Francesca Freemantle (trans.) '*The Sutra on the essence of transcendent knowledge*' in Trungpa Tulku (ed.) *Garuda III*, p.3.

27 Dowman, *Sky Dancer*, p. 220.

28 There are several *bardo* (gap or between) states, which the Tibetans elucidate as times between different states of reality. They are: the various phases between death and rebirth; whilst dreaming; whilst meditating; and the time between birth and death.

29 Toril Moi, *Sexual/Textual Politics* (Methuen, 1985), p.100–1.

30 Luce Irigaray, *Elemental Passions* (Athlone, 1992), p.3.

31 Luce Irigaray, *Sexes and Genealogies* (Columbia University Press, 1993), p.98.

32 Ibid.

33 Ibid., p.68.

34 Dorje Phagmo is the pig-headed goddess, loosely based on the ancient Tantric goddess Kali, and is visualised with an entourage of dakinis.

35 In Tibetan Buddhism there are three levels of divine manifestation: the *Dharmakaya* which is the non-dual sphere of supreme awareness; the *Sambhogakaya* which is the realm of the deity; and the *Nirmanakaya*, the realm of the incarnated deity. Kuntu Zangmo belongs to the *Dharmakaya*, and because of her association with emptiness is shown naked, without ornamentation. Even in the realm of the non-dual, the Tibetans puzzlingly create the *yab-yum*

symbolism of Kunto Zangpo with his consort Kunto Zangmo, their union being symbolic.

36 Arthur Anthony Macdonnell, *Practical Sanskrit Dictionary* (OUP, 1971), p.104.

37 Margaret Whitford, *Luce Irigaray* (Routledge, 1991), p. 35.

38 Dowman, *Sky Dancer*, p. 273.

CHAPTER 8:   THE QUESTION OF 'OTHERNESS' IN FEMALE REPRESENTATION

1 H.V. Guenther, *Buddhist Philosophy in Theory and Practice* (Shambhala, 1976), p.200.

2 Ibid.

3 Ibid., p.195.

4 Ibid., p.166.

5 Robert A. Paul, *The Tibetan Symbolic World* (University of Chicago Press, 1982), p.272.

6 'Local' deities are differentiated from divine deities by virtue of the fact that they are unenlightened and still chained to the samsaric cycle of existence, in the spirit realm. They haunt particular areas and have a demonic form, but are capable of being converted to Buddhist practice, and thereafter become protectors of the dharma.

7 Garma C.C. Chang, *The Hundred Thousand Songs of Milarepa* (Shambhala, 1977), vol.I, p.5.

8 Ibid.

9 Ibid.

10 Ibid., p.307.

11 Ibid., p.309.

12 Arnaud Desjardins, *The Message of the Tibetans* (Stuart & Watkins, 1969), p.80.

13 A full explanation of this important term is to be found in the *Prajnaparamita*, the Sutra taught by the Buddha concerning the insubstantiality of all phenomena. Tibetan Buddhist sources define 'emptiness' as the 'explicit negation: things do not exist as such apart from our labelling them to be this or that' (Guenther, *Buddhist Philosophy in Theory and Practice*, p.225).

14 Anne C. Klein, 'Primordial purity and everyday life' in C. Atkinson *et al.* (eds) *Immaculate and Powerful* (Crucible, 1987), p.134.

15 Ibid.

16 Luce Irigaray, *Speculum of the Other Woman* (Cornell University Press, 1985), p.165.

17 Margaret Whitford, *Luce Irigaray* (Routledge, 1991), p.154.

18 Ibid., p.155.

19 Ibid., p.153.
20 Ibid., p.71.
21 Irigaray, *Speculum of the Other Woman*, p.165.
22 The *Chöd* rites were reputed to have been begun in the eleventh century by the Tibetan female mystic, Machig Labdron. In the myth surrounding her life, a male yogi in India transferred his consciousness into the body of a female foetus in Tibet and she was born with miraculous powers. It was during her reading of the *Prajnaparamita* that she achieved insight pertaining to the emptiness of all things, and developed the practice which uses visualisations of demons to overcome fears and dispel the notion of a belief in a 'self'. In the practice, the meditator beats the rhythm of the chant with a large hand-held drum and simultaneously rings a bell, which is said to represent the feminine. At intervals a thigh bone trumpet is blown to summon the demons to a feast of the meditator's ego.
23 The Mandala offering involves the making of a symbolic offering of everything imaginable using a small plate and rice to mark out a mandala of the universe and everything in it.
24 Rita Gross, *Buddhism after Patriarchy* (State University of New York Press, 1993), p.162.
25 Ibid.
26 Ibid.
27 Ibid.
28 Ibid.
29 Ibid.
30 Ibid.
31 Ibid., p.221.
32 Ibid., p.222.
33 Kelly Oliver, *Reading Kristeva* (Indiana University Press, 1993), p.174.
34 Gross, *Buddhism after Patriarchy*, p. 165.
35 Ibid.
36 Dudley Young, *Origins of the Sacred* (Abacus, 1993), p.91.
37 Oliver, *Reading Kristeva*, p.177.
38 Val Plumwood, *Feminism and the Mastery of Nature* (Routledge, 1993), p.144.
39 Willy Fischle, *The Way to the Centre* (Robinson & Watkins), pp.33, 49.
40 Keith Dowman, *Sky Dancer* (Routledge & Kegan Paul, 1984), p.258.
41 Trungpa Tulku, *Glimpses of Abidharma* (Prajna, 1978), p.75.
42 Ibid., p.61.

43 Ibid., p.60.
44 Margaret Whitford, *The Irigaray Reader* (Blackwell, 1991), p.47.
45 Trungpa Tulku, *Glimpses of Abidharma*, p.61.
46 Plumwood, *Feminism and the Mastery of Nature*, p.146.
47 Luce Irigaray, *Sexes and Genealogies* (Columbia University Press, 1993), p.72.
48 David Black, 'The relationship of psychoanalysis to religion' in Ivan Ward (ed.) *Is Psychoanalysis another Religion?* (Freud Museum, 1993), p.12.
49 Dorje Phagmo is represented as wrathful in appearance and, like Kali, associated with blood, even menstrual blood, and is adorned with various ornaments and accoutrements which symbolise her raw female power. (See Tsultrim Allione, *Women of Wisdom* (Routledge & Kegan Paul, 1984). In particular her naked body with exposed genitals signifies the power of the female.
50 Ekajati is a one-eyed dharma protector of wrathful appearance. See Chapter 3 on eye symbolism.
51 In an interview with Davine Del Vale in 1992, Allione stated that the dakini practices had come to her in a vision, which the head of the Bön lineage later thought might be a *gongter* or 'treasure of the mind' (see Chapter 7). Her contention is that these female-specific practices are 'part of the coming of Buddhism to the West'.
52 Whitford, *Luce Irigaray*, p.157.

CHAPTER 9: PERSPECTIVES ON CULTURE AND GENDER
1 Peter Bishop, *Dreams of Power* (Athlone, 1993), p.35.
2 Ibid., p.41.
3 Ibid., p.30.
4 Ibid., p.46.
5 Ibid., p.130.
6 Ibid., p.122.
7 Ibid., p.96.
8 Ibid.
9 Ibid., p.60.
10 Ibid., p.130.
11 Val Plumwood, *Feminism and the Mastery of Nature* (Routledge, 1993), p.72.
12 Ibid.
13 Ibid., p.41.
14 Agehananda Bharati, *The Tantric Tradition* (Rider, 1992), p.212.
15 Ajit Mookerjee, *Kundalini* (Thames & Hudson, 1982), p.62.
16 Bishop, *Dreams of Power*, p.104.

17 Toril Moi (ed.) *The Kristeva Reader* (Blackwell, 1990), p.161.
18 Kelly Oliver, *Reading Kristeva* (Indiana University Press, 1993), p.139.
19 Trungpa Tulku, *Empowerment* (Vajradhatu, 1976), p.59.
20 Ibid. The Vajra Hell is one specifically reserved for practitioners who break their vows, and involves interminable suffering.
21 Geshe Ngawang Dhargyey, *Tibetan Tradition of Mental Development* (Library of Tibetan Works and Archives, 1974), p.243.
22 Ibid., p.244.
23 Trungpa Tulku, *Empowerment*, p.66.
24 Ibid., p.71.
25 Ibid., p.61.
26 See Introduction, Note 4.
27 Donna Haraway, *Simions, Cyborgs and Women* (Free Association, 1991), preface.

CONCLUSION

1 The Yogacharin school is epistemological and characterised by its 'one-mind', philosophy, in which there is no individual knower, and phenomena and intelligence are brought together in luminous cognisance. In this way the enlightened 'realise' the false dichotomy between mind and phenomena, whereas the unenlightened adhere to duality.
2 Nagarjuna was a tenth-century Indian philosopher who founded the Madhyamika or Middle Way, and who opposed the Yogacharin School, asserting that 'that any philosophical view could be refuted, that one must not dwell upon any answer or description of reality, whether extreme or moderate, including the notion of "one-mind"' (Trungpa Tulku (ed.) *Garuda III*, Shambhala, 1973, p.47). He was the major exponent of the *Prajnaparamita*.
3 Kelly Oliver, 'Politics of psychoanalysis' in Oliver (ed.) *Ethics, Politics and Difference in Julia Kristeva's Writing* (Routledge, 1993), p.12.
4 Jessica Benjamin, *The Bonds of Love* (Virago, 1990), p.181.
5 Barbara Adam, *Time and Social Theory* (Polity, 1990), p. 60.
6 Ibid., p. 169.
7 Victor Burgin, 'Geometry and abjection' in J. Fletcher *et al.* (eds) *Abjection, Melancholia and Love* (Routledge, 1990), p. 105.
8 Ibid., p. 119.
9 Miranda Shaw, *Passionate Enlightenment* (Princeton University Press, 1994), p.19.
10 Oliver, 'Politics of psychoanalysis' in *Ethics, Politics and Difference in Julia Kristeva's Writing*, p.12.

Bibliography

Adam, Barbara, *Time and Social Theory*, Polity Press, 1990.

Allione, Tsultrim, *Women of Wisdom*, Routledge & Kegan Paul, 1984.

Amadiume, Ifi, *Matriarchal Foundations: The Igbo Case*, Karnak House, 1987.

Angus, S., *The Mystery-Religions and Christianity*, John Murray, 1928.

Arens, W., *The Original Sin*, Oxford University Press, 1986.

Aris, M., *Hidden Treasures and Secret Lives*, Routledge & Kegan Paul, 1989.

Aris, M. and Aung San Suu Kyi (eds) *Tibetan Studies*, Aris & Phillips, 1980.

Atkinson, C. *et al.* (eds) *Immaculate and Powerful*, Crucible, 1987.

Bachofen, J., *Myth, Religion and Mother Right*, Routledge & Kegan Paul, 1967.

Bechert, H. and Gombrich, R. (eds) *Buddhism*, Thames & Hudson, 1984.

Benjamin, J., *The Bonds of Love*, Virago, 1990.

Berg, Elizabeth L. 'The third woman', *Diacritics*, 2, 2, 1982.

Berger, Pamela, *The Goddess Obscured*, Robert Hale, 1988.

Berzin, Alex (trans.) *The Mahamudra*, Library of Tibetan Works and Archives, 1978.

Beyer, S., *The Cult of Tara*, University of California Press, 1973.

Bharati, Agehananda, *The Tantric Tradition*, Rider, 1992.

Bhattacharyya, N.N. *Ancient Indian Rituals*, Curzon, 1975.

Bhattacharyya, N.N. *History of the Tantric Religion*, Manohar, 1982.

Bishop, Peter, *The Myth of Shangri-La*, Athlone, 1989.

Bishop, Peter, *Dreams of Power*, Athlone, 1993.

Black, David, 'The relationship of psychoanalysis to religion' in Evan Ward (ed.) *Is Psychoanalysis another Religion?* Freud Museum Publications, 1993.

Blofeld, John, *In Search of the Goddess of Compassion*, Mandala, 1990.

Bose, M.M. *Post Caitanya Sahajiya Cult*, Calcutta University, 1930.

Breaux, Charles, *Journey into Consciousness*, Rider, 1990.

Briffault, Robert, *The Mothers*, Allen & Unwin, 1959.

Bucknell, R. *Twilight Language Explorations*, 1986.

Burgin, Victor, 'Geometry and Abjection' in J. Fletcher *et al.* (eds) *Abjection, Melancholia and Love*, Routledge, 1990.

Campbell, Joseph, *Myths and Symbols in Indian Art and Civilization*, Pantheon, 1947.

Campbell, Joseph, *The Masks of God*, Secker & Warburg, 1962.

Campbell, Joseph, *Myths To Live By*, Paladin, 1972.

Campbell, Joseph, *The Power of Myth*, Doubleday, 1989.

Campbell, June, 'Beyond Duality : A Buddhist Reading of Bessie Head's *A Question of Power*', *Journal of Commonwealth Literature*, 24, 1, 1993.

Campbell, June (trans.) 'The 100 Verses of Advice to the People of Tingri by Padampa Sangye, *Kailash: Journal of Himalayan Studies*, 2, 3, 1974.

Chand, Attar, *Tibet: Past and Present*, Sterling, 1982.

Chang, Garma C.C. *The Hundred Thousand Songs of Milarepa*, 2 vols, Shambhala, 1977.

Cleary, Thomas, *Immortal Sisters*, Shambhala, 1989.

Cles-Reden, S. von, *The Realm of The Great Goddess*, Thames & Hudson, 1961.

Cumont, Franz, *The Mysteries of Mithra*, Kegan Paul, Trench, Trübner, 1903.

Dalai Lama, *Freedom in Exile*, Clio, 1991.

Daly, Mary, *Pure Lust*, Women's Press, 1984.

Daly, Mary, *Webster's First New Intergalactic Wickedary of the English Language*, Women's Press, 1988.

Das, Chandra, *A Tibetan–English Dictionary*, Rinsen Book Company, 1979.

Dasgupta, S.B. *An Introduction to Tantric Buddhism*, Shambhala, 1974.

David-Neel, Alexandra, *With Mystics and Magicians in Tibet*, Abacus, 1977.

Davis, Elizabeth, *The First Sex*, Penguin, 1971.

De Nebesky-Wojkowitz, *Oracles and Demons of Tibet*, Oxford University Press, 1956.

De Silva, P. *An Introduction to Buddhist Psychology*, Macmillan, 1979.

Desjardins, A. *The Message of the Tibetans*, Stuart & Watkins, 1969.

Dhargyey, Geshe Ngawang, *Tibetan Tradition of Mental Development*, Library of Tibetan Works and Archives, 1974.

Diop, C.N. *Cultural Unity in Black Africa*, Karnak House, 1989.

Douglas, N. and White, M. (eds) *Karmapa, the Black Hat Lama of Tibet*, Luzac, 1976.

Dowman, Keith, *The Divine Madman*, Rider, 1980.

Dowman, Keith, *Masters of Enchantment*, Arkana, 1988.

Dowman, Keith, *Sky Dancer*, Routledge & Kegan Paul, 1984.

Edkins, Joseph, *Chinese Buddhism*, Trübner, 1880.

Edwardes, Michael, *A Life of the Buddha*, Folio Society, 1959.

Eisler, Riane, *The Chalice and the Blade*, Pandora, 1990.

Eitel, E.J. *Handbook of Chinese Buddhism*, Trübner, 1888.

Eliade, Mircea, *Yoga*, Routledge & Kegan Paul, 1958.

Eliade, Mircea, *Myths, Dreams and Mysteries*, Harvill, 1960.

Eliade, Mircea, *Birth and Rebirth*, Harvill, 1961.

Eliade, Mircea, *Shamanism*, Routledge & Kegan Paul, 1964.

Eliade, Mircea, *The Encyclopoedia of Religion*, MacMillan, 1987.

Erndl, Kathleen, *Victory to the Mother*, Oxford University Press, 1993.

Evans-Wentz, W.Y. (trans.) *The Tibetan Book of the Dead*, Oxford University Press, 1960.

Evans-Wentz, W.Y. (trans. and ed.) *Tibet's Great Yogi Milarepa*, Oxford University Press, 1969.

Fischle, Willy, *The Way to the Centre*, Robinson & Watkins, 1982.

Fletcher, J. *et al.* (eds) *Abjection, Melancholia and Love*, Routledge, 1990.

Francke, A.H. *History of Western Tibet*, Partridge, 1907.

Francke, A.H. 'The meaning of *Om Mani Padme-Hum*', *Journal of the Royal Asiatic Society*, 1915.

Francke, A.H. *Antiquities of Indian Tibet*, 2 vols, Calcutta, 1914, 1926.

Frazer, James, *The Illustrated Golden Bough*, Macmillan, 1978.

Freemantle, Francesca (trans.) 'The Sutra on the essence of transcendent knowledge' in Trungpa Tulku (ed.) *Garuda III*, Shambhala, 1973.

Fuller, C.J. *Servants of the Goddess*, Cambridge University Press, 1984.

Gellner, David, *Monk, Householder and Tantric Priest*, Cambridge University Press, 1992.

Getty, Alice, *The Gods of Northern Buddhism*, Oxford, 1928.

Gimbutas, M. *The Goddesses and Gods of Old Europe*, Thames & Hudson, 1982.

Gimbutas, M. *The Language of the Goddess*, Thames & Hudson, 1989.

Goldenberg, Naomi, *Changing of the Gods*, Beacon, 1979.

Govinda, Lama Anagarika, *Foundations of Tibetan Mysticism*, Rider, 1972.

Graves, Robert, *Mammon and the Black Goddess*, Shenvel, 1965.

Gross, Rita, *Buddhism after Patriarchy*, State University of New York Press, 1993.

Guenther, H.V. *The Life and Teachings of Naropa*, Oxford University Press, 1963.

Guenther, H.V. (trans.) *Kindly Bent to Ease Us*, 3 vols, Dharma, 1975.

Guenther, H.V. *Buddhist Philosophy in Theory and Practice*, Shambhala, 1976.

Guenther, H.V. *Matrix of Meaning*, Shambhala, 1984.

Guenther, H.V. and Trungpa, C. *The Dawn of Tantra*, Shambhala, 1979.

Guntrip, Harry, 'My experience of analysis with Fairbairn & Winnicott (How complete a result does psycho-analytic therapy achieve?)', *International Review of Psychoanalysis*, 2, 1975.

Gyatso, Janet, 'Down with the demoness' in Janice Willis (ed.) *Feminine Ground*, Snow Lion, 1987.

Gyatso, Kelsang, *Guide to Dakini Land*, Tharpa, 1991.

Haraway, Donna, *Simions, Cyborgs and Women*, Free Association, 1991.

Hastings, James (ed.) *Encyclopaedia of Religion and Ethics*, 3 vols, T. & T. Clark, 1915.

Havnevik, Hanna, *Tibetan Buddhist Nuns*, Norwegian University Press, Oslo, 1990.

Hiltebeitel, Alf, *The Cult of Draupadi*, 2 vols, University of Chicago Press, 1991.

Hodgson, B.H. *Essays on the Languages, Literature and Religion of Nepal and Tibet*, Trübner, 1874.

Hoffmann, Helmut, *The Religions of Tibet*, Allen & Unwin, 1961.

Homayouni, M. *The Origins of Persian Gnosis*, Malvana Centre, 1989.

Irigaray, Luce, *Speculum of the Other Woman*, Cornell University Press, 1985.

Irigaray, Luce, *Elemental Passions*, Athlone, 1992.

Irigaray, Luce, *Sexes and Genealogies*, Columbia University Press, 1993.

Irigaray, Luce, *Je, Tu, Nous*, Routledge, 1993.

James, E.O. *Origins of Sacrifice*, John Murray, 1933.

James, E.O. *The Cult of the Mother Goddess*, Thames & Hudson, 1959.

Jardine, A.A., and Menke, A.M. *Shifting Scenes*, Columbia University Press, 1991.

Jäsche, H.A. *A Tibetan–English Dictionary*, Routledge & Kegan Paul, 1978.

Jayakar, P. *The Earth Mother*, Penguin, 1989.

Jung, C.G. *Psychology and the East*, Ark, 1978.

Jung, C.G. *Alchemical Studies*, Routledge & Kegan Paul, 1983.

Karmay, H. *Early Sino-Tibetan Art*, Aris & Phillips, 1975.

Karmay, Samten G. *The Treasury of Good Sayings*, London University Press, 1972.

Kemp, R. *The Potala of Tibet*, Stacey International, 1988.

Kerenyi, C. *Eleusis*, Routledge & Kegan Paul, 1960.

Klein, Anne C. 'Primordial purity and everyday life' in C. Atkinson *et al.* (eds) *Immaculate and Powerful*, Crucible, 1987.

Traveller in Space

Klein, Melanie, *The Psychoanalysis of Children*, Virago, 1989.

Knight, Richard, *A Discourse on the Worship of Priapus*, George Redway, 1883.

Kongtrul, Jamgon, *The Torch of Certainty*, Shambhala, 1977.

Krige, E.J and Krige, J.D. *The Realm of a Rain-Queen*, Oxford University Press, 1943.

Kristeva, Julia, 'Women's time' in Toril Moi (ed.) *The Kristeva Reader*, Blackwell, 1990.

Kristeva, Julia, *Language The Unknown* (trans. Anne M. Menke), Harvester Wheatsheaf, 1989.

Kuznetsov, B. 'Who was the founder of the "Bön" religion?, *Tibet Journal*, 1, 1, July/September 1975.

Landaw, J. and Weber, A. *Images of Enlightenment*, Snow Lion, 1993.

Lawson, E.T. and McCauley, R.N. (eds) *Rethinking Religion*, Cambridge University Press, 1990.

Lemesurier, Peter, *The Healing of the Gods*, Element, 1988.

Leroi-Gourham, A, *The Dawn of European Art*, Cambridge University Press, 1982.

Levy, G.R. *The Gate of Horn*, Faber & Faber, 1948.

Levy, G.R. *The Sword From the Rock*, Faber & Faber, 1951.

Lovelock, J. *Gaia*, Oxford University Press, 1987.

Lowe, Lisa, 'Des Chinoises', in Kelly Oliver (ed.) *Ethics, Politics and Difference in Julia Kristeva's Writing*, Routledge, 1993.

MacCulloch, J.A. *The Religion of the Ancient Celts*, T. & T. Clark, 1911.

MacDonald, K. *Buddha, Buddhism and Hinduism*, Traill, Calcutta, 1890.

MacDonnell, A.A. *A Practical Sanskrit Dictionary*, Oxford University Press, 1971.

Mackenzie, Vicki, *Reincarnation : The Boy Lama*, Bloomsbury, 1988.

Maitreya, Arya and Asanga, *The Changeless Nature*, Karma Kagyu Trust, 1979.

Majupuria, Indra, *Tibetan Women*, M. Devi (India), 1990.

Maraini, Fosco, *Secret Tibet* Hutchinson, 1952.

Matics, Marion L. (trans.) *Entering the Path of Enlightenment*, Macmillan, 1970.

Meyer, Johann, *Sexual Life in Ancient India*, Broadway Oriental Library, 1930.

Michael, Franz, *Rule by Incarnation*, Westview, 1982.

Mitchell, J (ed.) *The Selected Melanie Klein*, Penguin, 1986.

Moeller, W.O. *The Mithraic Origin and Meanings of the Rotas-Sator Square*, Leiden, 1973.

Moi, Toril, *Sexual/Textual Politics*, Methuen, 1985.

Moi, Toril (ed.) *The Kristeva Reader*, Blackwell, 1990.

Monier-Williams, M. *A Sanskrit–English Dictionary*, Oxford, 1899.

Mookerjee, Ajit, *Kundalini*, Thames & Hudson, 1982.

Mookerjee, Ajit, *Ritual Art of India*, Thames & Hudson, 1985.

Mookerjee, Ajit, *Kali, The Feminine Force*, Thames & Hudson, 1988.

Morgan, Robin, *The Demon Lover*, Mandarin, 1989.

Mullin, Glenn H. *Death and Dying*, Arkana, 1986.

Nye, Andrea, *Feminist Theories and the Philosophies of Man*, Croom Helm, 1988.

Oliver, Kelly, *Reading Kristeva*, Indiana University Press, 1993.

Oliver, Kelly (ed.) *Ethics, Politics and Difference in Julia Kristeva's Writing*, Routledge, 1993.

Onians, R.B. *The Origins of European Thought*, Cambridge University Press, 1987.

Orenstein, G. *The Reflowering of the Goddess*, Pergamon, 1990.

Orofino, Giacomella, *Sacred Tibetan Teachings*, Prism, 1990.

Paul, Diana Y. *Women in Buddhism*, University of California Press, 1985.

Paul, Robert A. *The Tibetan Symbolic World*, University of Chicago Press, 1982.

Plumwood, Val, *Feminism and the Mastery of Nature*, Routledge, 1993.

Pythian-Adams, W.J. *Mithraism*, Constable, 1915.

Rawson, Phillip, *The Art of Tantra*, Thames & Hudson, 1973.

Richardson, H.E. *Ancient Historical Edicts at Lhasa*, Royal Asiatic Society, 1952.

Rinpoche, Kalu, *The Foundations of Buddhist Meditation*, Kagyu Kunkhyab Chuling, 1972.

Rockhill, W.W. *The Land of the Lamas*, Longmans, Green, 1891.

Roerich, George, *Tibetan Paintings*, Gian, 1985.

Said, Edward, *Orientalism*, Routledge & Kegan Paul, 1978.

Said, Edward, *Culture and Imperialism*, Chatto & Windus, 1993.

Samuel, Geoffrey, *Civilized Shamans*, Smithsonian Institution, 1993.

Sax, William, *Mountain Goddess*, Oxford University Press, 1991.

Shaw, Miranda, *Passionate Enlightenment*, Princeton University Press, 1994.

Sjöö, Monica, *The Great Cosmic Mother*, Harper & Row, 1987.

Snellgrove, D. *Buddhist Himalaya*, Cassirer, 1957.

Snellgrove, D. *The Hevajra Tantra*, Oxford University Press, 1959.

Snellgrove, D. *Nine Ways of Bön*, Oxford University Press, 1967.

Snellgrove, D. *Indo Tibetan Buddhism*, Serindia, 1987.

Talim, M. *Woman in Early Buddhist Literature*, 1972.

Tarthang, Tulku, *Time, Space and Knowledge*, Dharma, 1977.

Thompson, W.I. *The Time Falling Bodies Take To Light*, Rider/Hutchinson, 1981.

Thondup, Tulku, *Buddhist Civilization in Tibet*, Routledge & Kegan Paul, 1987.

Trungpa, Tulku, *Empowerment*, Vajradhatu, 1976.

Trungpa, Tulku, *Glimpses of Abidharma*, Prajna, 1978.

Trungpa, Tulku, *Born in Tibet*, Unwin, 1979.

Trungpa, Tulku, *Shambhala, the Sacred Path of the Warrior*, Shambhala, 1984.

Trungpa, Tulku, (ed.) *Garuda III*, Shambhala, 1973.

Tsong Ka Pa, *Tantra in Tibet*, Allen & Unwin, 1977.

Tucci, G. *Transhimalaya*, Barrie & Jenkins, 1973.

Tucci, G. *The Religions of Tibet*, Routledge & Kegan Paul, 1980.

Ulansey, David, *The Origins of the Mithraic Mysteries*, Oxford University Press, 1989.

Usher, Jane, *The Psychology of the Female Body*, Routledge, 1989.

Walker, Barbara, *The Woman's Encyclopedia of Myths and Secrets*, Harper & Row, 1983.

Walker, Barbara, *The Crone*, Harper & Row, 1985.

Ward, Ivan (ed.) *Is Psychoanalysis another Religion?* Freud Museum Publications, 1993.

Wayman, Alex, *The Buddhist Tantras*, Routledge & Kegan Paul, 1973.

Werner, E.T.C. *Myths and Legends of China*, Sinclair Browne, 1984.

Werner, Karel (ed.) *Symbols in Art and Religion*, Curzon, 1990.

Whitford, Margaret, *Luce Irigaray*, Routledge, 1991.

Whitford, Margaret (ed.) *The Irigaray Reader*, Blackwell, 1991.

Williams, C.A.S. *Outlines of Chinese Symbolism and Art Motives*, Dover, 1976.

Willis, J.D. (ed.) *Feminine Ground*, Snow Lion, 1987.

Willis, J.D. 'Dakini: some comments on its nature and meaning' in *Feminine Ground* 1987.

Wittig, Kurt, *The Scottish Tradition in Literature*, Mercat, 1978.

Young, Dudley, *Origins of the Sacred*, Abacus, 1993.

Index